M... Plays: 2

Benefactors, Balmoral, Wild Honey

'You can classify plays in any number of ways,' writes Michael Frayn in his introduction to this second volume of his work for the theatre: 'as comedies or tragedies; as verse or prose; as high comedies, low comedies, black comedies, tragi-comedies; as art or entertainment. But however you do it they all fall into two even more fundamental categories – they are all hits or flops. The present collection contains one example of each, and one that was at different times both.'

Benefactors: 'Dazzling . . . This prismatic work circumscribes the disillusionment of an era.' *New York Times*

Balmoral: 'A sophisticated drollery, an educated amusement.' *New Statesman*

Wild Honey, a reworking of Chekhov's first play: 'A brilliant piece of theatre bearing the stigmata of genius . . . a farce with the smell of sulphur: a character-study of a man who achieves self-knowledge through suicidal despair.' *Guardian*

Michael Frayn was born in 1933 in the suburbs of London. He began his career as a reporter on the *Guardian*, then became a columnist, first for the *Guardian* and then for the *Observer*. Two volumes of his columns have been published: *The Original Michael Frayn* (Methuen, 1990) and *Speak After the Beep* (Methuen, 1995). He has written eight novels: *The Tin Men*, *The Russian Interpreter*, *Towards the End of the Morning*, *A Very Private Life*, *Sweet Dreams*, *The Trick of It*, *A Landing on the Sun* and *Now You Know*, together with a volume of philosophy, *Constructions*. He has written two original screenplays – one for the cinema, *Clockwise*, and one for television, *First and Last* – as well as numerous plays for the stage, including: *Alphabetical Order*, *Donkeys' Years*, *Clouds*, *Make and Break*, *Noises Off*, *Benefactors*, *Look Look* and *Here*. He has translated Chekhov's last four plays, and dramatised a selection of his one-act plays and short stories under the title of *The Sneeze*. He has also translated a modern Russian play, Yuri Trifonov's *Exchange*. All his plays and translations have been published by Methuen.

MICHAEL FRAYN

Plays: 2

Benefactors
Balmoral
Wild Honey
(from the untitled play by Anton Chekhov)

with an introduction by the author

Methuen Drama

METHUEN CONTEMPORARY DRAMATISTS

This edition first published in Great Britain in 1991
by Methuen Drama
Reissued with a new cover design 1994; reissued in this series 1997
by Methuen Drama
Random House UK Limited
20 Vauxhall Bridge Road, London SW1V 2SA
and Australia, New Zealand and South Africa
Distributed in the United States of America by Heinemann,
a division of Reed Elsevier Inc,
361 Hanover Street, Portsmouth, New Hampshire NH 03801 3959

Random House UK Limited Reg. No. 954009

Benefactors first published in 1984 by Methuen London Ltd
Copyright © 1984, 1985 by Michael Frayn

Balmoral first published in 1987 by Methuen London Ltd
Copyright © 1987 by Michael Frayn

Wild Honey first published in 1984 by Methuen London Ltd
Copyright © 1984, 1985 by Michael Frayn
Introduction copyright © 1984, 1985 by Michael Frayn

This collection copyright © Methuen Drama 1991
Introduction copyright © 1991 by Michael Frayn

The author has asserted his moral rights

ISBN 0-413-66080-X

A CIP catalogue record for this book is available from the British Library

Printed and bound in Great Britain by
Cox & Wyman Ltd, Reading, Berkshire

CAUTION

Contents

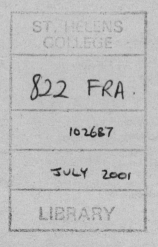

Michael Frayn

A chronology of first performances

Translations and adaptations

Introduction

You can classify plays in any number of ways – as comedies or tragedies; as verse or prose, as high comedies, low comedies, black comedies, tragi-comedies; as art or entertainment. But however you do it they all fall into two even more fundamental categories – they are all hits or flops. The present collection contains one example of each, and one that was at different times both.

This way of looking at plays may seem crass, even corrupt. But a play as written is not a finished product. It's merely a prospectus, a scheme for a proposed event. That event, when it occurs, is a transaction between the play's makers and its audience, an offer accepted or rejected. The success that the play has, or fails to have, may be critical or commercial, or both, or neither; and it may change, of course, from production to production. Whatever form it takes, though, it's the nature of the response that characterises a play most distinctly, and colours everything about it.

What's so alarming, if you have to watch the evolution of a play from draft to draft, from production to production, even from night to night, is how fine the divide is that sends the waters this way or that way, to end up so far away in the frozen north or the sunlit south, and how difficult it often is to tell from one moment to the next which way things are going to go. Audiences have communal responses, and communal responses are unpredictable and violent because they are self-reinforcing. You begin to warm to what you're seeing; your warmth warms the people around you; their warmth warms you back; your corporate warmth warms the performers; you all warm to the performers' warmth. Or you chill, and the chill spreads around, then up to the stage and back. In all responses in the theatre there is an element of either love or hate. Love encourages and cherishes and overlooks faults; hate discourages and wishes for failure. Loved performers respond with love; performers who feel the audience's antagonism reply in kind. And as always, love and hate lie close together, ever ready to change places. The history of every drama, when you come to look at it, is a drama in itself, with the same tendency to sudden shifts of feeling and reversals of fortune.

First the unequivocal hit. *Benefactors* was a success in both London and New York, and all that comes immediately to mind now of its genesis is a steady upward path, difficult but continuously rewarding. If I think harder, though, it wasn't quite as simple as that. I recall a moment of panic at the first read-through, for example, when the whole complex structure that I thought I had created seemed to have shrivelled to dust at its first exposure to the air. And another at the first preview, which coincided with some unfortunate public event – a Tube strike or a freak storm, or just possibly both, I can't remember – as a result of which the theatre was almost empty. The events of the play, which had grown dense and absorbing in the close confines of the rehearsal room, seemed suddenly lost and tiny in all that space.

And I'm completely forgetting the play's appalling heredity. It was the offspring of an earlier play called *Up*, written some ten years earlier and never even produced. This in its turn was the rewritten son of my second play, *The Sandboy*, which was produced at the Greenwich Theatre in 1971. It opened during some kind of dispute in the newspaper industry, as a result of which only one review appeared the following morning, a shattering dismissal in *The Times* by Irving Wardle. I realise with hindsight that it was probably a fair enough assessment, and I've just braced myself to open my files and see precisely how fair. But it's not there. I've suppressed it, even from myself. The story of this particular play's life is one of trying to conceal and extirpate humble origins. The cheering and uplifting conclusion is that it can be done.

The thorough-going flop in this collection is *Balmoral*. Even this, though, in the course of its tangled and painful history, seemed for one wild moment to be heading towards a happy ending.

It was first produced, under its present title, at Guildford, in 1978, with a distinguished cast, and with Michael Codron waiting to take it into the West End; and it was terrible. I withdrew it and completely rewrote it. The new version was done in the following year at the Greenwich Theatre, under a new title: *Liberty Hall*. It was a wonderful production, one of the best I have ever had. George

Cole played Skinner, the great Scottish comedian Rikki Fulton came south to play McNab, and the director was Alan Dossor, who is among other things a master of physical comedy. It's painful to recall one's failures in life, but there were things about that production that still come back to me and make me laugh. One of them was built into Poppy Mitchell's set – the visible track that the regular passage of McNab, on his thieving journeys over the years across the Balmoral breakfast-room, had worn in the tartan linoleum. Another was the great panic-stricken clearing up, when Godfrey Winn (Julian Fellowes), running to answer the door, skidded wildly in the pig-swill spread out over the floor by McNab for Skinner's inspection – and skidded not once but every night, each time as helplessly and unforeseeably as the first. Also the moment when Skinner, bowed and staggering under the great weight of the expired Walpole, sat down on the hot paraffin stove . . .

We had one single preview before we opened, and at once, on our very first time in front of an audience, we stepped into the realms of theatrical gold. I don't think my memory is playing me false when I recall that in Act One, at any rate, the audience became hysterical. The startled cast lost control. For minutes at a time the proceedings on stage became completely inaudible. When the evening ended I believed that I had done what I had been trying to do for so long – I had written a farce that worked.

The next night, as so often happens after a particularly good first preview, the show was down. In fact it was down to nothing, as flat as a flat tyre. Again I don't think my memory is overdramatising the occasion when I recall that the evening passed in absolute silence, with not a single laugh from beginning to end. This was the press night, and the reviews next morning were lacklustre. The glow we had seen at the preview had been fool's gold.

As the run went on we got quite a lot of our laughs back, though we never quite recovered that first wild glory. But any prospects of further life for the play had been killed by the press night. One of the practical lessons I learnt from this is that you might settle for very few previews, or none, but that in no circumstances must you compromise on a single one.

I subsequently rewrote the play yet again, and then again, and it's been produced once or twice since. But it's never had much success.

I see now, with hindsight, that it couldn't possibly work, because it's based upon an entirely abstract notion, a pure counterfactual – a past that never happened, that never *could* happen. This is of course the subject of the play – the idea that things could be other than they are, the notion of imposing a fiction upon reality, of making the dead alive, of reading servitude as liberty – and of altering reality in the process. In the first place I think this was simply too oblique to grasp – people were heard coming out at the end saying to each other in bewilderment 'But there *wasn't* a revolution in this country . . .' And in any case it's not a possible basis for farce. Farce, I now realise, has to be rooted in immediately believable reality. Desperation may eventually drive the characters to the most fantastic and improbable lengths, but the desperation has to be established first, and its source has to be the threat of an embarrassment so familiar that the audience's palms sweat in sympathy.

No, it's more complicated than that. Your palms *don't* in fact sweat in sympathy when you watch the ignoble terrors and strategems of the characters in a farce. You refuse to let yourself identify with the characters, or feel their feelings. You reject absolutely the idea that it could be you up there, so idiotically embarrassed, so transparently mendacious. Their situation is too humiliating to be owned up to. They are somebody else, somebody who could never be you.

This is what gives farce its hysterical edge. Your refusal to recognise yourself has an element of violence in it. You know perfectly well that, just like your scapegoats up there, you *do* on occasion tell lies to avoid social embarrassment to yourself or others. You know that in your dreams you *are* discovered with your trousers round your ankles, performing acts which in waking life you take great if usually unconscious pains not be discovered performing. You are attempting by your laughter to demonstrate, both to the rest of the audience and to yourself, that you do not lie, or fear public exposure. And in this you are lying once again, and risk being found out, and must laugh louder to show you are not lying. You are like the bully who conceals the despised characteristic in himself by persecuting it in others. You have to shut off your brain and behave like a madman.

Farce is a brutally difficult form. It is also of course a despised one. In laughing at it you have lost your moral dignity, and you don't like to admit it afterwards – you don't like to concede the power of the people who have reduced you to such behaviour.

So *Balmoral*, I now realise, was doomed from the first by a fundamental conceptual error. It was a Titanic searching for its iceberg.

In which case how could it have made people laugh that once . . .?

Well, all theories of comedy and farce break down at some point, some sooner than others. This particular theory fails at the very first performance, which suggests that it may be even more inherently defective than the play itself.

The play that fell into both categories at different times was *Wild Honey*; it was a great hit in London, and a failure in New York.

Its history, like that of the other two plays, was long, but for most of it, as in the history of the Russian provinces where it's set, little happened. The National Theatre first sent me the Russian text, at Christopher Morahan's suggestion, in 1978. I had seen and enjoyed his television production of Dmitri Makaroff's Royal Court version, with Rex Harrison, back in the early sixties, but had never read the original before, and could remember nothing but the image of Platonov asleep with his hat over his face. Chekhov's text, I discovered, was 150 pages long – at least six hours worth of material – untitled, and, in the version which the NT had found and photocopied, bristling with the hostile thickets of now near-obsolete hard signs that characterise the old orthography. The first chance I got to read it was while I was in bed with influenza. Slowly, through the veils of my fever and the limitless tangled undergrowth of Chekhov's first two acts, the most wonderful characters and scenes began to emerge. I at once longed to work on it, and sent the National Theatre my detailed proposals for adapting it, down to the title itself. I even included a twenty-page scene-by-scene synopsis of the original so that they would know exactly how much I intended to change – not realising, in my headlong rush of enthusiasm, that there was a translation of it by Ronald Hingley available in the Oxford Chekhov. The response from the National to all this was appropriately Russian: no response. Nothing. Not so much as a printed postcard of acknowledgement.

So that was Act One of this particular meta-drama. Act Two was constructed on a time-scale entirely suitable to the leisurely exposition of Chekhov's original; another four years elapsed before the play was actually commissioned. When it was finally produced, in 1984, it followed a converse course to *Balmoral*. Performances started with a dress rehearsal so awful that I made plans to emigrate before press night, and then matured steadily through a week of previews. Ian McKellen told me later that it was only from the audience reaction during the previews that he had discovered the play was a comedy. The press night, by the time we got to it, was one of those occasions you dream of, when cast and audience together seem to catch fire, and produce a warmth and glow that linger for hours afterwards.

It had a very good run at the National. And then it failed in New York. Success and failure in the New York theatre are particularly immediate, dramatic, and total. First nights in London are fraught occasions because the critics are there to pass judgment; first nights in New York are even more fraught because they are not. Everyone is in a great state of dinner jackets and celebrity, but the critics have been and gone – they've seen the show at one of the previews, and their notices are already printing in the first editions that will hit the streets shortly after the final curtain. There is a traditional first-night party afterwards at Sardi's, halfway through which some mysterious messenger brings the traditional early copy of the *New York Times*. Its judgment is as absolute and final as God's. The verdict spreads through the room like a stain through water, imperceptibly and immediately colouring everything rose-pink or ash-grey. If it's good someone gets up on a chair and reads it aloud. There are stories of people launching excitedly into a public reading only to find halfway through that it is in fact the order for execution. There are other stories of the waiters removing all the bottles of wine from the tables as soon as the word reaches the kitchens, and of the whole party melting wordlessly away into the night. There is even one story about a cast who heard what the review was going to be in the interval, and who didn't bother to perform Act Two.

With *Wild Honey* I can't remember much about the performance itself, except that someone introduced me to Jackie Onassis in the interval, and I failed either to recognise her or to catch her name. The party afterwards, though, was a spectacularly sumptuous occasion, even by New York standards, held not in Sardi's but in the oyster bar under Grand Central Station. Somewhere around midnight the shadow of Frank Rich's review in the *Times* passed across the room like the Angel of Death. 'Rich is bad,' someone whispered to me. It had the ring of an unanswerable moral principle, like 'Black is beautiful'. My disappointment was tempered by my curiosity to see what would happen. It was my third play in New York, and after two successes I half-expected, as at the end of one's third wish in a fairy story, to see not just the champagne disappear but the whole oyster bar with it, and to find myself suddenly transported back to my humble woodcutter's shack in the outer suburbs of London. But, exactly as in a play, even these expectations were reversed, and we roystered, not to say oystered, on through the night undeterred. Rich is bad, no doubt about it, but rich can also be rather pleasant while it lasts. The play closed three weeks later; the principal producer told me he had lost about a million dollars.

I suppose, looking back, that the glorious first night in London marked the climax of my career in the theatre. *Benefactors* had opened three months earlier at the Vaudeville, *Noises Off* was still running across the road at the Savoy; for just over a year, until August 1985, when *Wild Honey* closed, I had three plays on in London. Since then I have done almost nothing in the theatre but straight translations, and one new play, *Look, Look*, too humiliatingly unsuccessful even to reproduce here in the flops department. Someone told me recently, with many convincing examples, that few playwrights' careers last longer than fifteen years. My first play, *The Two of Us*, was produced in 1970, so maybe my grand climax was also my final curtain.

Including *Wild Honey* in a collection of my own plays may seem to imply unjustifiable claims about the extent of my contribution to it. I decided to put it here, though, rather than in my collection of Chekhov translations, simply to avoid any possible confusion between translation and adaptation. The introduction I wrote to the first single-play edition of the text, which is reproduced later in this volume, gives not only the fullest possible account of Chekhov's original, and of all the considerable mysteries and uncertainties that surround it, but also attempts to make clear what my adaptation involved.

Not clear enough, though, I realise with hindsight. When the play was produced some playgoers, even some reviewers, credited me with (or blamed me for) the more farcical elements. They supposed, in other words, that it began as more or less pure Chekhov and finished as more or less impure Frayn. The converse (sadly) is true. Most of the liberties I took were in getting the action of the play under way with reasonable despatch. It's true that I have emphasised the farce in what follows rather than the moralising and melodramatic elements which are also present in the original. But the farce is essentially Chekhov's own handiwork, and I have focussed the play around it because it seems to my (perhaps corrupt) taste to be by far the most successful, characteristic, and original element of the play that Chekhov wrote. I have reorganised and tightened the sequence of farcical encounters in Anna Petrovna's garden at the end of Act One, and around Platonov's house in the early part of Act Two. In general, though, the more farcical the play becomes the closer it is to the original. Most of the wonderful black farce towards the end – the great confrontations in the schoolroom between the drunken and demoralised Platonov and each of the women in turn with whom he is involved, is pure Chekhov. I wish I had written it, but I didn't. I merely trimmed it and fitted it all more tightly and securely together. And, of course, translated it. I shouldn't like to forgo the credit for that.

I don't know why anyone should be reluctant to recognise this aspect of Chekhov. He after all began his career as a professional humorist, and became a serious writer only by quite gradual evolution. The surprise is that he was writing scenes as funny and profound as these even before that career had started. This I find not just surprising but incomprehensible; and having seen them actually played in production I find it even less comprehensible now than when I first read them, shining like buried treasure among all the muddle of the original. In these scenes Platonov becomes in my view one of the great comic characters of the world's theatre, and this volume would be worth the price for them alone.

Michael Frayn, 1991

Benefactors

Benefactors was first presented by Michael Codron at the Vaudeville Theatre, London, on 4 April 1984, with the following cast:

DAVID	Oliver Cotton
JANE	Patricia Hodge
COLIN	Tim Pigott-Smith
SHEILA	Brenda Blethyn

Directed by Michael Blakemore
Designed by Michael Annals
Lighting by Rory Dempster

Benefactors was first presented in New York by James M. Nederlander, Robert Fryer, Doublas Urbanski and Michael Codron in association with MTM Enterprises, Inc. and CBS Productions at the Brooks Atkinson Theatre on 22 December, 1985 with the following cast:

DAVID	Sam Waterston
JANE	Glenn Close
COLIN	Simon Jones
SHEILA	Mary Beth Hurt

Directed by Michael Blakemore
Settings by Michael Annals
Costumes by John Dunn
Lighting by Martin Aronstein
Production State Manager: Susie Cordon

ACT ONE

Three entrances — left, right, and centre.
Left: a large wooden kitchen table and half-a-dozen chairs, with other comfortably worn kitchen furnishings. Right: a single bleak upright chair.

DAVID *and* JANE.

DAVID. Basuto Road. I love the name!

JANE. Basuto Road. How I hate those sour grey words!

DAVID. Basuto Road, SE15. And you can practically see it. Victorian South London. Two-storey terraces with tiny front gardens and tessellated front door steps. You can practically smell the grey lace curtains in those little bay windows. Don't you think?

JANE. You look back in life and there's a great chain of cloud-shadows moving over the earth behind you. All the sharp bright landscape you've just travelled through has gone grey and graceless.

DAVID. Basuto Road. But when you think how fresh and hopeful that must have sounded once, back in 1890! I suppose we'd just annexed Basutoland. East Africa was as new as outer space. The Empire was as desirable as television. There's the whole history of ideas in that one name.

JANE. Basuto Road. There it is, on the box-files all along the shelf. Grey-faced reproachful words, shuffling towards you out of the shadows. I look away — and there it is again, all the way down the chest where he keeps his old drawings.

DAVID. Also Bechuana Road and Matebele Road and Mashona Road and Barotse Road.

JANE. Then ten years, fifteen years away behind you the land's out in sunlight again. You can see everything small and shining in the distance — so clear you feel you could reach out and touch it

DAVID. Plus Maud Road, Daisy Road, Frances Road, and Phoebe Road. I suppose they were the builder's daughters. Rather sad — it's all coming down. About fifteen acres. What do you think?

JANE. Basuto Road. It started in the sunlight. He was happy then. Yes! He was! He was happy! He came back in the middle of the day to tell me about the job, and he was like a child with a new bicycle. Ten years ago? No, twelve or more. But that day, at any rate — that's out in the sunlight again.

DAVID. It's probably an impossible site. It's jammed between a railway line and a main road. What do you think?

JANE. He couldn't sit still. He couldn't stop talking about it

DAVID. It's zoned at 150 to the acre. I bet it's more like 200. I'll need you to check that for me.

JANE. We were both still children. Middle-aged children.

DAVID. But that would mean housing for 3,000 people. It's probably not possible. What do you think? If it's possible the council wouldn't be asking me — they'd be doing it themselves. It would be a huge job — I'd have to double the size of the office. But that's where the work is, Jane, in local authority housing. That's where the real architecture's being done. So what do you think?

JANE. What *did* I think? I don't know. I can't remember. I expect I was against it. I expect I raised all kinds of sensible objections. That was the way we operated then. David was for things; I was against them. Government and Opposition. And we'd always settle the question democratically. One for, one against — motion carried.

DAVID. I'll go and have a quick look at the site. Ring Bill, oh, and Geoffrey Lewin. Tell them I've been called away. Emergency. Job falling down.

Exit DAVID *centre.*

JANE. And that was fair. Because when I voted against I was really voting for. In those days. Anything David was for I was for. I wasn't going to tell *him* that, of course. Why not? I can't remember. Not that I needed to tell him. He knew perfectly well. Anyway, I had to come out in favour of this project soon enough, because Colin was against it.

Enter COLIN *left*.

David was for it, so Colin was against it. Colin was against it, so I had to be for it. It was like the start of a game.

COLIN. I gather David's landed one of these great slum clearance jobs. Changing the face of London. So he's on his way up in the world.

JANE. Not that Colin cared much. Not then. He was mildly sardonic. But then he always was. He didn't think about it. We none of us thought about it.

COLIN. What do you think about it, Jane?

JANE. King opposite king. Queen on her colour.

COLIN. I said what do you think about it?

JANE. A twilight area.

COLIN. A twilight area?

JANE. Not a slum clearance scheme, Colin. Not a slum.

COLIN. A twilight area. It sounds very beautiful.

Enter SHEILA *and* DAVID *left*.

JANE. Isn't that right, David?

DAVID. What's that, my love?

JANE. Basuto Road — a twilight area.

DAVID. It's certainly not a slum, whatever a slum is. No worse than this neighbourhood, really. Or no worse than it used to be. A bit grey and exhausted, that's all. Little weary shops where they sell maroon cardigans and dusty sanitary fittings. Little places under the railway arches where they respray cars and stable rag-and-bone men's ponies. You get a few surprises, too. There was a brand-new red Mercedes parked in Bechuana Road yesterday.

COLIN. A rival architect.

DAVID. A richer one than me, obviously.

COLIN. Or some demolition contractor sizing the job up. Like the hangman taking a look through the peephole.

DAVID. It's got to be done, though, Colin.

COLIN. Oh, it's got to be done. Otherwise the areas where architects and demolition contractors live will start to look a little grey and exhausted again.

DAVID. I don't know why I put up with you, Colin. Everybody else takes me seriously.

COLIN. I take you seriously, David. You're building the new world we're all going to be living in.

DAVID. You sit at my table eating my food and drinking my wine . . . Where's your glass?

COLIN. Sheila takes you seriously, anyway. She thinks the future's right there inside your head, like a chick about to burst out of an egg.

DAVID. I might as well have my father round all the time.

COLIN. Though she might feel rather at home in a sunset area.

JANE. A twilight area.

COLIN. Wouldn't you, my love?

DAVID. And don't start on Sheila, for God's sake.

JANE. Anyway, Colin, it's got to be done. You know that in your heart. We've got to rebuild areas like that.

COLIN. You're going to be working on this one, are you, Jane? Down there with the clipboard? Knocking on doors, doing the market research?

JANE. I don't do market research.

COLIN. Good morning, madam. Would you like your house pulled down?

DAVID. They're going to get their houses pulled down whether they like it or not. And we don't need to ask them what they want instead because we know.

COLIN. Nice little semis with nice little gardens.

DAVID. The best popular housing so far devised.

COLIN. But you're not going to build them nice little semis with nice little gardens.

DAVID. I can't! I've got to show a net housing gain, not a colossal housing loss. What do you get with semis?

COLIN. Aesthetic typhoid, I expect.

DAVID. You get about thirty persons to the acre. I've got to house something more like 200. I'd have to cover the site with one solid fused mass of semi-detached house.

COLIN. Sheila thinks that sounds wonderful.

DAVID. Work it out for yourself. You were Senior Whatsit.

COLIN. Was I?

DAVID. I thought you were Senior Whatsit? At Eton, or wherever it was?

COLIN. Senior Classical Whatsit. Not Senior Town Planning Whatsit, like you.

DAVID. Difficult to rise above Senior Milk Monitor at my school.

COLIN. Wake up, Sheila. It's the barefoot boyhood again.

DAVID. Sheila's all right. Sheila's awake.

COLIN. She's not saying very much. Are you, my pet?

DAVID. She's talking more sense than some people.

COLIN. If only we could find out what Sheila wanted we'd know what everyone wanted.

JANE. Over dinner, this would be. The children out of the way. Occasional clicks and whimpers on the baby-alarm from their two across the street. Colin and Sheila — I don't know — they seemed to live round here. She'd leave the children here at some point in the day. That's what usually happened. Then when she came to collect them she'd sit down for a cup of coffee and sooner or later she'd be saying, 'This is awful — I haven't done anything about the children's tea.' And I'd say, 'That's all right — they can have something here.' And then next thing I knew it would be, 'This is terrible — I haven't done anything about getting a meal for Colin.' And I'd say,

'Give him a ring — we've got plenty.' And she'd say, 'This is awful — we seem to live round here.'

DAVID. They're not here *again*?

JANE. Your friends, not mine.

DAVID. Sheila's *your* friend.

JANE. Sheila's *not* my friend.

DAVID. They seem to live round here!

JANE. You were the one who told them that house was coming up.

DAVID. *That* house! Not *this* house!

JANE. Anyway, I thought we were supposed to be helping them?

DAVID. I've been helping people all day. I've been helping 200 people to the acre. I don't want to help people all evening.

COLIN. How's Basutoland?

DAVID. Don't *ask* me . . . Sheila . . . I don't want to talk about it. I've spent most of the day with the Regional Architect and the Regional Quantity Surveyor, and they say it may take a year just to establish the budget with the Ministry. All I know so far is that I've got to get the furthest door within range of a ninety-foot firehose and that I've got to provide lifts deep enough to accommodate stretchers and coffins. Also that the site's next to a trunk road, and the Ministry of Transport say categorically no access. So there we are. 14,000 people on the housing list, and no access to the site.

COLIN. All right, then, David — don't.

DAVID. Don't what?

COLIN. You said you didn't want to talk about it.

DAVID. I don't want to talk about it. I've been talking about it all day. Have you opened some wine? I'm not going to go high. But if I don't go high we won't qualify for the high-rise subsidy, and if I don't get the high-rise subsidy we won't be rising at all, high or low. And of course I'll fight. We'll reach compromises, I'll get waivers. But when I think of the struggle it's going to be! When I think of all the words, all the paper, all the anger, all the dust, all the mud . . . Because I'm not going to build towers. No one wants to live in a tower.

COLIN. I'd like to live in a tower.

JANE. Colin, why won't you ever be serious?

COLIN. I am serious. You build a really high tower, David, and I'll come and live at the top. Surrounded by silence. Silence and empty sky.

DAVID. Don't be silly, Colin.

JANE. The lifts would keep breaking down. You know what these places are like.

COLIN. Perfect.

DAVID. You'd never meet your neighbours. You wouldn't see a living soul from one week's end to the next.

COLIN. This isn't a block of flats you're describing, David. This is paradise.

JANE. No, we liked them. We really did. I wasn't just running a soup-kitchen. Well, we liked him. David liked him. But he did actually urge David to build tower blocks! Quite funny when you think what happened later. It was just part of the game, of course. David was against them, so Colin was for them. He wasn't serious. David pretended not to be serious, but in fact he was. That's why Colin could always get a rise out of him Colin one end of the table, grinning. David the other end, frowning. Me putting in a word here and a word there, trying to redress the balance. And Sheila sitting there like the Dormouse, not saying anything at all.

COLIN. Come on, my love. You've talked enough for one evening.

DAVID. More wine? More coffee? More something?

COLIN. Which of us has the harder task, do you suppose? You, getting rid of us; or us, getting away from you?

COLIN *and* DAVID *go off centre.*

JANE. I can't think now which year that would have been. Sixty-nine, I suppose, or seventy . . . Mind Jake's frog farm thing in the hall . . . !

Exit JANE *centre.*

SHEILA. Sixty-eight. That was the year. He started on Basuto Road in April, just after Lizzie's birthday. They were such good friends, it was lovely. You felt you could always pop across the road for a chat. I used to go flying over there at all hours. I'd just slip a coat round my shoulders and push their front door open, and — Hoo-hoo! And Jane would be rushing around, doing fifteen different things at once, and I'd sit there in the kitchen and watch her and I'd think, Oh, if only I could be like that! If only I'd got her energy! And the colours of everything in the kitchen were so warm and friendly. And David would come popping in for a moment on the way to one of his sites, and the children were lovely, and they'd all make you feel you belonged there.

Enter JANE *left.*

I cry sometimes now when I think about it.

JANE. Poor old Sheila.

Exit SHEILA *right.*

Always flying over with some new disaster. The washing- - machine had overflowed — the lavatory was blocked — Matt or Lizzie was ill. Matt and Lizzie were always ill. You'd be working in the kitchen, say, and you'd suddenly become aware that there was this little voice somewhere in the house going 'Hoo-hoo . . . hoo-hoo . . . '

Enter DAVID *left.*

DAVID. I wish she wouldn't say hoo-hoo.

JANE. She's got to say something.

DAVID. We could lock the front door.

JANE. No, we couldn't.

DAVID. Some people lock their front doors.

JANE. Not us.

SHEILA (*off*). Hoo-hoo!

DAVID. If only she'd say, 'It's me', or, 'Anyone at home?'

Enter SHEILA *centre*.

SHEILA. Anyone at home?

JANE. Hello! Just in time for coffee!

SHEILA. Oh, Jane, I can't. Hello, David.

DAVID. You're looking lovely. Big kiss. See you later, I expect.

Exit DAVID *centre*.

SHEILA. I've got to get Matt to the hospital. He's got an appointment at eleven.

JANE. Eleven? I'd better run you there in the minibus.

SHEILA. Oh dear. This is awful. I must learn to drive.

JANE. We'll get David to teach you.

SHEILA. Colin would never buy a car, of course.

JANE. I hate them, too.

SHEILA. Then on Saturday I've got to get the children to my mother's.

JANE. Learn to drive, Sheila. Then you can borrow the minibus. Hold on, I'll get the keys.

Exit JANE *left*.

SHEILA. She must have thought I was awful, now I look back on it. I practically lived over there! The children would come looking for me, and they'd be hungry, and before I knew what was happening Jane would be making them baked beans and egg soldiers. Things they'd never eat at home they'd tuck into perfectly happily over there. Her children were older, of course. I suppose Matt and Lizzie being there was almost like having two more in the family.

Enter JANE *left*.

They'd all disappear upstairs to watch television together, and the next thing I knew there'd be a glass of wine on the table in front of me, and Jane would be urging me to ring Colin and stay for supper.

JANE. Well, you didn't get to the shops today, did you?

SHEILA (*into phone*). Hello, Colin? It's me.

Enter COLIN right.

COLIN. You're at Jane's.

SHEILA. I'm at Jane's.

COLIN. She's inviting us for supper.

SHEILA. She says why don't you come over and have some supper.

COLIN. You're in love with that woman.

SHEILA. She thought the children could have a bath here. They could sleep in the spare room.

COLIN. Did you hear what I said? I said you're in love with her.

SHEILA. He says that would be super.

Exit COLIN right.

JANE. She sometimes invited us back, of course.

Enter DAVID left.

DAVID. Oh no! No, no, no, no! I can't! I'm ill! I've got architect's elbow!

JANE. David, we have to make the effort once in a while.

DAVID. It'll be all cold and dark brown, and Colin'll be in a funny mood, and there'll be trouble with the potatoes.

JANE (*into phone*). Sheila, I'm terribly sorry. David's got a meeting on Wednesday evening.

SHEILA. Thursday? Or Friday? Or the following week some time?

JANE. Sheila, why don't I give you a ring when we've got clear of work and holidays and children and parents and things?

SHEILA. They came to us sometimes. A few times. But we went

on walks together, we went on picnics. We always used to say, 'If we're going with the Kitzingers we know the weather will be fine!' And it was! It always was!

JANE. The children always complained about it, of course. 'Do we *have* to go with the Molyneuxs?' — 'Yes, we *do*!' '*Why* do we have to go with the Molyneuxs?' — 'Because we've got a car and they haven't.' — 'But they're so *boring*! And Matt and Lizzie smell.'

SHEILA. And once, when we were on our way back from somewhere, David took us to see Basuto Road. I can't remember what it looked like now. All I can remember is David making a great gesture with both arms, like a magician commanding up a vision. And me feeling terribly happy. I don't know why.

DAVID. Forget all these houses, Sheila. Forget all these little streets. What we've got is very roughly a triangle. Main road — Bechuana Road — railway. I'll tell you what I'm thinking of doing, Sheila. I'm thinking of a courtyard. Two sacrificial slab blocks . . .

Enter COLIN *right.*

COLIN. Two what?

DAVID. Sacrificial slabs. All right, Colin, all jokes in writing, please, on the back of a postcard. Two long slab blocks that sacrifice daylight on the outside to protect the rest of the scheme from the noise of the road and the railway. Six or seven stories high. Blind walls on the outside, and all the flats facing inwards into the morning and afternoon sun, on to the gardens and play areas, on to the life of the community.

SHEILA. It sounds a bit like your old college at university.

DAVID. Exactly, Sheila! Absolutely! I predict a first!

SHEILA. My God, have I said something right for once?

JANE. You've put your finger on the basic principle of all modern British architecture.

COLIN. The college wasn't seven stories high. We didn't have a railway running down one side of it.

DAVID. No, but she's got the general point. We felt like a community because the building had turned its back on the rest of the world.

JANE. What did the rest of the world feel like?

COLIN. Yes! Poor Jane!

DAVID. Why poor Jane? She was in another college.

JANE. That's what I mean.

DAVID. Well, of course you were in another college! We were in a men's college! You're not a man! Don't be silly.

COLIN. How wonderful — a row! Don't stop!

DAVID. *I'm* not rowing.

JANE. *I'm* rowing.

COLIN. Sheila's withdrawn to a tactful distance.

SHEILA. No, no.

COLIN. Just a little chat about the old days, my pet. Look, she's feeling all excluded.

SHEILA. No, I'm not. I'm very interested.

DAVID. Come here, Sheila. My favourite pupil.

SHEILA. No, I was just thinking, it must be wonderful to change things. It must be magical to look at some new thing that wasn't there before and think, *I* did that!

DAVID. No, it's not, Sheila. It's heartbreaking. It's always just warped windows and condensation problems. It was going to be so new and amazing, and it never is, it's always just like everything else. I'll tell you what's wonderful, Sheila . . . I'm not talking to you two . . . I'll tell you what's really magical. A bare building site. Something still quickens in me when I smell that raw damp smell of green brickwork and wet cement. When I feel the loose hardcore shift and grind under my shoes. I love those huge holes in the ground when people are going to go really high. Amazing emptiness, like the emptiness of a conjuror's hat, because you know that marvels will come out of it. I love looking at the site when it's like this, even — all other houses, all clutter waiting to be cleared.

COLIN. Some elegant new concrete block in the East End blew up last week.

DAVID. One flat blew up. There was a gas escape.

COLIN. The whole lot came down like a pack of cards.

DAVID. One side came down.

COLIN. Progressive collapse.

DAVID. Because it was system-built. The walls were holding up the floors. I shall use a steel frame.

JANE. Come on. The children will be screaming with hunger.

COLIN. The words will outlast the building, even so.

DAVID. What words?

COLIN. Wonderful words. 'Progressive collapse.'

JANE, DAVID *and* COLIN *go off right.*

SHEILA. I knew what David meant, though. Something coming — yes. Something new. Everywhere we went with them the trees were alight with fresh green. And yes, we had rain sometimes, of course we had rain — but a warm spring rain, with something new and marvellous in the wind behind it.

Enter JANE *right.*

JANE. Then on Monday morning I'd be back down there. David thought the council's figures were wrong. So I was up and down those dull grey streets every day with my clipboard, trying to find out how many people there actually were to be rehoused. There was never anyone in. Ring the bell. Wait. Silence . . . Ring another bell. Dog barking. Wait. Next house. Ring. Silence . . . And then, as you turn to leave some doorstep, you realise there are two faded, ancient eyes inspecting you through the letter-box. You bend down and speak to them. 'Good morning. I'm doing a survey of housing requirements in the district.' The eyes gaze at you for a long time. Then they speak. 'Oh, no, love. We're all Labour here.' Bang. Try the next house. A black face looks round the door.

Black faces. A woman covered in children like an apple tree with apples. 'Good morning. I'm doing a survey of housing requirements in the district.' She laughs. Oh dear. Never mind — plough on. 'I wonder if you could tell me how many people there are in your household?' She puts her hand to her mouth and laughs like a bird singing; she can't understand my dialect. 'I see. Thank you.' In the next house some huge wild animal flings itself against the other side of the door, audibly slavering. Across the street I wait for minutes on end while infirm and elderly footsteps struggle downstairs towards the door. An ill grey face appears. 'Good morning. I'm doing a survey of housing requirements in the district.' — 'It's my mother, you see.' 'I beg your pardon?' — 'She's fallen out of bed. I can't lift her.' And of course when I get up there it's not just lifting she needs. So that's the morning gone.

SHEILA. I do admire you, Jane. I wish I could do something really worthwhile like you.

JANE. Sorry, I've only just got back.

SHEILA. I do envy you, having the chance to get out of the house.

JANE. Do you want a quick cup of coffee before you fetch Lizzie?

SHEILA. I'll do it.

JANE. Sit down!

SHEILA. But then you're good with people, aren't you.

JANE. People. I don't think I like people very much.

SHEILA. You're so good at helping people.

JANE. I ought to be. That's all I ever do. Help David. Help the children.

SHEILA. But that little boy down at Basuto Road. The one who'd been locked out by his mother.

JANE. Well, I couldn't just leave him standing there in the rain.

SHEILA. I wish I was like you, Jane.

JANE. Look, I'm not trying to help anyone down at Basuto Road.

I'm just trying to count them. I keep my eyes shut as much as I can.

SHEILA. It's what I always wanted to be — someone who helped other people.

JANE. You are. You do. Don't be silly, Sheila.

SHEILA. I did, when I was nursing. I never seem to have the time to do anything these days. I think I *am* other people.

DAVID (*off*). Only me.

Enter DAVID *centre.*

Where are my Wellingtons? I'm supposed to be out at Finchley . . . Sheila . . .

SHEILA. It's like the wind rushing into the house.

DAVID. They should be in the car. They're *never* in the car . . . ! The wind, yes — that's what I'm going like today. Ten to three. Aren't you fetching Lizzie?

SHEILA. Oh my God! One day I'm going to forget her completely!

JANE. Coffee . . .

SHEILA. I'll have it when I come back . . .

Exit SHEILA *centre.*

JANE. Twenty to three. Do you want her coffee? You lent your boots to Daisy.

DAVID. That was a long speech.

JANE. What?

DAVID. Sheila just then. Oh, yes, Daisy. I think Sheila's a bit happier, isn't she? I think things are a bit better over the road.

JANE. Are they?

DAVID. Funny when he lived in that terrible flat, and we weren't supposed to know she existed. I'll never forget dropping him outside the door one day, and there was this unexplained pregnant belly trying to conceal itself behind the side of the porch.

JANE. I expect she'd locked herself out.

DAVID. I expect she had. I sometimes think he only married her because we happened to meet her.

JANE. We didn't *happen* to meet her. She came knocking on the door, saying Colin was in Durham and she was in labour.

DAVID. My first sight of *him* was saying grace in Hall. Very grave and unsmiling. Collar and tie, yellow flower in his buttonhole, scholar's gown; no shoes or socks. It was our first term. I can still remember the shock. The world wasn't really serious after all!

JANE. Imagine being married to him, though.

DAVID. Imagine being married to Sheila. Where did he pick her up?

JANE. Outside Lugano railway station.

DAVID. Thirty, and he was giving English lessons.

JANE. She'd had her rucksack stolen.

DAVID. Senior Classical Whatever-it-was, and he was giving English lessons in Lugano.

JANE. He's got a perfectly good job now.

Enter COLIN *right.*

There's no need to feel sorry for him.

DAVID. Working on a women's magazine?

JANE. Yes, but then he's got that encyclopaedia thing he does in his spare time. He's the editor of that.

DAVID. He's the entire staff, isn't he?

COLIN. Fornication . . . Fetishism . . . Frigidity . . .

Enter SHEILA *right.*

SHEILA. He'd spread it out over the living-room floor at night.

COLIN. Foreplay . . . Femininity . . . Fallopian tubes . . .

SHEILA. I'd just watch him sometimes. I couldn't have the television on.

COLIN. Father . . . Father-figure . . . Fun . . . I'll do Fun myself . . .

SHEILA. Did you say Femininity? I could do Femininity.

COLIN. What?

SHEILA. I mean, if you wanted me to.

COLIN. That's an idea. Jane could do Femininity.

DAVID. What's it called? Happy Families?

JANE. I don't think he chose the title.

DAVID. I mean, the bits you do are fine.

JANE. I think he takes it all quite seriously.

DAVID. But then you've got a degree in anthropology.

COLIN. How about the kids? Would they like to do a bit? Fathers? Foot fetishists?

DAVID. All the same, a lot of people are going to find something like this genuinely helpful.

COLIN. Yes, you might benefit yourself. You might try looking under D for Domination.

DAVID. I'm always longing to be done good to.

COLIN. Symbols of male potency; towers, high-rise, getting the thing up — you'll find most of your professional life in there.

SHEILA. The trouble would be afterwards, when we got home.

You'd never know which way Colin was going to jump. Sometimes we'd sit down and laugh about them.

COLIN. What should we do without them, my pet? What should we talk about together, if we didn't have David and Jane?

SHEILA. When you said about putting towers into holes in the ground! He didn't know where to look!

COLIN. He wasn't always so tamed and righteous. He was like a wild hare — quick and timid and wide-eyed and cunning — and he laughed and he smelt, and we were going off to Greece together, and he came to my rooms one night and he said, I'm not going to marry her — I'm not — I'm not!

SHEILA. Do you think they're sitting there talking about us?

COLIN. What would they do without us? We make them feel good. It's our one contribution to the world.

DAVID. It's unpleasant for *her*. That's what I hate.

JANE. I think she rather enjoys it.

DAVID. Those little embarrassed laughs of hers.

JANE. I shouldn't worry about Sheila.

DAVID. I wish we could do something to help them.

JANE. We do! We just about keep that marriage together! What do you think they're doing at the moment?

DAVID. You mean, talking about us? Talking about us talking about them, probably.

JANE *and* DAVID *go off left.*

SHEILA. And sometimes he'd sit down, and I wouldn't know whether he wanted to talk or not. I'd just know that whatever I did it would be wrong.

COLIN. What?

SHEILA. Nothing. I was just thinking.

COLIN. Just thinking what?

SHEILA. Just thinking it was funny when he said about having these, you know, by his Finchley site.

COLIN. These what by his Finchley site?

SHEILA. Strange erections.

COLIN. Don't try to make smutty remarks. It doesn't please me. Why do you think it would please me?

SHEILA. I'm sorry. I thought . . . I mean, you often . . .

COLIN. Don't try to ape me. Why do you think it would please me to see myself aped?

SHEILA. Don't be like this, Colin.

COLIN. You think I'm so pleased with myself going out that I want to see myself coming back?

SHEILA. I just thought it was funny.

COLIN. Yes, I heard you laugh.

SHEILA. I didn't laugh.

COLIN. You're always laughing. You're the only one of us without a sense of humour, and you're the only one who laughs. But you don't know *when* to laugh, you see.

SHEILA. I didn't think I was laughing.

COLIN. You don't know *how* to laugh.

SHEILA. Please, Colin, please!

COLIN. You wouldn't start singing in public. You know you're tone-deaf. But you're deaf to all shades of relation and meaning. Go away. Go to bed. You disgust me.

Exit SHEILA *right.*

DAVID (*off*). Problems! Problems, problems!
  Enter DAVID *centre.*

  That's all my life consists of!

  Enter JANE *left.*

  I get to the office — there's a message from the site agent at Finchley. They've driven their ten-ton crane on to the children's play area. To their great surprise, their ten-ton crane is now in the drains underneath the children's play area. I get back to the office and there's this waiting.

SHEILA (*off*). Hoo-hoo!

DAVID. I can't build anywhere within six feet of that thing. So I've lost about a fifth of the site.

JANE. Couldn't they divert it?

SHEILA. Hoo-hoo!

  Exit COLIN *right.*

DAVID. Oh, that bloody woman! Divert it? Yes, they could divert it, but that's going to cost about a thousand pounds a metre!

JANE. Couldn't you get them to cut back on parking-space?

Enter SHEILA *centre.*

DAVID. Hello, Sheila . . . Cut back on parking-space? What good would that do . . . ? Come in, come in.

SHEILA. Sorry.

JANE. If you didn't have to provide a hundred per cent off-street parking you'd have a bit more space and money to play with.

SHEILA. I thought David would be at the office.

DAVID. I'm just on my way down to see the Borough Architect about *this*!

JANE. The electricity people have got a 275,000-volt cable running across the Basuto Road site.

DAVID. So what — I have to go to eleven stories?

SHEILA. Oh dear. Poor David.

DAVID. You wouldn't believe what goes on under that site. Wires, pipes, sewers. It may not be buildable. Seriously. I may be building a piece of unbuildable land.

JANE. Back for lunch?

DAVID. I may not be back at all.

Exit DAVID *centre.*

SHEILA. Poor David.

JANE. It's his element. If you don't like problems don't take up architecture.

SHEILA. It must be awful for him, though.

JANE. Anyway, if you don't like problems don't take up living.

SHEILA. Poor David . . . Poor David . . .

JANE. Sheila, love, what's the matter?

SHEILA. Nothing.

JANE. Come on — you'll make me cry too. It's not the children?

SHEILA. No.

JANE. Colin?

SHEILA. No, no.

JANE. You haven't had a row?

SHEILA. No, no, no.

JANE. Sheila, we can't both stand here crying if I don't even know what we're crying about.

SHEILA. It's not anything. I don't know what it is. I'm sorry. I'm all right. I'm sorry, Jane. I'm fine. Everything's fine. It's just that . . .

JANE. Just what, love?

SHEILA. Just that . . .

JANE. I'll get us some coffee.

SHEILA. Jane, what should I do if he left me? How should I cope? I can't manage the children on my own! And what about the money? I can't help worrying about the money. What would I do? I can't go back to nursing — I have to collect Lizzie at three o'clock every afternoon. I just stand there in the kitchen after the children have gone off to school, and my thoughts go round and round — what should I do? — how should I manage? — and I can't get anything done, I don't know where to start, and I think, he can't come home again and find everything like this — I haven't even made the beds — and then I think, it's awful — I can't go running over the road again!

JANE. Sheila, take a deep breath.

SHEILA. I know you've got David's problems to worry about.
JANE. Sh.

SHEILA. You've got your own work to be getting on with.

JANE. Come on. Coffee. Still warm. Lots of sugar.

SHEILA. Oh, Jane . . . Oh, Jane . . . Whatever should I do without you?

JANE. Now, come on, love, don't start crying again. Just tell me. Has Colin said something about leaving you . . . ? There isn't anyone else, is there . . .? I think it's all inside your head, Sheila. You're shut away on your own all day so you start to imagine things.

SHEILA. I watch Colin in the evening sometimes. He looks round at the home we've made — that brown sideboard, those brown chairs — everything's brown! And I know what he's thinking.

JANE. Does he say what he's thinking?

SHEILA. No, he's very kind. He tries to be kind. But I know. And he's right! It *is* hopeless! *I'm* hopeless! I'm no use to him! He was lovely once. He was shining and dark and fearless and frightening. He didn't care if people hated him. Some people do hate him, you know. You don't hate him, do you, Jane . . . No, you're his only real friends. Oh, Jane! Isn't life cruel? He could have done anything. I've held him back somehow, I don't know how. I've held him down.

JANE. He loves you, Sheila.

SHEILA. I should have gone off and had the baby on my own. I could have coped then. I wasn't always like this, Jane! Because he's pulled me down, too! And then I think, perhaps I *want* him to go. Maybe that's why I keep thinking about it. Maybe that's why I'm so frightened of it.

JANE. Sheila, he loves you. I know he does.

SHEILA. Yes, well . . . Are *you* happy, Jane?

JANE. Oh, don't worry about me.

SHEILA. *I* think you're happy. Aren't you?

JANE. Heavens, I don't know. I'm not sure I've ever stopped to consider it.

SHEILA. You must be!

JANE. Must I?

SHEILA. Someone's got to be happy! It doesn't make sense otherwise. I just stand there in the kitchen sometimes and hold on to the table and think, Well, *Jane's* happy, at any rate.

JANE. You'll be happy again. I promise you.

SHEILA. *Are* you happy, Jane?

JANE. I've been very lucky. I realise that.

SHEILA. You won't say it, will you.

JANE. Sheila, love, it's not something you can *ask* anyone to say.

SHEILA. Nobody will ever say it. Sometimes I think it's because they're frightened to admit it. And then sometimes I think it's because no one is.

JANE. You know what, Sheila? We must get you out of that house during the day. You're going a bit mad over there. We must find you a job. Now, come on, I'll drive you down to the shops and you can get something amazing to give Colin for dinner . . . Where are my keys?

Exit SHEILA *centre.*

What else could I have done? The last thing I wanted was to get involved in Sheila's troubles. I just didn't have any choice! I couldn't have covered my ears! I didn't have much choice about the job I found her, either. I only knew one employer in those days.

Enter DAVID *left.*

DAVID. Work for *me*? Sheila?

JANE. Two or three hours a day, that's all.

DAVID. Doing what?

JANE. Doing all the things *I* do for you. Phone. Letters. Filing . . .

DAVID. So what would you be doing?

JANE. I could spend more time down at Basuto Road

DAVID. There's less and less you can do there now.

JANE. There's more and more! There's that woman who's being evicted. There's that couple I promised to take down to Ashford to see their son. They'll never go if I don't drive them.

DAVID. No good asking you to help me. You go off and help everyone else in the world instead.

JANE. I don't want to help anyone. I hate helping people. I want to study them. I'm an anthropologist, not a social worker.

DAVID. You'll have to learn to pass by on the other side occasionally.

JANE. You pass by on the other side and there's someone in that gutter.

DAVID. Jane, I'm really under pressure.

JANE. Yes, you need more help.

DAVID. Don't you want to help me?

JANE. Not forever. I've always said that. I'm not a secretary.

DAVID. *She's* not a secretary. She's a nurse.

JANE. You need a nurse.

DAVID. Oh, Jane. You know what I love? I love dropping in at the house in the middle of the day, and there you are.

JANE. I hear your step in the hall, and my heart leaps.

DAVID. When I worked at home — that was the best time. When we both worked in the same room all day, because there wasn't anywhere else. Or anyone else. That was the best time of all.

JANE. Things have to change, though, love.

DAVID. Do they?

JANE. That's your profession, isn't it, changing things?

DAVID. My absurd and foolish profession.

JANE. And when you think about poor Colin and Sheila . . .

DAVID. I suppose we still live in one room, by comparison.

JANE. Anyway, it'll only be for a couple of hours a day. You'll hardly see her.

DAVID. Do we have to?

JANE. That's what the children always ask.

DAVID. And do we?

JANE. Yes, we do.

DAVID. What the children always ask then is, Why do we have to?

JANE. And what we always answer is, Because you do.

 Enter SHEILA *right.*

DAVID. I'm only going to pay her what I'd pay anybody.

JANE. Oh, love, she'll be so thrilled.

Exit DAVID *left.*

SHEILA. Work for *David*? Me? Oh, Jane, no, no, no.

JANE. David would be so thrilled if you would.

SHEILA. Jane, I couldn't! I haven't touched a typewriter since I was at school. I'd get in such a muddle. I'd be terrified.

JANE. It's only for David.

SHEILA. I'm terrified of David!

JANE. Sheila!

SHEILA. I am! I don't think you understand what it's like for me. I used to be terrified of you.

JANE. I should have thought David and I were very tame after Colin.

SHEILA. Yes, then there's Colin. What would Colin say?

JANE. It wouldn't affect him. He'd be out at work. So would David, so would I. You could just sit here and have the house to yourself.

SHEILA. Oh, Jane, what's he going to say?

Enter COLIN *right.*

COLIN. How much is he paying you?

SHEILA. Paying me? Oh, we didn't . . . I didn't ask.

COLIN. He is proposing to pay you?

SHEILA. Oh, yes. I think so. I suppose so.

COLIN. Because your qualifications make you quite a catch for the job. You are a State Registered Nurse.

Exit JANE *left.*

SHEILA. So I'll say yes, shall I?

COLIN. As long as you're not doing it out of charity, my pet. As long as you're not just helping her to get out of the house because he's so beastly to her and she's going mad cooped up on her own all day.

SHEILA. Anyway, I'll try it for a week or two, shall I?

COLIN. I shall expect you to come home each day with a wonderful fund of David-and-Jane stories.

SHEILA. All right. If you think I should.

Exit SHEILA *right.*

Enter DAVID *centre.*

DAVID. I don't believe it! They couldn't do this to me! I think in this one small area of South London they have now finally managed to stamp out the practice of architecture!

SHEILA (*off*). Hoo-hoo!

DAVID. Come in.

Enter SHEILA *centre.*

Exit COLIN *right.*

There's no need to say hoo-hoo. This is where you work now.

SHEILA. Sorry. I thought you were talking to someone.

DAVID. I was. I was talking to myself. They've now scheduled part of the site as a public open space. I give up. I really do. Anyway, you're in charge. The house is yours. Jane's out. I'm just going . . . I'll have to go to eighteen stories . . . Sorry. Letters — on the machine. You know how to use one of these things? Articles, catalogues — I've marked them for filing. Coffee, food — you know where it is — help yourself. Oh, and would you pay the milkman?

Exit DAVID *centre.*

SHEILA. Now . . . Machine . . . Typing paper — where's the typing paper? I don't know where they keep the typing paper! No typing paper! No *typewriter* . . . ! (*Into phone.*) Hello . . . ? He's not here . . . I'm sort of his, I'm his secretary . . . Did he get a letter from you this morning? I don't know, I haven't seen the, I don't know what letters, I don't . . . Well, yes, I

don't know where he keeps his engagement diary. Could you
ring back when . . . ? Oh . . . (*Puts phone down.*) Oh God. Oh
God . . . ! (*Into phone.*) Hello . . . ? No, she's not here . . . No,
Daisy's at school. I'm David's sort of secretary. I mean
Mr Kitzinger's sort of . . . Sorry . . . ? You were just what . . . ?
Laughing, oh, yes . . . Yes, I'll tell him. Bernie who . . . ?

JANE (*off*). It's only me.

SHEILA. Sorry — I missed that . . . Cousins. Mr Cousins, right . . .

   Enter JANE *centre.*

JANE. Just looking in to see how you're getting on.

SHEILA. Mrs Kitzinger's here now if you want to . . . Oh, he's
   rung off.

JANE. Who was that?

SHEILA. That was Mr Cousins. Bernie Cousins. In Romford.

JANE. Oh, *Bernie*. His cousin . . . Come on, Sheila, love. Don't
   give way. You're doing fine. Didn't David tell you who might
   call? Oh, he *is* hopeless. He's no imagination about other
   people at all. Come on, I'll make you a list of everyone in his
   office — all the people who might call about the jobs in hand
   — all his relatives — all my relatives. You're going to be the
   best-organised secretary in the business . . . Here are the
   tissues, look . . . (*Into phone.*) Hello . . . ? I'll take this — you
   make us some coffee . . .

   Enter DAVID *left.*

DAVID. 'Thank you for your kind and thoughtful litter . . . I
   shall indeed be seeking to reduce the provision for barking —
   space . . . ' Still, she's quick to learn. She's got everyone's
   name straight already.

JANE. I expect you helped her a bit, didn't you?

DAVID. Not really. She also reminded me about my sister's
   wedding anniversary.

JANE. I wonder how she knew about that.

DAVID. No idea. Did she tell you?

JANE. Did she . . . what?

DAVID. I told her to tell you. You always forget to send my sister a card.

JANE and DAVID go off left.

SHEILA. It's funny. I never thought about Colin while I was over at the Kitzingers'. I didn't even think much about Matt or Lizzie. Isn't that awful? Not even when I found I could do everything after all. Or even when I found there wasn't all that much to do. Some mornings there was nothing at all. I'd creep out of the kitchen and look into the other rooms. I'd go right through the house, very softly, just opening all the doors, and looking into each room in turn. The children's bedrooms. The bathroom. I'd go into David and Jane's room and very gently slide open the drawers. Not touch anything. Just look. Crisp folded sheets; soft folded shirts; shiny folded slips. And up out of each drawer would come the fresh tidy smell of clean clothes. And the only sound would be the quiet ticking of the clock on the table by their bed. I know people look at me and think, what a misery she is! But I can be happy. I have been happy. I was happy then. I'd go downstairs and find ironing waiting to be done in the basket on top of the washing-machine, and I'd get out the iron and do it. There'd be a whole mountain of stuff waiting at home, and I'd be over at the Kitzingers', doing theirs! Isn't that awful? But there was more time there. Isn't that absurd? Then David would come flying in — or Jane — or both of them.

Enter DAVID centre.

DAVID. Sheila, love, it's early closing. Could you possibly run down to the cleaners and fetch my grey suit?

SHEILA. Suit, right. And Mr Harding rang. I pretended not to know what Mr Perry had told the Chairman of the Housing Committee. Was that right?

DAVID. Perfect. Brilliant. Tell Jane I've gone to County Hall.

Exit DAVID centre.

SHEILA. Don't forget you're seeing Mr Judd at four.

Enter JANE *left.*

JANE. Sheila, love, could you be an absolute angel? Could you stay on and give the children their tea?

SHEILA. I'd love to.

JANE. I've got to take Mrs Peck in for a big showdown with the Housing Officer.

SHEILA. David's gone to County Hall.

JANE. I can't find my car keys. Where do we keep the spare ones?

SHEILA. On top of the fridge. In the Oxo tin.

JANE. How did we ever survive without you?

Exit JANE *centre.*

SHEILA. And after I'd collected Lizzie at three I'd come back and give the children their tea. All five of them — Matt and Lizzie as well — all round the table together. And I wouldn't just get a packet of fish fingers out of the freezer. I'd make them toad in the hole, or I'd fry up all the leftovers into some great concoction of my own. And little Poppy's eyes would light up, and even Jake once said, 'That was great, Sheila.' And I'd sit there at the head of the table, being Mum, making them wash their hands and lay and clear, and I'd feel so pleased with myself. Isn't it . . . I don't know . . . pathetic, I suppose.

Enter COLIN *right.*

Then I'd have to go back and cook dinner for Colin.

COLIN. I must say, that steak and kidney pie was a triumph. Even with the crust beginning to char, the centre was still frozen. Steak and kidney Alaska.

SHEILA. I'm sorry — I couldn't get back any earlier. David came home from this meeting and he was in a great state about it. You know how he gets. Apparently the planning department are being absolutely rigid about daylight angles.

COLIN. What was that girl in Ibsen called?

SHEILA. What?

COLIN. The one who made the old boy climb up the scaffolding?

SHEILA. No, but it means he can't put a five storey slab along the railway.

COLIN. Inspired by her youth and vitality, he climbed to the top of his new high-rise.

SHEILA. No, but that means he can't meet the Yardstick with the point blocks at eighteen stories.

COLIN. And fell off and broke his neck.

SHEILA. I'm not going to give it up, you know. I'm not. You've taken everything else away from me. You've laughed me out of everything I ever had. But not this! I'll fight you about this! I will, Colin! I'll fight you! I'll fight you!

COLIN. Apricots.

SHEILA. What?

COLIN. I'll have a tin of apricots.

SHEILA. Pears or raspberries. There aren't any apricots.

COLIN *and* SHEILA *go off right.*

Enter DAVID *centre.*

DAVID. Right. Site plan. Sketch pad. Pencils . . . Peace. Quiet . . . Let architecture commence. Forty whole minutes — thirty-five whole minutes — of actual architecture . . . Now, where are we? Six eighteen-storey blocks . . . Can't go there — cable. Can't go there . . . overshadowing. Can't go there, because then the vehicular access has to go *there*, and that's within fifty metres of the junction. Start again. Five twenty-four storey blocks . . . Not losing any units . . . ? Gaining forty-eight units. Right. Six extra stories, so they'll have to go back how far? Where are the daylight protractors . . . ? Hold on. Now I'm overshadowing the low-rise . . . ! Oh, it's such a battle! I can't fight shut up in this little kitchen . . . ! Sheila!

Enter SHEILA *left.*

SHEILA. Sorry.

DAVID. I thought you'd gone home.

SHEILA. I was upstairs.

DAVID. Talking to myself, was I?

SHEILA. It's lovely seeing you work.

DAVID. I can't work.

SHEILA. I won't disturb you. I've got to go out and get Lizzie, you see.

DAVID. I couldn't work in the office. I can't work here . . . I think I'll walk round the block . . . Lizzie?

SHEILA. It's three o'clock. I've got to fetch her from school.

Exit SHEILA *centre.*

DAVID. Hold on. I'll come with you. Anything's better than working.

Exit DAVID *centre.*

Enter SHEILA *right.*

SHEILA. That's why we first went for a walk together — to fetch Lizzie. Funny, when you think about it. After that we went to the park two or three times. Once or twice we went as far as the woods. Sometimes he'd talk about Basuto Road, or one of his other schemes. Sometimes he'd just mooch along in silence, with his hands in his pockets and his shoulders hunched up, scuffing his feet through the piles of fallen leaves like a boy coming home from school.

Enter COLIN *left.*

Once in the woods a leaf came spinning slowly down from the bare branches right in front of me. I've chased after falling leaves with the children sometimes; I can never catch them. But this one — I just opened my hand, and it settled like a bird. A year's happiness.

Exit SHEILA *right.*

JANE (*off*). Hello! It's only me!

Enter JANE *centre.*

I've been sitting in that damned hospital with the Swain boy for nearly two hours . . . Colin! I thought you were Sheila!

COLIN. I found some fish fingers in the fridge. I gave the children those. They're upstairs watching television.

JANE. Funny to see you sitting at the kitchen table again. You haven't been for ages.

COLIN. No.

JANE. How long have you been here?

COLIN. Most of the afternoon.

JANE. Where's Sheila?

COLIN. Where indeed? The school rang at half-past three to say that Lizzie was still standing outside the gates.

JANE. I'm sorry, Colin. I know what you feel about Sheila working here.

COLIN. Do you?

JANE. Have you asked David where she is?

COLIN. No.

JANE. Isn't he here?

COLIN. No.

JANE. I'll ring the office.

COLIN. The office say he's here.

JANE. His stuff's here.

COLIN. So I observe.

JANE. I expect they've gone for a walk, then.

COLIN. Gone for a walk?

JANE. David likes to wander round the neighbourhood when he's brooding about a scheme. I think Sheila sometimes tags on.

COLIN. Taking dictation as they go?

JANE. I don't suppose David says very much. He just likes to have someone there.

COLIN. So they're walking about the neighbourhood in silence. For three hours. In the rain.

JANE. Taken shelter. Gone to the pictures. *I* don't know.

COLIN. You know she's in love with him?

JANE. Colin. Dear Colin . . .

COLIN. Not news to you, I'm sure.

JANE. News. That's right. That's just what it is — news. David says he doesn't know how you became a journalist. I know. Because that's your trade. You look as if you don't care what anyone thinks, but you do, you care a lot, you want us all to be surprised and shocked, you want to get a reaction.

COLIN. Got a reaction this time, anyway.

JANE. Yes. I'm sorry. But it makes me angry, Colin, when you talk like that. David wants everyone to love him . . .

COLIN. And apparently everyone does.

JANE. . . . And you want everyone to hate you. Or perhaps you don't. Perhaps you want to test them. You want them to love you in spite of being hateful.

COLIN. Don't worry, Jane. I don't suppose he's in love with her.

JANE. If you want to know the truth, she's frightened of him.

COLIN. Of course. She's frightened of you, too.

JANE. She used to be.

COLIN. She used to be in love with you.

JANE. You are a fool, you know, Colin. You only get one life. You can't go back and say, Please, Miss, I've spoilt this one, can I have another?

COLIN. A twinge of jealousy there, I thought. Just for an instant. Odd how reflexive it is. I'm sure you weren't in love with her.

JANE. You always want to pull everyone down. You pull her down. That's what makes her so insecure.

COLIN. Why, what did she say to you?

JANE. Nothing. She doesn't need to say anything.

COLIN. Did she say, 'Jane, I think he's going to leave me'? Did she . . . ? I see she did.

JANE. *Are* you going to leave her?

COLIN. Jane, I have a quiet laugh sometimes when I think about you going down there to Basutoland and helping people. I can't imagine what you make of the Basutos. You don't seem to understand the plain, everyday folk across the street. You haven't grasped one basic general principle — that other people's lives are at least as complicated as your own.

JANE. You haven't answered my question.

COLIN. I am answering it. Sheila and I have been through all this business before, you see. The falling in love. The running across the road. The 'Help me, help me.' The 'I'm going mad.' The 'Oh God, he's going to leave me.' Last time it was a couple of music teachers. This is when we were living in that flat, before you kindly found us the house. She started with Mrs. Got Mrs driving her everywhere, giving her meals, looking after the baby. Then she announced that she wanted to take up singing. Mrs taught singing. Give her an interest, take her out of herself. So for six months she had singing lessons. Practised, too. An hour a day, without fail. Have you heard Sheila singing . . . ? Then she said she wanted to learn the oboe. Mr taught the oboe. And she would have done it, too, Jane! She would have practised the oboe!

JANE. Poor Sheila.

COLIN. She's tone-deaf.

JANE. So you stopped her?

COLIN. I had a word with Mrs. Life goes round like a wheel, Jane. What we've done once we do again. Round and round. We don't change. We never escape.

JANE. She may not be good at music, but she's good at helping David and me. So that's a change from last time.

COLIN. Good, is she? What, efficient? Well-organised?

JANE. I don't know what we'd do without her.

COLIN. I can believe that, as a matter of fact. How absurd things are.

JANE. I hope she'll go on working here. So that's another change from last time. And *are* you going to leave her?

COLIN. She used to be frightened of me once, of course. She used to be in love with me. I've got to have one stick left in the rack.

JANE. That you?

DAVID (*off*). Only me.

Enter DAVID and SHEILA centre.

DAVID. Only us . . . Colin!

SHEILA. What are you doing here?

DAVID. We got caught in the rush-hour.

SHEILA. Where are the children? *Where's Lizzie?*

COLIN. Standing outside the school, I presume.

JANE. She's upstairs, watching television. They're both upstairs.

DAVID. We got caught in the rain.

SHEILA. Didn't they get my message?

DAVID. So we found a teashop and had four lots of tea.

SHEILA. I rang the school! I told them to tell Lizzie to come home with Matt! Upstairs . . . ?

Exit SHEILA left.

DAVID. Then we got caught in the rush-hour . . . You're not going? Stay for supper. We haven't seen you for months . . .

Exit COLIN centre.

Have a drink . . . I'll open some wine . . .

Exit DAVID centre.

Enter SHEILA right.

SHEILA. Early in the new year, that was. Cold. Wet. A terrible start to a terrible year. Why do I say that? Amazing things happened that year! I wouldn't go through that year again . . . Lizzie never got my message for one very simple reason. I never sent it. I was lying. I'd forgotten all about her. Isn't that

awful? I mean truly awful . . . As soon as I came into the
kitchen and saw Colin and Jane sitting at the table like that I
knew what he'd been telling her. And yes, I was in love with
David. And no, I was never in love with the oboe-teacher, nor
with the oboe-teacher's wife. But it's true that I was in love
with David. And that it was absurd, now the words had been
said, now the thought had been thought. Absurd and painful
and humiliating. Because David certainly wasn't in love with
me. Why should he have been? No one has ever been in love
with me, except Colin, for three months by that lake in
Switzerland and one month back in London afterwards. I
don't really know what David thought about me. I think he
quite liked me being round the house. I was better than no
one. That's how I was the first to hear about his idea for
Basuto Road.

JANE. Colin was right, of course, She *was* a bit in love with
David. Poor Sheila. Poor silly Sheila. I don't think David even
realised. Or perhaps he did know.

Enter DAVID *centre.*

I look at him from so much further off these days. I see all
kinds of things I didn't see then. Perhaps he did know. He
certainly liked having someone around to talk to about his
work. He told her some things before he told me. He told
her about his big idea. How could he have been such a fool?

Exit JANE *left.*

DAVID. Skyscrapers, Sheila. That's the answer. That's the *only*
answer. I've tried every other solution, and it doesn't work.
I'm going to build 150 low-rise walk-ups for families with
young children, and then 600 units for all the rest in twin
skyscrapers. What do you think? I don't mean eleven stories,
or eighteen, or twenty-four. I mean fifty stories. The highest
residential buildings in Europe. What do you think? There'll
be endless problems, there'll be endless objections, but I'm
going to do it, Sheila. Because in the end it's not art —
it's mathematics. A simple equation. You collect up the terms,
you get rid of the brackets and there at the bottom of the page

on the righthand side is the answer; 150 low-rise walk-ups and two socking great skyscrapers. I feel dizzy just thinking about them. When the clouds are low they'll be *above* the clouds. When it's clear you'll be able to see the whole length of the North Downs, from Hampshire into Kent. They'll be a hazard to aircraft, Sheila! So what do you think? Half of South London's going to be in their rain-shadow! They'll change the whole climate! I'm joking, Sheila, I'm joking. Do you realise you'll be able to stand on the Chilterns and see my skyscrapers over the top of Hampstead Heath! Won't you? Where's the map? In the office. Back at six.

Exit DAVID *centre.*

Enter COLIN *right.*

COLIN. Sheila, my love, I've poured you a small glass of the whisky you gave me for Christmas. We're not dead yet, Sheila. We can still enjoy ourselves from time to time. We can still have a laugh together.

SHEILA. But why is it so funny, if it's the only way he can do it?

COLIN. To all low-flying aircraft in the vicinity of SE15.

SHEILA. But if it's going to give people a good view . . .

COLIN. To a more abundant rainfall on the plains of Basutoland.

SHEILA. I suppose it is a bit funny, after everything he's said.

COLIN. To bed, then, my love. And to David, who does what he can to bring the semi-detached a little closer together.

COLIN *and* SHEILA *go off right.*

Enter JANE *centre.*

JANE. It's only the evening paper. I thought you'd better see it, though.

Enter DAVID *centre.*

Where did they get the story? That's what I don't understand.

DAVID. 'Residents in South-east London spoke out today against plans to build New York-style skyscrapers as part of a local council redevelopment scheme . . . ' Plans? What plans? I haven't even done the outline proposals yet! I haven't set pen to paper! 'The two skyscrapers would be the highest residential buildings in Europe . . . ' I haven't told anyone apart from you! ' "No one has consulted us," said old-age pensioner Mr William Pavey . . . ' Of course no one's consulted them! There's nothing to consult them about yet! 'There are fears that they could be a hazard to aircraft, and they could even affect South London's weather . . .' Oh my God.

JANE. You told Sheila?

DAVID. I told Sheila.

JANE. She'll have to go, David.

DAVID. She can't possibly have picked up the phone and rung the newspapers!

JANE. No, it would have been Colin who told the newspapers.

DAVID. What, picked up the phone . . . ?

JANE. Talked to someone somewhere. It's his profession! And then he's jealous of you. He's always been jealous of you.

SHEILA (off). Hoo-hoo!

JANE. And she colludes with him. She buys him off by feeding him amusing little titbits about you and me. She sells us to him! I know how they work, those two!

SHEILA. Hoo-hoo!

JANE. She'll destroy you, David. She'll destroy us both. You'll have to tell her. Now! While the paper's still in your hand!

Enter SHEILA *centre.*

SHEILA. It's me . . . Sorry . . . I've got the children — we've got cases and bags . . . Oh, Jane! I've left him!

JANE. Bring the children in, then, Sheila.

DAVID. I'll get the bags.

SHEILA *and* DAVID *go off centre.*

JANE. They looked like two little refugees. All white faces and wide eyes. They cheered up, though. They watched television, they played pelmanism all over the floor with Poppy, and Poppy let them win. Then they drank their cocoa and went to bed as if they'd always lived in our house. Which of course they pretty much had. Sheila was a rather more difficult case. She kept saying she couldn't possibly stay, so could we drive her to a hotel. She made us lock the front door and promise not to let Colin in. She couldn't eat. Then after we'd washed up and put everything away she suddenly felt weak and dizzy with hunger. She cried a bit. She also laughed a bit.

Enter SHEILA *centre.*

She kept saying it seemed so normal sitting at our kitchen table. Which of course it was. And she couldn't stop saying how awful she felt about letting David down.

Enter DAVID *centre.*

SHEILA. The phone went, and as soon as he said he was from the newspapers I knew what had happened. It was like one of those dreams where you just suddenly know this awful thing has gone wrong. He asked to speak to you — I said you were out all afternoon. So he said, could I help him because they'd heard this report that you were designing two skyscrapers in the path of aircraft coming into London Airport.

DAVID. It's not important, Sheila. It won't make any difference. All my fault for saying anything.

SHEILA. Well, I panicked. I just put the phone down. It rang again. I picked it up and it was the same man, so I just put it down again without saying anything. I suppose that must have made it seem worse. But I couldn't think what to do. All I could think was, This is Colin! Colin did this to me!

DAVID. Skyscrapers. That was a joke, too, calling them skyscrapers.

SHEILA. When he came in last night I didn't say anything. But I could see from the way he looked at me. He knew I'd found out. I felt as if a mouthful of scalding coffee was going down my throat. I've been sitting here all day today thinking about it. I won't let him take this away from me! I won't! I won't! So then I went back to get his dinner, and I took the remains of yesterday's stew out of the fridge, and I saw him sitting there at the table, looking at me, and I could smell the stew, and it was cold and brown, all cold and brown, and I suppose I threw it at him, because I was shaking and sobbing and there was this foul brown stuff all over everything.

JANE. She went to bed eventually.

DAVID. You've got everything you need? Anything you want, Sheila, just tell us.

Exit SHEILA *left.*

JANE. David and I stayed up for another hour or more, talking about it. Or not talking about it. We'd started to feel uneasy about Colin by this time.

DAVID. We should have given him a ring and told him they were all right.

JANE. It's after midnight now.

DAVID. I suppose he's going to think this is all our doing.

JANE. Well, it isn't.

DAVID. Isn't it?

JANE. David, we did everything we could to help them. We did. Both of us. We truly and sincerely did.

DAVID. Yes. If we *hadn't* tried to help them they'd still be together. Perhaps I should go round. What do you think?

JANE. We rang him in the morning. There was no reply. We rang him in the evening. We rang him next day, and the next. Then his office rang us; he hadn't been in all week. He'd vanished! So in the end I went to look for him.

Enter SHEILA *left.*

I didn't say anything to Sheila. I just quietly took their spare key out of the tin on the refrigerator, and went across the road. It was a kind of brown twilight inside their house. The curtains were still drawn; they'd been drawn all week. There were children's toys underfoot, and overturned cardboard boxes. I opened the living-room door, and there was the life they'd shared, abandoned at one muddled arbitrary moment in time. Clothes waiting to be mended; more toys; open newspapers; two unwashed nursery mugs. Everything gone cold and still . . . I opened the kitchen door . . . I can feel even now that sudden wave of cold spreading up from my stomach, shrinking the skin on my face, then the scalp over my head. Because there it was — the unmistakeable stench of putrefying flesh . . . Funny, when I look back on it. I'd worked out what it was by the time I managed to see anything. It was just like Sheila had said — foul and brown and everywhere. But it *was* me who found him in the end. In a derelict house in Frances Road, in the middle of David's redevelopment area. The council had just started to move people out. I saw this front door standing ajar, and I pushed it open. I don't know why. I suppose I thought there might be something bad inside. And there he was.

Enter COLIN *centre.*

COLIN. Come in. Welcome to the battlefront.

Curtain.

ACT TWO

The same.

DAVID

DAVID. Basuto Road. Those sour stale words. You look up from your work, and there they are along the files. Or you're going down some other path in your mind altogether — and suddenly they're coming towards you. The same shabby sad-eyed pair. And before you know what you're doing you've turned and crossed the street to avoid them. Why? What could they say that hasn't been said?

Enter JANE *and* SHEILA *centre.*

SHEILA. In Basuto Road?

JANE. In Frances Road, to be precise.

DAVID. After all, the Basuto Road scheme included our very successful redevelopment of Colin and Sheila. We should have had awards for our work on them, we should have had bronze plaques to put up.

SHEILA. 'Welcome to the battlefront'? What battlefront?

JANE. He's going to stop the scheme.

DAVID. I mean that. Jane used to say that when she opened the front door in Frances Road she didn't recognise him for a moment. He seemed taller. His eyes were fully open. He was alive. And I say, good for him.

SHEILA. And he's|*living* there? He's got himself a flat on David's site?

JANE. It's a squat.

SHEILA. A *squat*?

JANE. The council have started clearing the houses. As the tenants move out so the squatters move in.

DAVID. And I wouldn't have recognised Sheila when she heard the news. All of a sudden she was — well, yes, she was *alive*. And I say, good for her.

SHEILA. What sort of squatters?

JANE. I don't know. Young people.

SHEILA. Colin hates young people.

JANE. Rather tired old young people, so far as I could see.

SHEILA. He hates old people. He hates everyone.

JANE. They've got electricity and water, and one or two bits of furniture. It's not too bad.

SHEILA. I don't care if it is too bad. I hope it's terrible. I hope he's infested with lice.

DAVID. No, if we still had offices I'd put up photographs of Colin and Sheila in reception. The sort that architectural photographers take through ultra-violet filters. Dreamlike white sunlit shapes towering against black skies full of summer clouds. Perhaps Sheila would be the low-rise part of the development, the family walk-ups. But Colin . . . Colin would be towering.

SHEILA. He's gone mad! What does he think he's doing?

JANE. Organising a campaign against the scheme.

SHEILA. Organising a campaign? How can he organise a campaign? He can't even organise his own children!

JANE. Well, he's organised all this lot out of their sleeping bags.

SHEILA. He's never lifted a finger for them!

JANE. He's got them all painting posters.

SHEILA. He can't organise himself!

JANE. They were all smoking animatedly.

DAVID. A twilight area. That's what Colin and Sheila were when we started work on them. They were like Basuto Road — full of hidden sewers and geological faults. We got them stood up in the sunshine. They fell down again later, of course, the way some buildings of the period did. But that wasn't the design —

that was defective materials. No, seriously, we helped them, we did them some good. I haven't done all that much good in this world, it seems. But I did give Colin and Sheila a purpose in life. In fact I gave them two. I gave them one each.

SHEILA. You don't know what he's like! He's hopeless! He can't even do his job properly! They'll be ringing up again — I know they will! He'll be sacked! He's been sacked before!

JANE. He won't be this time, Sheila. He's resigned.

SHEILA. I knew it! I knew he would, sooner or later! What are we going to live on? Has he forgotten he's got a family to support?

DAVID. Sheila, love, don't worry, don't get upset. You can always rely on us. You know that.

SHEILA. You don't understand what he's like! He comes here and smiles and you think he's someone like you. But he's not. He's evil. All he can do is to pull down and destroy. He hates you. You don't understand what that is, someone hating you. He's going to pull you down and destroy your scheme. I know he is! He's destroyed me, and now he's going to destroy you. I'm nothing. I don't count in his eyes. But he's used me to get at you. That's what I shall never forgive myself.

SHEILA *and* JANE *go off left.*

DAVID. She kept coming back to that all evening. That and the money. That and the money and how she couldn't go on staying with us now she'd let us down like this and how she couldn't afford to live anywhere now there was no money. We didn't get her to bed until one o'clock. Then we sat up talking to each other. It was the only time we were ever alone together.

Enter JANE *left.*

JANE. She's still in a great state.

DAVID. Was that all right, saying she could work full time? I thought it might make her worry less about the money.

JANE. Funny, though, isn't it. You're supporting Colin's family so that he's free to destroy your livelihood.

DAVID. Not much he can do, really.

JANE. Isn't there?

DAVID. Well, is there? I don't think the Housing Committee's going to pay much attention to some wretched squatter. Is he all right down there?

JANE. Having the time of his life, so far as I could see.

DAVID. Is there anything we can do for him, do you think?

JANE. You mean, *help* him?

DAVID. We're helping Sheila. We don't want to take sides.

JANE. David, sides have been taken! Colin's taken them! Whatever side we're on, he's on the opposite one!

DAVID. He's still a friend.

JANE. No, he's not — he's an enemy!

DAVID. Look, he may have decided he hates us — I don't know — but we don't have to hate him back.

JANE. Sheila's right — you don't understand what it is, being hated. You think everyone else in the world is like yourself . . . I suppose that's what Colin said about me.

DAVID. Be no good if I went to see him? What do you think?

JANE. It's not a virtue, David. It's a sort of moral blindness.

DAVID. Or if *you* went back?

JANE. I'm not going anywhere near him. I feel the same as Sheila. I hope he starves. I hope he's eaten by rats.

Exit JANE *left.*

DAVID. They all took it so personally! Even Jane. The blood rose to her cheeks, her eyes sparkled. The Basuto Wars had started. My wars, of course, but I still felt like a bemused neutral observer. I didn't understand Colin's feelings. But then I'd never understood anything about him, from the first moment I'd met him. I didn't think he was driven by jealousy, or bitterness that we'd broken up his marriage. I thought really he was against the scheme because he was against the scheme. Why shouldn't he be against it? Why shouldn't he try and stop it? It's a free country, and anyway there was nothing he could do. That's how it seemed to me. That's how it seemed to me then. I suppose. Where had we got to by that stage? I finished the outline proposals in July. That must have been April. Well, early days.

Exit DAVID *left.*

Enter COLIN *right.*

COLIN. May. The beginning of May. I'd wake soon after five each morning, when it started to get light, because of course there were no curtains at the window. I'd feel the slippery nylon of the sleeping-bag around me, and the narrow canvas of the camp-bed, and I'd remember where I was. I'd look round the room. One suitcase of clean clothes; a single wooden chair; a few books on the shelf in the corner. Nothing else. Bare boards, bare walls. And I'd feel a lightness, a physical lightness. I'd laugh sometimes for sheer physical pleasure. Though there were times when I wept. That was for the children. For their endless colds and their nagging coughs, for their desolate vomitings and helpless retchings, for the feel of them sitting in my lap wrapped in eiderdowns, with hot muddled aching heads leaning against my chest. Always ill. But if you're a nurse, like Sheila, someone has to be a patient. And that would make me think of David, and I'd laugh again. Sooner or later he'd be coming to see me, full of concern. Concerned about Sheila, of course — even more concerned about me. Perhaps just a little concerned about his scheme. He'd look all hurt and puzzled. He'd want to know why I'd done it. What could I say? Public spirit? Jealousy? Pique? I didn't know why I'd done it! Perhaps just to see the look on his face when he came to ask me. But I was wrong about that.

Enter JANE *right.*

JANE. Your mail.

COLIN. Jane.

JANE. It's all right. I'm not staying.

COLIN. I thought it would be David.

JANE. I was passing the door.

COLIN. Does David know you're here?

JANE. No.

COLIN. A clandestine meeting.

JANE. Why did you do it, Colin?

COLIN. Why did I do it? I should have guessed it would be you. David looks concerned; you're the one who has to run around and *be* concerned.

JANE. Why did you marry her?

COLIN. Why did I *marry* her?

JANE. It was a cruel thing to do.

COLIN. Leaflets?

JANE. What?

COLIN. Do you want to fold some?

JANE. You won't stop it. You know that. You won't have any effect at all.

COLIN. How are the children?

JANE. *Your* children?

COLIN. Yes, my children.

JANE. All right.

COLIN. How are *your* children, then? How's Sheila? How's David?

JANE. Sheila says you can see the children on Saturday.

COLIN. Perhaps you could drive them over?

JANE. That's not a serious suggestion. I hope.

COLIN. I've no car, Jane. I'm out of work. I'm homeless. I'm one of your Basutos now!

JANE. A squat. So this is what you want, is it, Colin?

COLIN. What do you think I've been living in for the last ten years? Actually it reminds me of school. Bare boards and cold water and smelly feet.

JANE. And a lot of admiring fourth-formers.

COLIN. Yes, and something serious to do.

JANE. Folding leaflets?

COLIN. Another house to beat for the house shield. Someone to defeat. And you want to know why I married Sheila? Out of kindness, Jane. Out of the kindness of my heart. My one crime.

JANE. Colin, can I tell you something I've never told you before? Something I've never said to anyone, ever.

COLIN. A secret.

JANE. Yes, a secret.

COLIN. This is why you've come to see me, is it?

JANE. Possibly.

COLIN. You're in love with me.

JANE. More secret than that. I don't like you.

COLIN. Oh, Jane.

JANE. I never have liked you.

COLIN. Jane, Jane, Jane.

JANE. So now I've said it.

COLIN. After twenty years. Does David know?

JANE. He does now. And what a stupid farce it was, pretending I did like you! Because now you don't even like David! You hate him!

COLIN. I like you, Jane.

JANE. No, you don't.

COLIN. Oh, yes. I like you because I see in you a little of the blackness I have in me. That's why you don't like me. Because you know I can see it.

JANE. Yes. Well.

COLIN. Anyway, you have more hot soup to distribute. I'll tell you another secret, though, Jane. You're the expert on helping the Basutos, and you know the scheme's not going to help them. You loathe it as much as I do. You won't tell David that, of course. Don't worry — I won't tell him. That really *is* a secret . . . Or do you mean it was even a secret from yourself?

JANE. Saturday — I'll leave the children at the door.

Exit JANE *right.*

Enter DAVID *and* SHEILA *centre.*

DAVID. Where's Jane?

SHEILA. She's gone to see some people in Wandsworth.

DAVID. I still haven't finished the elevations.

SHEILA. I'll wait dinner for her, shall I? It's only stew.

DAVID. They've got to be at the Borough Architect's office in the morning.

SHEILA. I'll take them in.

DAVID. I'm not going to get to bed at all. Wandsworth?

SHEILA. SW something.

DAVID. There. What do you think?

SHEILA. I think it's brilliant, David.

DAVID. How about the new walkways?

SHEILA. They're brilliant. Everything. It's all, I don't know, absolutely . . . well . . .

DAVID. Brilliant, yes, but don't cry, Sheila. It's not that brilliant. Just get the dinner on the table. I'll eat and work at the same time. You know what it's missing, though, Sheila . . . ? Handkerchief . . . One small element in the design? People. No people! Where are the people? Ah, whole packet of people. Very nice class of tenant you get from Letraset. Well-dressed. Don't write on the walls. Don't stuff old mattresses down the rubbish-chutes.

JANE (*off*). Only me.

DAVID. And they don't over-eat. Nothing like fat people for throwing the architecture out of scale.

Enter JANE *centre.*

So what do you think?

JANE. Very good . . . I meant to say use up the cold chicken.

SHEILA. I've made sandwiches with it for the children's lunch.

DAVID. Sheila thinks it's brilliant.

JANE. Spot of grease. You shouldn't work in the kitchen.

DAVID. I'll put someone over it. Actually, you could have fat people standing at the bottom of these things and no one'd ever notice. No one'd ever *see* them . . . What?

JANE. Nothing. Just looking.

DAVID. Has he managed to stir up the Basutos yet?

JANE. I've been over in Wandsworth.

DAVID. Don't worry — it can't possibly affect us. This'll be in front of the Housing Committee tomorrow. With any luck I'll have the full scheme design in front of the council next winter — and that's the first the Basutos will know about it. Suddenly there'll be a huge scale model on display at the Town Hall, with little cars on the roads and lots of trees made out of green loofah . . . What?

JANE. Nothing. Just thinking.

DAVID. I'm telling Sheila. You don't have to listen.

JANE. You're very up today.

DAVID. Up all day. Up all night.

JANE. Up all month.

DAVID. Anyway, Sheila, by the time we get to scheme design it'll be too late, because (a) everyone loves a scale model, and (b) no one's going to notice it's there, and (c) the council will have spent a hundred thousand pounds, and no one's going to persuade them they've spent it all for nothing . . . Jane, don't listen if you don't like it! Don't look! Go and call the children!

JANE. They offered me a job.

DAVID. Who offered you a job?

JANE. These people I've been talking to.

DAVID. What people?

JANE. These people in Wandsworth. It's a kind of housing trust.

DAVID. You've stopped working for me altogether?

JANE. I haven't decided whether to take the job yet.

DAVID. I mean, if it's housing you're interested in, that's what I'm doing — housing. That's what this trust does, is it? It builds houses?

JANE. It preserves houses. It rehabilitates them, so they don't have to be pulled down.

SHEILA. I'll call the children, shall I?

JANE. David, I can't always think the same as you about everything.

DAVID. No. Think what you like. Do what you like. Free country.

SHEILA. I'll get the children.

JANE. *I'll* get them.

   Exit JANE *left.*

DAVID. Put another happy little family group on the concourse here, look. Husband walking left, wife walking right.

COLIN. Only one thing I learnt at school turned out to be much use in life, and that was writing Greek hexameters. If you can get some aspect of human destiny into five dactyls and a spondee then you can get the headline on a magazine article into thirty points across two. You can also get a programme of political action on to a piece of cardboard small enough to be held up and waved about in the air. I took real pleasure in the work. 'Don't scrape the skies — just sweep the streets.' A whole philosophy of government in eight syllables!

DAVID. Amendments. Re-drawings.

SHEILA. Night night.

DAVID. Off to bed?

SHEILA. It's nearly twelve. Don't get up.

   Exit SHEILA *centre.*

DAVID. Some of the more half-baked members of the Housing Committee thought people might get dizzy if they looked over a balcony with a 450-foot drop underneath it. Been got at by someone, I suppose. Well, why shouldn't he? Free country.

COLIN. We also wrote on lavatory walls. The Town Hall lavatory walls. 'Living in the sky is strictly for the birds.' 'Spread a little sogginess — give a cloud a home.' These were the high-rise slogans, designed to accommodate disaffected social workers. Most of the campaign was rather more low-rise. 'Hands off our homes!' 'Save our streets!' Some of it was lower still. 'Town Hall *Sieg Heil*.' 'Skyscrapers = SS.' We had all kinds of supporters by this time. Not all of them had heads.

DAVID. But the sheer labour of it! This is when the problems with the foundations began to emerge. They'd have to be bigger — we'd have to divert the Generating Board's megavolt cable after all. I'd sit hunched over the drawing-board late into the night, struggling with all the problems, and I couldn't help laughing sometimes. There were people out there in the night somewhere struggling to make the problems harder!

COLIN. But the sheer pleasure of it! We sprayed walls — we shouted council meetings down. We didn't have to worry about being fair or truthful or tidy. That was the great liberation. Fairness and tidiness and truth are for people who've got what they want already. We had nothing; we could do anything.

DAVID. I felt no resentment for Colin, though. Nothing but sadness. It was like seeing someone destroy himself with drink. Deliberately blunting his own intelligence and feeling. Deliberately dissolving his life in waste and futility.

COLIN. I sometimes thought about David, hunched over his drawing-board far into the night, and I couldn't help laughing. He was using up his life designing a scheme that was never going to be built. That everyone but him knew was never going to be built. That he knew was never going to be built.

DAVID. I could have done with some help from Jane. No, that was unfair. No reason why she should have to work for me if she didn't want to. Better for her to have her own job. And if she was going to start preserving things, better for her to be preserving them over in Wandsworth.

Exit DAVID *left.*

COLIN. I did one fair and tidy thing, though. I suggested the name of an excellent field-worker to our friends in Wandsworth. I gave Jane her start in life, at any rate.

Exit COLIN *right.*

Enter JANE *centre.*

JANE. David not back?

Enter SHEILA *left.*

SHEILA. He's over the road. He's measuring the kitchen. Oh, Jane, I do feel awful about him working on my house when he's so busy already.

JANE. If you're busy you can always do more. It's having too little to do that makes you feel like doing less. Are they washed?

SHEILA. I'm going to fold them.

JANE. I'll help you. Quite funny, really, David doing a rehab. Rehabilitating your house. Why doesn't he pull it down and start again? Why didn't we pull this one down?

SHEILA. It is different, though, isn't it, Jane?

JANE. Is it?

SHEILA. Jane, there are lots of people who haven't got homes at all. We've got to build them *something*. I know you worry about it, Jane, but it's got to be done. You know it has.

JANE. It's like a bonfire, isn't it. Faith, I mean. It flares up here — it dies down there. You never know where or when.

SHEILA. Jane, perhaps I shouldn't say this, but I see you and David every day and I know you don't really agree with what he's doing, and I can't help worrying about it. Because I know what you think. You think we ought to ask people more what they actually want. But, Jane, it's no good asking people what they want, because they don't know what they want until they've got it. No one asked them if they wanted Basuto Road the way it is now. Probably in the first place they didn't! It may have been years before they realised they wanted it like that! People aren't all as clever as you, Jane! *I'm* not! I didn't want to work for David. You made me. And you were right, and I'll be grateful until the day I die!

JANE. This is what David's been telling you?

SHEILA. David doesn't know what people want, but I do, because I know what *I* want. I don't want David to ask me what colour my kitchen should be. I want him to tell me. I don't want him to ask me whether I want the house redesigned. I just want him to do it. And when I say I feel awful about it and he shouldn't be doing it I don't want him *not* to do it! That's what people are like, Jane! That's what most people are like. Colin doesn't know what he wants! I know you feel sorry for him and you take his part — but he doesn't know what he wants any more than I do! Or he didn't, until he saw somebody else who did, and then he knew he wanted to stop it and smash it. Because it's all part of the same old battle between good and evil, the same old war between light and dark. I know you won't like my saying that. But it is, Jane, and you mustn't let him win you over!

JANE. I'll put these things in the airing cupboard.

SHEILA. He's only doing it to get at David. He's broken up our marriage. Don't let him break up yours as well.

Exit JANE *left.*

Jane . . .

Exit SHEILA *left.*

Enter COLIN *right.*

COLIN. And then one morning you wake up, and it's November, and it's still dark at eight o'clock, and there's nothing in the room but a broken wooden chair, and a few old clothes, and a shelf of unread books, and there's nothing to get up for but the same old struggles and the same old quarrels, and you think, why bother? Who cares what they do to a few grey and grimy houses? What does it matter what happens to a few grey and grubby people? If he wants to build a monument to himself, why shouldn't he?

Enter JANE *right*.

JANE. I've brought your winter overcoat. I'm not staying. I'm not talking. Scarves and pullovers and things in here . . . You look terrible. Are you all right?

COLIN. Fine.

JANE. You're not ill, are you?

COLIN. No.

JANE. What's the matter, then?

COLIN. Loss of appetite. How's David? Is he still enjoying his food?

JANE. I'm not talking about David.

COLIN. I know what he thinks. He thinks he's life and I'm death. But I'm not the one who's sealing the earth with concrete. I'm not the one who's putting up gigantic monumental tombstones.

JANE. It's freezing here. Haven't you got a heater?

COLIN. Or maybe I am death. But how meaningless life would be, if death weren't there to stop it.

JANE. You might feel better if you had a bit more light in here.

COLIN. He's the light, and I'm the dark.

JANE. I suppose I should say thank you for my job. I've only just found out.

COLIN. You and I, Jane. We're both the dark. But then you look up on a clear night and you'll see there's only a dusting of light in all creation. It's a dark universe!

JANE. I'll bring the children on Saturday.

Exit JANE *right*.

Enter DAVID *centre*.

DAVID. Holes. Black holes. Every time I talk to the structural engineers the foundations get bigger! The whole scheme's getting sucked down into these two yawning black holes!

Enter SHEILA *left*.

SHEILA. Or do you just want to be left in peace?

DAVID. Jane not back?

SHEILA. She said she'd be late.

DAVID. Why do I go on with this rotten scheme? I know what it'll be like. The concrete will spall and the ceilings will crack. There'll be condensation under the balconies and leaks in the roof. And the people who live in it will do nothing but complain. They'll hate it. They'll hate me for building it.

SHEILA. You'll feel differently tomorrow. You know how one's feelings change.

DAVID. Yes. I suppose that's why I go on with the scheme. Because if I can get these two towers up that will be something fixed. Two pieces of space will have an outline. As long as those two buildings stand they'll stand in the same place, they'll stand in the same relationship to each other. They won't melt into different shapes. They won't move round each other in the night, or lean against each other for support, or turn their backs on each other, or knock each other down.

SHEILA. It's all my fault, isn't it?

DAVID. They won't feel sorry for each other.

SHEILA. It would be better if I'd never met you.

DAVID. They won't even feel sorry for themselves.

SHEILA. Better if I'd never been born.

DAVID. Anyway, I don't have any choice. I can't just give it up. That's my livelihood. That's my life.

SHEILA. She'd never do anything to hurt you, David. I'm sure of that. She'd never do anything disloyal. You know she wouldn't. Her feelings haven't changed.

DAVID. I wonder if he ever has any doubts.

SHEILA. I couldn't bear it if anything happened to you two. I love you both. *Both*! And that's *my* life. And if anything ever came between you I can't *think* what I'd do! I daren't *think* what I'd do!

JANE (*off*). Me . . .

Exit SHEILA *left.*

Enter JANE *centre.*

I thought I heard Sheila?

DAVID. Went upstairs.

JANE. What?

DAVID. Would you stop it if you could? The scheme. If you could press a button to stop it, and I'd never know, would you press it?

JANE. David . . . All I've said is that I think you're going to have a struggle.

DAVID. I am having a struggle. Would you stop it, Jane?

JANE. I think public opinion has changed since that block collapsed in the East End.

DAVID. That was system-built. These are steel-frame buildings. Would you stop it?

JANE. I think public opinion has changed. That's all I'm saying!

DAVID. I suppose you don't need to say more. You *are* public opinion. Sheila, are you coming in or aren't you?

Enter SHEILA *left.*

SHEILA. I'm sorry.

JANE. I'll go and say hello to the children. I think it's a brilliant scheme, David. Brilliant. Brilliant!

SHEILA. I'm sorry, Jane. I'm so sorry.

JANE *and* SHEILA *go off left.*

DAVID. And then it was spring again. Up came the bright forgotten green. Back came our spirits. A General Election was called, and I was working late and early to finish the scheme design before there were any policy changes at the Ministry. And suddenly there was Colin, sprouting up everywhere like the weeds in the garden. He was in the papers. He was on television. A hero of the Resistance.

Enter SHEILA *centre.*

SHEILA. He's standing now! In the election!

Exit COLIN *right*.

'The most colourful candidate here, though, is undoubtedly
Colin Molyneux (Independent). A familiar figure to television
viewers in his jeans and tee-shirt with the legend *Get 'em down!*
emblazoned across the chest . . . '

DAVID. Wonderful!

SHEILA. ' . . . Molyneux is a former classical scholar who gave
up a successful career in journalism . . . '

DAVID. 'Successful career in journalism.' Perfect! Progressive
collapse! Get on to 'progressive collapse'.

SHEILA. 'The slogan refers to the notorious twin skyscrapers
planned by the local Housing Department . . . '

DAVID. Progressive collapse! Progressive collapse!

SHEILA. 'Molyneux warns that a progressive collapse fifty
floors up could bring concrete débris raining down over
several acres . . . '

DAVID. 'Several acres.' Good. It's growing. Go on.

SHEILA. 'Molyneux delights his street-corner audiences with
gibes at what he calls "North London cultural imperialism"
. . . '

DAVID. More! More!

SHEILA. 'There are cheers when he talks about "rarefied
Hampstead architects . . . "'

DAVID. Hampstead? I'm going up in the world!

SHEILA. '" . . . of foreign extraction . . . "'

DAVID. He didn't say that! He can't have said that!

SHEILA. '" . . . who see districts like this as nothing but vacant
lots where they can erect monuments to themselves, as giant
boneyards for their own monstrous tombstones."'

DAVID. Tombstones? Tombstones . . . He hates me, doesn't he?
He actually hates me.

JANE (*off*). Sorry! Have you eaten . . . ?

Enter JANE *centre.*

Sheila . . . You must be starving . . . Well, first time for everything. I sacked a man today. Terrible! Terrible . . . ! What's the matter?

SHEILA. Colin. He's standing for Parliament now!

JANE. I shouldn't worry. He won't get there.

DAVID. You knew, did you?

JANE. Knew? What, that he was standing? Yes. Didn't you?

DAVID. No. You didn't tell me.

JANE. David, not now. Not this evening. I've had a long day. I'm going to have a long evening.

SHEILA. Well, I ought to be getting back.

JANE. You just came running across to tell him the good news, did you?

SHEILA. I just happened to see it.

DAVID. Don't blame *her*!

JANE. It's funny, though, isn't it? Every time I come in, she goes running out.

DAVID. Don't start on *her*!

JANE. And every time she runs out she leaves a row behind.

SHEILA. Anyway . . .

JANE. Well, now you've started it you might as well stay and enjoy it.

SHEILA. Jane, please, I can't bear this.

DAVID. Go on, Sheila, go home.

JANE. No! She can stay!

DAVID. Sheila . . .

JANE. I said she can stay! So, all right, I didn't tell you Colin was standing. I'm sorry. It didn't seem of any great moment. He won't get in. He'll get sixty-five votes. I'm sorry, though. All right? I've apologised. What else? Is that all? May I sit down now and eat my supper? I've got work to do afterwards.

DAVID. Where's he getting the money from?

JANE. What money?

DAVID. For the Election. Posters, halls, deposit. He's living on social security.

JANE. How should I know?

DAVID. He's not getting it from you? You're not giving him money? It's not our money?

JANE. Is that what you're worrying about?

DAVID. *Is* it our money?

JANE. No!

DAVID. Is he getting it from the people you work for?

JANE. He's getting a little from the Trust.

DAVID. So you do know, then?

JANE. It's not *my* idea! In fact I've consistently opposed it!

DAVID. You said you didn't know. But you do know. Why did you say you didn't know?

JANE. David, I'm not going to be cross-examined like this.

SHEILA. Please!

DAVID. That's the first time you've ever lied to me.

SHEILA. Please! Please!

JANE. Listen, David. Not once, not once have I ever done or said anything that could possibly be disloyal! Not once! I mean, it's ridiculous! I hate the man! I've always hated him! That's all I ever concealed from you!

DAVID. You hate the scheme, too.

JANE. All right, I'll tell you what I think about the scheme. I've never said it to anyone, and I'll never say it again. But if you want to know, I'll tell you. I think those towers of yours are two giant tombstones.

DAVID. Tombstones?

JANE. One for each of us. Anyway, now I've said it.

DAVID. Now you've said it.

JANE. So now you're happy. And don't start snivelling now, Sheila! The row's over!

Exit SHEILA *centre.*

DAVID. Tombstones. It was a coincidence, of course. She'd never heard him use the phrase. She was certain of that. All the same, she wouldn't go and see him again.

Enter COLIN *right.*

The phone rings.

JANE (*into phone*). Hello?

COLIN. Where were you? I've been waiting in all morning.

DAVID. She wouldn't take the children over on Saturday.

COLIN. Can't you hear me, Jane? I said, Where were you?

JANE. I'm sorry, I couldn't come.

DAVID. She should have gone and told him. She shouldn't have waited for him to go out to a phone-box and ring her.

COLIN. Why — is David making difficulties?

JANE. I just couldn't.

COLIN. He's there now, is he?

DAVID. There was no reason not to go and tell him. I certainly wasn't stopping her.

COLIN. I said, He's there now, is he?

JANE. I heard you.

COLIN. I see. Well, tell him we had a torchlight procession last night. Tell him there were five thousand people marching down Basuto Road. From all over London, Jane. All singing. It was like the end of the war. *I* was singing, Jane. You wouldn't have recognised me.

JANE. I'm sorry about the children. I can't bring them any more. You'll have to make some arrangement with Sheila.

Exit JANE *left.*

DAVID. I thought of going to see him myself. I don't know what I was going to say.

Exit COLIN *right.*

I suppose I thought I'd be very generous and understanding. Tell him they were both perfectly free to do everything they could to stop the scheme. We didn't all have to hate each other. I certainly didn't hate him. Something along those lines. Made some contact. It would have been a ridiculous scene. Perhaps I should have gone, though. If I'd gone to him he wouldn't have come to us.

Enter COLIN.

Things might have turned out quite differently. South London might have had another skyline altogether.

Enter JANE *centre.*

JANE. What are you doing here?

DAVID. He wants to see Matt and Lizzie.

JANE. Where are they?

DAVID. Upstairs.

JANE. Where's Sheila?

DAVID. She's upstairs. They're all upstairs. Sheila's in rather a state.

JANE. You shouldn't have come here, Colin.

DAVID. What else could he do?

JANE. Stupid inviting him in.

DAVID. I didn't invite him in! He walked in! He was here when I got back!

JANE. We'll have to start locking that door. You can't just walk in here now, Colin. Things have changed. All it can do is to make trouble. Get him out of here, will you, David? I'm going to see Sheila.

DAVID. Jane, I can't put him out! He's not a cat!

JANE. Well, I don't want him here! I don't want him in my house!

Exit JANE *left.*

DAVID. Colin, I'm sorry. She's right, though. Things *have* changed. We can't all sit round the table together now . . . Colin, look, I don't know how to say this. I know you resent me. I know things haven't always gone well for you in the last few years. I know I've had a certain amount of luck in life . . . Colin, what can I do? I can't apologise for being lucky! And I worked for that luck, and all right, I like my work, but that's not even true — most of my work I don't like! I don't like it anymore than you ever liked yours, because most of it isn't work, it's fighting, and I'm not a fighter! You know that. You're a fighter — I'm not a fighter. I hate fighting . . . Colin, I'm trying to make peace.

Enter JANE *left.*

JANE. I told you to get him out of here.

DAVID. Jane, listen . . .

JANE. Do *I* have to do it?

DAVID. Jane, he won't go until he's arranged something about the children.

JANE. Well, Sheila won't come down until he's gone.

DAVID. And he won't go until he's seen Sheila.

JANE. David, I don't understand. Why are you taking his side?

DAVID. Why am *I* taking his side? *I'm* not taking his side! *I'm* not the one who paid him money to wreck my work! *I'm* not the one who kept creeping off for little chats, and then came back and announced I was turning London into a graveyard!

JANE. David, once and for all, I did *not* give him money! I did *not* discuss your work with him! Ask him, if you don't believe me! He's your friend! Ask him! Ask him!

DAVID. *Me* taking his side! My God!

JANE. Ask him! Ask him! Ask him!

Enter SHEILA *left.*

SHEILA. Shut up! Both of you! Shut up! The children are crying
. . . You see what you've done . . . ? Fight *him*! He's the one!
He's the destroyer! Look at him, sitting there grinning with
pleasure at his handiwork! That's all he can do! Smash and jeer!

JANE. Sheila, go back upstairs.

SHEILA. It's not laughter. You don't know how to laugh. You
don't know what laughter's for.

JANE. Sheila, get out of here! Out! Out! Out!

DAVID. Don't start on her now!

JANE. Don't start on her? She's the cause of it all!

DAVID. Sheila? *Sheila's* the cause of it all?

COLIN. She's in love with you.

SHEILA *picks up a steaming stewpan.*

DAVID. Sheila!

JANE. Hot!

DAVID. Don't!

COLIN. Agh!

JANE. Water! Cold water!

DAVID. Here! Towel!

JANE. Phone! Quick!

DAVID. Car! Car! Get him into the car!

JANE. I'll take him. You see to her.

JANE, COLIN *and* DAVID *go off centre.*

SHEILA (*drops pan*). Oh . . .

Enter DAVID *centre.*

He shouldn't have said that.

DAVID. In his face, Sheila. In his face!

SHEILA. He shouldn't have said it.

DAVID. No . . . I suppose Jane knew all along.

SHEILA. I'm sorry.

DAVID. Not very clever, am I? Though I don't know quite what I could have done.

SHEILA. You've been so kind to me.

DAVID. Not much use to anyone.

SHEILA. I'll get the children.

DAVID. You don't have to go. This doesn't change anything, does it? You'll go on working. I'll go on working . . .

SHEILA. Always so kind.

DAVID. Now you've burnt your hands.

SHEILA. I'm sorry.

DAVID. I suppose I should find something to put on them . . . In his face, though. I don't know how you could have done that. I don't know anything about anyone.

SHEILA. I'll go and see to the children.

Exit SHEILA left.

Enter COLIN right.

COLIN. It was worth a few votes, anyway. A mask of surgical dressing, and stories in all the papers — 'Ban-the-towers Colin in mystery attack'. And when polling day came, the outraged electorate rose as one man. Or to be precise, as 173 men. 'Colin Molyneux, Independent, 173 votes'. 173! I wonder what I should have got without the bandages? Poor David, though. My face was painful enough for him. My lost deposit must have been almost more than he could bear.

Enter SHEILA left.

DAVID. Don't worry about Colin. He's all right — I saw him again today . . . And don't worry about the children — they know people have fights . . . Don't worry about Jane and me. We're fine. We're going away for a few days together. It doesn't matter if the scheme's a bit late. We know where we stand now . . . 173 votes! Poor Colin. I'll go over and see him again tomorrow — I'll take the children over . . . Don't worry, Sheila!

Exit DAVID centre.

COLIN. He'd stand there on the doorstep with my two children held out in front of him like a couple of placatory bottles of wine. He smiled a lot of concerned smiles. Reminded me of some occasion he'd found very affecting when I'd worn a flower in my buttonhole but apparently forgotten my shoes and socks. He was like a dog wanting to be taken in and loved. He gave up in the end, though.

Doorbell. Exit SHEILA *centre.*

Sick visiting, child ferrying — it all stopped the day the scheme stopped.

Enter JANE *and* SHEILA *centre.*

SHEILA. *Stopped?*

JANE. They rang him this morning. Didn't he tell you?

SHEILA. I knew it! I knew it! This was the Housing Committee last night?

JANE. Apparently the Ministry had rejected the revised estimates. I thought you'd know all about it.

SHEILA. David was sure the council would fight them!

JANE. Apparently not.

SHEILA. Oh, Jane, it's all my fault! I held him up! If he'd got the drawings finished a month earlier . . . A week earlier, even . . . !

Enter DAVID *centre, with keys.*

Oh, David! It was me, wasn't it? It was me!

DAVID. No, no. It's all in here. ' "We Did It!" says Giantkiller Colin.'

SHEILA. Colin? Colin did it?

DAVID. ' "I always knew we'd wear them down in the end," grinned lone campaigner Colin Molyneux today.'

SHEILA. Colin?

JANE. I thought it was the electricity people? I thought they said it was going to cost another half-million pounds to divert the cable?

DAVID. Yes, or else it was the Ministry, because they wouldn't pay the Generating Board. Or the council, because they wouldn't fight the Ministry. Or that block in the East End. No, it was Colin. Among others. Why wouldn't the Ministry pay? Why wouldn't the council fight them? Because no one believes in going high anymore. Because public opinion has changed.

SHEILA. Not *my* opinion, David.

DAVID. No, not your opinion.

JANE. I'm going to put dinner on the table. I've got to work afterwards.

SHEILA. I shall always blame myself.

DAVID. I was too late, that's all. A week, a year — who knows?

SHEILA. It was me.

DAVID. It was people. That's what wrecks all our plans — people.

SHEILA. I can't imagine how you must feel, David.

DAVID. How *I* must feel? I don't know. Like dinner, mostly . . .

COLIN. And that was the end of the Basuto Wars. Basutoland was saved! They didn't pull it down. They did it up.

JANE. We rehabilitated the whole area.

COLIN. The very first improvement they made was to evict me.

SHEILA. I suppose that's when everything changed.

JANE. I suppose that's when we ceased to believe in change.

SHEILA. It was a terrible time. I don't know what David would have done if Jane hadn't had a career. He *knew* he was right about the towers. He wouldn't let go. The practice just went to pieces.

DAVID. Jane, can I slide your stuff back and put dinner on the table?

JANE. Just a minute.

COLIN. We all depended on Jane. At least, I assume it was her influence that got me my job. I assume it was Jane who rehabilitated me.

SHEILA. He got one tower built eventually. It took him seven years. It's only half the height he wanted, and it's not local authority housing, it's private offices. But it's a beautiful building — it won a prize. That didn't help him, though, because it was the recession by then, and there was no work to be had.

DAVID. I've changed my ideas in life. More than once. I never wanted to build high. But you had to then! I never wanted to come down to earth again. But I had to. I'm not ashamed of that. We all have to change, we all have to give. Someone has to, anyway. Nothing would happen in the world otherwise.

COLIN. Rehabilitation schemes. That's what I write about. That's what I live in — a rehab. A new word. A new world of tastefully uniform front doors and tastefully paved pedestrian precincts. I sometimes feel I'd like to demolish the lot, and put up a few skyscrapers. So I suppose *I* haven't changed.

DAVID. We all change. Everything changes. I'm rather proud of some of those rehab schemes I've done for Jane. I'm happy enough, anyway. We're happy enough . . . Look, I can't keep the meal hot indefinitely.

JANE. Just coming.

SHEILA. I see David's building sometimes when I'm on my way to my sessions with Dr Medtner. It makes me think of . . . I don't know — summer coming, the feeling that things are going to change.

DAVID. The only one who never changed was Sheila. She went on believing to the end, like some old Stalinist. Still does, for all I know. She moved away when they divorced. I couldn't keep her on, of course — I couldn't keep anyone on. It was best for her, anyway — she'd got completely dependent on us. I think Jane found her a job somewhere.

COLIN. Even Sheila's being rehabilitated. Or so I gather from my daughter. Lizzie's nineteen now. She says Sheila goes to see some woman of Central European extraction in Hampstead.

SHEILA. Dr Medtner says I can learn to change. I have the

capacity for happiness, she says.

COLIN. Apparently this woman's got a husband who's a doctor, too. An eye-specialist, according to Lizzie. 'Lizzie,' I said, 'have the white stick ready.'

DAVID. Shall I put something over it to stop it drying up? What do you think?

JANE. I suppose I've changed. I've learnt one thing from working with people, anyway: they want to be told what to do.

DAVID. Or do you want to eat as you work?

JANE. That's what I long for. I know that. Just to be told what to do . . . Dinner? Well, slide this stuff back and put it on the table, then.

DAVID. I drove down Basuto Road the other day. The sun was shining, and some woman was standing in a doorway with her children and laughing, and it all looked quite bright and cheerful.

SHEILA. Basuto Road. Yes, and at once it's summer, and everything is about to change.

COLIN. I did one good thing in this world, anyway. I helped poor old David. I saved him from a lifetime of public execration.

JANE. Basuto Road? It's strange; the cloud moves on, and there's the landscape out in sunshine again.

DAVID. Basuto Road. There's the whole history of human ideas in that one name.

JANE. And yes! I was! I was happy!

DAVID. Laughing and laughing, this woman was. But what she was laughing about I never discovered.

Curtain.

Balmoral

An earlier version of *Balmoral*, with the same title, was first presented at the Yvonne Arnaud Theatre, Guildford, on 20 June 1978, in a production directed by Eric Thompson. A version close to the present one was first presented under the title *Liberty Hall* at the Greenwich Theatre on 24 January 1980, with the following cast:

WINN	Julian Fellowes
DEEPING	Anthony Sharp
BLYTON	Rowena Cooper
MCNAB	Rikki Fulton
SKINNER	George Cole
TRISHA	Jill Meager
KOCHETOV	Oliver Cotton

Directed by Alan Dossor
Designed by Poppy Mitchell
Lighting by Nick Chelton

The present version was first presented, under the title *Balmoral*, at the Bristol Old Vic on 8 May 1987, with the following cast:

WINN	Mark Tandy
DEEPING	Anthony Pedley
BLYTON	Helen Ryan
MCNAB	Kevin Lloyd
SKINNER	Bernard Lloyd
TRISHA	Lysette Anthony
KOCHETOV	Kevin Wallace

Directed by Leon Rubin
Designed by Sally Crabb
Lighting by John A Williams

ACT ONE

Balmoral. 1937.
A room in the castle.
Tartan furnishings; antlers; Landseers. A baronial fireplace,
and three doors, left, right, and centre. Armchairs, a dining table,
and a sideboard with breakfast things on it.
As you look at the room, however, slight discrepancies become
apparent. A small electric fire burns in the great fireplace. There
is an odd assortment of kitchen chairs round the dining table. A
notice-board is fixed on one of the doors.
WINN is standing in front of the hearth, warming his backside
at the little electric fire. He is 29, and is wearing plus-fours and a
Fair Isle sweater. He has a newspaper under his arm and he is
smiling reflectively.
Enter DEEPING, centre. He is 60, and is wearing an old
well-cut suit, with a muffler round his neck. He has a folder of
papers under his arm. He is a gentleman.
He stands just inside the door, looking round the room and
rubbing his hands gloomily. After a moment WINN glances at
him, then continues to smile to himself.

WINN. Strange world. Strange, strange world.

> DEEPING *does not rise to this. He continues to rub his hands,*
> *then turns to consult a thermometer hanging on the wall.*

> Forty-eight. The temperature. In here. Freezing hard outside.

> DEEPING *turns to the sideboard and helps himself without*
> *enthusiasm.*

WINN. I was out before breakfast, sniffing the air. I thought one
might get a spot of shooting today. We could have a whack at

the grouse. Perfect day for it.

DEEPING sits down at the table with his kedgeree, and looks round for something.

Paper?

Hands DEEPING the newspaper he had been holding behind his back. DEEPING smooths it out and reads as he eats.

Strange world, though, Warry.

DEEPING continues to read.

No, but seriously. Did you ever think, when you were a child, did you ever think for one moment that you would wake up one sparkling cold winter's morning in the years to come, and find the world outside all covered in white, and a tureen of steaming kedgeree on the sideboard, and realise you were a guest at Balmoral?

No response.

No, I believe this is going to be an awfully good year for me. When you think it's still only the fourth of January . . . I believe 1937 is going to be my year.

Enter BLYTON, centre. She is 40, and is wearing several layers of cardigan. She stands just inside the door, where DEEPING stood before, looking round the room and gloomily rubbing her hands.

Enid, did you ever think, when you were a little girl, did you ever so much as dream, that you might come downstairs one crackling frosty January morning, and find that you were standing in the breakfast room of a royal residence?

BLYTON gives no sigh of having heard. She shivers.

DEEPING (*glances up at her*). Forty-eight. To be absolutely precise.

BLYTON gazes at him. She stops rubbing her hands.

WINN. Alternatively, Warry, you and I could join forces and have a wallop at the poor old deer.

BLYTON turns sharply to look at WINN.

DEEPING (*explains*). Godfrey wants to shoot something.

WINN. Well, we are at Balmoral. That is the life here.

DEEPING (*quietly*). Do you ever want to shoot something, Enid?

WINN. No, seriously. We could get McNab to ghillie for us.

DEEPING. I sometimes want to shoot something.

WINN. No, all I'm saying is, here we are at Balmoral, and perhaps we should make a bit more effort to enjoy it.

DEEPING. Put another head up over the mantelpiece.

WINN *looks at* DEEPING, *surprised. Pause.*

BLYTON. Forty-eight?

Pause.

DEEPING. What?

BLYTON. Who is forty-eight?

DEEPING. *Who* is forty-eight? What do you mean, *who* is forty-eight?

BLYTON. You're not saying *I'm* forty-eight?

DEEPING. *It* is forty-eight.

BLYTON. It?

DEEPING. In here. In this room.

BLYTON (*looks slowly round the room, bewildered*). What *is* everyone talking about this morning?

She goes to the sideboard and helps herself to kedgeree.

DEEPING (*quietly*). *Two* more heads up over the mantelpiece.

WINN. Warry, all I'm saying is this . . .

DEEPING. Godfrey, all your immense labour is in vain.

WINN. All right — how about trying for a few rabbits?

DEEPING. I mean, Godfrey, that even if you preside over the hearth-rug in that maddening way until the seat of your trousers bursts into flame — even if you go out and slaughter all the rabbits, deer, grouse, budgerigars, and white mice in the entire Scottish Highlands, you will not succeed in convincing Enid and me that you are a gentleman.

Silence. WINN *gazes at* DEEPING. DEEPING *reads the paper.* BLYTON *sits down and begins to shovel kedgeree into her mouth.* WINN *looks at her, then back at* DEEPING.

WINN (*quietly*). Warry, that is a frightful thing to say. It's hurtful and mean and it also runs directly counter to the whole spirit of the Sixteenth Party Congress.

DEEPING. On the contrary, Godfrey. My remark was very much in line with the spirit of the Sixteenth Party Congress. You won't catch me like that.

WINN. Warry, why do you think we had a Revolution in Britain in 1917?

DEEPING. Not to turn you into a gentleman, surely?

WINN. To do away with class distinction. That process is now complete. We are at last living in a classless society. That was spelled out in resolution after resolution at the Sixteenth Party Congress.

Enter MCNAB, *right. He is 53, and is wearing a flat cap, a kilt, and Wellington boots. He is carrying an empty champagne bucket, with a handle improvised out of a piece of rope, and is trailing a shovel. The champagne bucket is full of coal. No one pays any attention to him.*

DEEPING. Exactly. There are no gentlemen, Godfrey. The species is extinct.

WINN. That's not *my* interpretation of the Sixteenth Party Congress.

DEEPING. What is your interpretation?

WINN. My interpretation is that we are *all* gentlemen.

Exit MCNAB *left.*

DEEPING. Gentlemen of the world, unite!

WINN. Marx and Engels were German. The Revolution didn't happen in Germany. It didn't happen in France or Italy or Russia. It happened in England. This is an English classless society. I mean, be reasonable, Warry! Look at us. Living in luxury. Waited on hand and foot. That's why Balmoral has been made over to the people — so that the people can live like kings.

DEEPING. We're not the people. We're writers.

WINN. Writers are people, Warry! Goodness me, we're dashed important people! That's why we're given the chance of a few weeks' break in a place like Balmoral.

Silence.

BLYTON. What are we eating?

DEEPING. Porridge.

BLYTON. Porridge?

DEEPING. I assume.

WINN. Kedgeree.

DEEPING. This isn't kedgeree. Kedgeree is made of rice. This isn't rice.

WINN. Well, it's certainly not oats.

DEEPING. It's some kind of barley.

WINN. Porridge is made of oats.

DEEPING. It's barley gruel.

WINN. Barley kedgeree.

BLYTON. It's got turnips in.

WINN. Barley and turnip kedgeree.

DEEPING. Or turnip soup with barley.

Enter MCNAB, left. He is carrying the champagne bucket and trailing the shovel, as before, but the bucket is now empty, and he is wearing a green baize apron under his jacket and over his kilt. He heads towards the righthand door.

WINN. Why don't we ask McNab? John, what are these good people eating?

MCNAB. Kedgeree.

WINN. Kedgeree. And what sort of kedgeree?

MCNAB. Barley and turnip kedgeree.

WINN. Thank you, John.

DEEPING. McNab, what leads you to suppose that this is kedgeree?

MCNAB. I cooked it.

DEEPING. But, McNab, why do you assume the result is called *kedgeree*?

MCNAB. Because it's Wednesday.

DEEPING. Thank you, McNab.

WINN. Thank you, John.

   Exit MCNAB, *right.*

   All I'm saying is we ought not to sit on our backsides and work all the time.

DEEPING. Walpole's still not down. He seems to have given up breakfast entirely these days. I wonder why.

WINN. All right, we all want to work.

DEEPING. He scarcely leaves his room from one day's end to the next.

WINN. *I* want to work. I *do* work. I did two hours work in here before breakfast.

DEEPING. He has a warm room, of course.

WINN. All I'm saying is that if they send you off to spend the winter season in a royal residence, and then you turn round and make no effort at all to enjoy it, then it does seem to me just a shade ungrateful, if not downright counter to the whole spirit of the Sixteenth Party Congress.

DEEPING. Hugh Walpole has the kitchen flue running through the wall of his bedroom. But then Hugh Walpole has a cousin running through the upper echelons of the Party.

   Silence.

BLYTON. My hot water bottle has gone.

DEEPING. Everything goes in this place.

WINN. Only if it's left around.

BLYTON. I can't sleep without a hot water bottle.

DEEPING. Half the lead off the roof has gone.

WINN. Let's not exaggerate, Warry. There's a lot still there.

DEEPING. All the bath plugs have gone.

BLYTON. I can't work without a hot water bottle.

DEEPING. The whole castle is going bit by bit.

WINN. You'll have to work in here, like the rest of us.

DEEPING. Apart from Hugh.

BLYTON. I can't work in the same room as other people.

WINN. It's only Warry and me.

DEEPING. Think what it's going to be like in the summer when this place is full. Imagine twenty or thirty writers living and working in here.

WINN. All complaining about the food.

DEEPING. All saying they can't work in the same room as other people.

BLYTON. I shall be dead before the summer.

Enter MCNAB, right, with the champagne bucket and the shovel. But the bucket is now full of coal, and he is no longer wearing the green baize apron. He heads towards the lefthand door.

(*to* MCNAB.) Have you seen a hot water bottle anywhere?

MCNAB. No.

WINN. John, is there a gun about the place?

MCNAB. No.

WINN. How about a pair of skates?

MCNAB. No.

DEEPING. Were you ever savagely punished, McNab, for talking in school?

MCNAB. No.

Exit MCNAB.

WINN. He has a lot to contend with, though. He has all the cooking to do, for a start.

DEEPING. I shouldn't call that cooking.

WINN. Remember he has all the cleaning, as well. All the washing. All the gardening.

DEEPING. All the stealing.

WINN. All the maintenance to the castle.

DEEPING. Fancy trying to run a place this size with one under-coachman!

WINN. He's not an under-coachman.

DEEPING. Before the Revolution he was an under-coachman.

WINN. Well, now he's a butler.

DEEPING. You can't seriously think of him as a butler!

WINN. Give him time. People grow to fill their jobs. Everyone knows that.

DEEPING. What about Skinner?

WINN. The Warden? The Warden is exactly the kind of case I'm talking about . . .

Enter SKINNER, *centre. He is a man of about fifty, and is wearing a neat dark suit, with a dark shirt and tie. He is holding a selection of ledgers.*

DEEPING. Good morning, Skinner.

WINN. Hello, Warden!

DEEPING. We were just talking about you.

SKINNER *does not respond. He slaps the ledgers down, and runs a sombrely assessing eye over the room.*

WINN. Anything I can do, Warden . . .? Are you looking for something?

SKINNER *crosses to the sideboard and picks up a half-empty milk bottle.*

Tea? Can I pour you a cup of tea, Warden?

Enter MCNAB, *left, with the champagne bucket. He is wearing the green baize apron, but is trailing a mop instead of the shovel, and the bucket is full of water.* SKINNER *watches the bucket narrowly as* MCNAB *crosses to the righthand door.*

SKINNER. Fetching more coal, McNab?

MCNAB. Washing down the hall.

SKINNER. With a champagne bucket?

MCNAB. With the coal bucket.

SKINNER. That's a champagne bucket.

MCNAB. Only bucket left.

SKINNER. All right.

MCNAB. All right?

SKINNER. All right.

Exit MCNAB, *right. Exit* SKINNER, *centre holding the milk bottle.*

DEEPING. You were saying?

WINN. I was saying the Warden is exactly the kind of case I'm talking about. Do you know what he was before the Revolution?

DEEPING. Cashier at the Clapham Junction Home and Colonial.

WINN. Yes, and within twelve years he was running the entire British tram-building industry.

DEEPING. And now he's sunk to being Warden of a state writers' home.

WINN. That's nothing to sneer at.

DEEPING. But he can't do it, can he. It's beyond him! They'll be coming for him one of these days. A ring at the doorbell at six o'clock in the morning. Then we'll come down to breakfast and — no Skinner!

WINN. Honestly, Warry! That's not the kind of thing to joke about.

DEEPING. What's he doing with that milk?

Enter SKINNER, *right, with the milk bottle. The milk has been emptied out, and a single bare twig put in its place. He gazes round the room, trying to see where it would create most effect.*

WINN. Oh, look, we've got a twig this morning! That'll brighten the place up.

SKINNER *tries the milk bottle in various locations. He stands back and sombrely assesses the effect.*

DEEPING. Is it the inspection today, then, Skinner?

WINN. How can he know whether it's today or not? It's going to be a surprise inspection. That's the whole point.

DEEPING. He may have had a tip-off.

WINN. Is it today, Warden?

DEEPING. They've done the painters and graphic artists at Sandringham. I had a letter from Spencer.

WINN. They've done the opera people at Holyrood. They arrested the catering manager and two baritones.

DEEPING. It'll be Skinner's turn sooner or later.

WINN. Anyway, the twig's nice.

Having settled the position of the twig, SKINNER *sits down and opens his ledgers.*

SKINNER. Right, let's get this meeting out of the way.

DEEPING. Meeting? What meeting?

SKINNER. Don't you ever look at the timetable?

WINN. Oh, the union meeting!

SKINNER. Right, minutes of the last meeting?

WINN. I move they be taken as read.

SKINNER. Seconded?

WINN (*prompting*). Warry?

DEEPING *shrugs and raises his arm.*

SKINNER (*signs the minutes*). Treasurer's report?

WINN. I move the report be received,

SKINNER. Seconded?

DEEPING. Your turn, Enid.

BLYTON (*suddenly becoming conscious of the world*). What?

WINN. Treasurer's report. We need a seconder.

BLYTON. What is everyone talking about?

DEEPING. Just raise your arm, Enid.

She raises her arm blankly.

SKINNER. Three. This branch will send a delegation to the Smash Tsarism rally in Edinburgh on Sunday, with the branch banner. Proposed?

WINN (*gently*). Warry . . .

DEEPING raises his arm.

SKINNER. Seconded?

WINN. Enid . . .

BLYTON raises her arm.

SKINNER. Four. This branch warmly welcomes the regional committee's call for increased production and a higher level of labour enthusiasm . . .

Enter MCNAB, right, with the champagne bucket, empty, the mop, and no baize apron. He crosses towards the left-hand door.

. . . and pledges an increase of six hours a week in voluntary unpaid overtime. Proposed?

WINN. Enid . . .

BLYTON raises her arm.

SKINNER. Seconded?

WINN raises his arm.

Five. Someone has stolen the ping-pong ball.

WINN. Oh my God.

DEEPING. What next?

MCNAB. The bellrope's gone.

Exit MCNAB, *left.*

SKINNER. I sit in my office in there working on the books. Keeping the books straight. I can't watch the ping-pong ball, the bellrope, the frying-pan, the billiard cue . . .

DEEPING (*to* WINN). We're going to be losing our half-holiday.

WINN. Warry, this is serious.

SKINNER. Look, any inspectors coming here, they're going to find these books in apple-pie order. If the books say I have one billiard-cue and four writers, then by heaven . . . Just a moment. Where's Deeping?

WINN (*indicating*). Here.

SKINNER. Then where's Blyton?

WINN. Here. It's Walpole, Warden. He never came down to breakfast.

SKINNER. Six. This branch condemns the brutal suppression of the strikes by motor industry workers in St. Petersburg, and calls upon the Russian Imperial Government to recognise trade union freedom.

Enter MCNAB, *left, without mop or shovel, but wearing the green baize apron and carrying the champagne bucket. It is now full of kitchen swill.*

Proposed?

WINN *raises his arm.*

Seconded?

DEEPING *raises his arm.*

Any other business? No other business. Are you building a swimming pool out there, McNab?

MCNAB *stops on his way towards the righthand door.*

Another bucket of water?

MCNAB. Bucket of swill.

SKINNER. You're washing the floor with swill?

MCNAB. Feeding the pigs.

SKINNER. Oh, yes, you're feeding the pigs. With a bucket of swill. And who knows what sins are concealed in a bucket of swill?

He gets up and goes over to MCNAB.

You see now why I've nailed up the back door? So that everything comes past me, McNab. Buckets of water, buckets of swill — they all pass before my beady eye. You're not the first person in the world to have tried putting it across on me, McNab. During my years in industry I had many thousands of men working under my management, and I can tell you — you don't know what thieving is. I have seen entire factories dismantled virtually in front of my eyes. I have seen complete grand hotels get up and walk out through the service entrance. I have seen a crack express leave Manchester Victoria complete with dining-car, Pullmans, and Pullman waiters, and turn up one week later at Wolverhampton High Level stripped to the bogies. So don't expect me to be impressed because you stole the doorbell last Thursday. Don't expect me to be amazed because the bell-rope's gone now.

MCNAB. Went ten times or more.

SKINNER. Never mind the bell rope. I want to see what you've got in that bucket.

MCNAB. In the bucket? Swill.

SKINNER. Show me, McNab.

MCNAB. Show you?

SKINNER. Show me.

MCNAB tips the swill out on the floor. SKINNER gazes at it unseeingly. Another thought has struck him.

Went ten times?

MCNAB. What?

SKINNER. The bellrope. How it could go ten times?

MCNAB. Because this fellow on the doorstep keeps pulling it! I saw him with my own eyes! Up and down, up and down it goes! Then this fellow looks through the letter box at me and he starts pulling it again.

SKINNER. What fellow looked through the letter box?

MCNAB. This fellow in the peaked cap.

SKINNER (*awestruck*). Peaked cap?

MCNAB. Driver of the car.

SKINNER. There's a car outside! An official car? And you've left them standing in the snow?

MCNAB. 'Let no one in!' Your words, Mr Skinner. No one to come in without the say-so from yourself.

SKINNER. Let them in.

MCNAB. You want them in?

SKINNER. Not you. (*To* WINN.) You.

WINN (*goes to the righthand door, in a flutter*). Oh dear. This is the inspector, is it?

SKINNER. Come back, come back. I'll go. You get this place straight. Breakfast! Breakfast! Get it out of here!

WINN *goes to the sideboard and begins clearing up the remains of breakfast.* MCNAB *stands where he was left, watching the activity all around.*

(*to* BLYTON *and* DEEPING.) You two — don't stand about like a bread queue. Get down to some work.

DEEPING. What about the ping-pong ball?

SKINNER. Leave all the thinking to me. You just get on with the writing.

DEEPING *and* BLYTON *prepare to write.*

No, go and fetch the paraffin stove out of my office.

They rise.

SKINNER (*to* BLYTON). Sit down!

Exit DEEPING, *centre.* WINN *takes the plates towards the lefthand door, leaving the tureen of kedgeree behind on the sideboard.*

WINN. In the kitchen?

SKINNER (*indicates the kedgeree*). The other thing! Take the other thing! (*To* BLYTON.) Pen open! This is a writers' home! *Somebody* be writing!

WINN. The kedgeree?

SKINNER. *That* stuff! Get it out of here! Put it in the kitchen!

WINN *returns to the sideboard, puts down his armful of plates, picks up the kedgeree, and heads back towards the lefthand door.* SKINNER *meanwhile is discovering a suspiciously clean patch on the wallpaper.*

Antlers! A set of antlers missing! (*To* WINN.) Plates!

WINN *returns to the sideboard and struggles to hold both plates and tureen of kedgeree.*

(*To* BLYTON.) Antlers! Another set of antlers!

BLYTON *gets up and begins to search hopelessly for some extra antlers.*

Enter DEEPING, *centre, carrying a paraffin stove.*

(*To* DEEPING.) Antlers! Antlers!

DEEPING. Antlers?

He puts down the paraffin stove, and takes down one of the other sets of antlers.

SKINNER (*to* BLYTON). You — start writing!

BLYTON *goes back to the table.*

(*To* MCNAB.) What do you think *you're* doing? (*Indicates the swill on the floor.*) Put it back!

DEEPING (*holding the antlers*). Put it back?

SKINNER (*to* MCNAB). Put it back!

MCNAB *begins to pick up handfuls of swill and put them back in the bucket.* DEEPING *starts to put the antlers back on the wall.*

(*To* DEEPING.) Not there! There!

DEEPING *takes the antlers across to the clean patch. MCNAB takes the directions as applying to the swill, and carries a handfull of it across the room. WINN struggles towards the lefthand door, beginning to drop his load of breakfast things.*

(*To* WINN.) Oh, for heaven's sake! Put it back where you found it!

DEEPING *takes the antlers back to where he found them. MCNAB takes the swill back to where it was.*

(*To* DEEPING.) Not you! Him!

WINN *struggles to pick up the items he has dropped. MCNAB, now totally confused, holds the dripping handful of swill over anything except the bucket.*

(*To* WINN.) Leave it! Sit down!

MCNAB *sits down, still holding the swill.*

(*To* DEEPING.) You — get the books out of my office!

DEEPING (*runs to the centre door, still holding the antlers, then stops*). What books?

SKINNER. 'What books?' Can't you people do *anything*? Sit down! (*To* MCNAB.) Stand up! (*To* WINN.) Let them in!

WINN. Let them in?

SKINNER. Let them in!

WINN *hurriedly dumps the kedgeree and the rest of the breakfast things on the nearest armchair, and goes out, right.*

(*To* DEEPING *and* BLYTON.) Write! Write!

(*To* MCNAB.) Wipe that swill off the floor!

Exit SKINNER, *centre.*

DEEPING *and* BLYTON *bend over their work —* DEEPING *still encumbered by the antlers.*

MCNAB *dumps his handful of swill in the bucket. Then he rips a piece of loose tartan wallpaper off the wall, gets down on his hands and knees, and begins to wipe the floor.*

DEEPING (*quietly*). Hide your eyes, Enid.

BLYTON. What?

DEEPING. Murder is going to be done at this inspection. Friend Skinner is going to be minced fine and fried in batter. Trussed and stuffed and roasted.

MCNAB. We're all in the same pan. If they roast the goose they'll roast the potatoes, too.

Enter TRISHA *and* KOCHETOV, *right, followed by* WINN. TRISHA *is 20, and is wearing a warm overcoat and a woolly hat.* KOCHETOV *is 26, and is wearing an expensive winter overcoat trimmed with fur. His is Russian, but speaks perfect English, with only a slight Russian intonation. His surname is stressed on the first syllable — KAWCHETOV.*

DEEPING *and* BLYTON *get to their feet.*

TRISHA. Hello. Mr Skinner?

DEEPING. No, no.

WINN. This is Mr Deeping. Mr Skinner will be here in one moment.

The three writers gaze at KOCHETOV *and* TRISHA, *overawed;* MCNAB *wipes the floor and listens.*

KOCHETOV (*entirely at his ease*). Charming room.

WINN. Yes.

DEEPING. Yes.

KOCHETOV. You must tell me where you get your tartan linoleum. Three writers — and you all work happily together in the same room?

WINN.
DEEPING. } Yes.
BLYTON.

KOCHETOV. The perfect community. Please — write, write. write!

WINN. Oh.

DEEPING. Well.

BLYTON. Thank you.

WINN, DEEPING *and* BLYTON *sit down simultaneously.*

KOCHETOV. I've seen people writing with a quill. I've never seen anyone writing with antlers before.

DEEPING. Oh yes. (*He puts the antlers aside.*) We were rearranging the room.

KOCHETOV. I have a feeling that we have taken you somewhat by surprise.

DEEPING. Not at all.

WINN. Yes, entirely.

TRISHA. I'm sorry, I should explain — this is Mr Kochetov.

WINN, DEEPING *and* BLYTON *rise, in unison.*

KOCHETOV. Please, please.

They sit, in unison.

Perfect.

TRISHA. Mr Kochetov is a Russian journalist.

KOCHETOV. The capitalist press, I'm afraid. Vulgar, sensational, and appallingly readable. And this is my mistress.

TRISHA (*deeply embarrassed*). Mr Kochetov, please!

KOCHETOV. My future mistress. Yes? My mistress-to-be.

TRISHA. Honestly . . . ! Mr Kochetov is a terrible tease.

KOCHETOV. Well, my love, it's impossible. You're like a shiny new rosy-cheeked apple. I can't help wanting to sink my teeth into you.

TRISHA. I'm Mr Kochetov's guide from the Board of Trade.

KOCHETOV. Her job is to stop me seeing all the things I'm not supposed to see.

TRISHA. That's not true! You can see anything you like! I've told you before — freedom of the press is guaranteed under the constitution. I'm just here to help you.

WINN. Just a moment. This gentleman is a *journalist?*

TRISHA. Yes, and he's a complete cynic.

WINN. A *Russian* journalist?

KOCHETOV. Oh, but I had a most excellent English governess.

TRISHA. He tells everyone we meet about his English governess.

KOCHETOV. No, but she prepared me very well for understanding this country, you see, because she was entirely held together by safety pins. So whenever I look at something here and I can't believe my eyes, I simply remember my old governess. Of course, I think. Safety pins! It's all held together by safety pins! This, I need hardly say, will be the first paragraph of my article.

WINN. But — sorry — you're not the inspector?

KOCHETOV. Inspector? (*To* TRISHA.) Am I the inspector?

TRISHA. I don't know anything about inspectors. Mr Kochetov is simply here to interview Hugh Walpole for the Russian newspapers.

WINN. Interview . . . ?

KOCHETOV. May we sit down?

WINN. Yes. Yes.

Without looking he indicates the chair where he put the breakfast things.

Newspapers? Russian newspapers?

He realises that KOCHETOV *is gazing at the breakfast things.*

Oh, I'm so sorry!

WINN *picks up the tureen of kedgeree and hands it to* MCNAB, *who is standing waiting with the bucket of swill beside him, then picks up the rest of the breakfast things.*

Enter SKINNER, *centre with a stack of ledgers.*

SKINNER. I do apologise! But I know you'll want to look at the books before you do anything else. Oh dear. Has no one even taken your coats? Writers, I'm afraid! Heads in the clouds. Feet not quite on the ground. How do you do?

TRISHA. This is Mr Kochetov.

KOCHETOV. How do you do?

SKINNER. Skinner, Skinner.

WINN (*urgently, still holding the breakfast things*). Warden . . .

SKINNER (*to* WINN). I don't want them! (*To* KOCHETOV.)
May I . . .?

> He helps KOCHETOV *off with his coat, cunningly turning him
> away from* WINN *and the breakfast things as he does so, which
> brings him instead face to face with* MCNAB *and the tureen of
> kedgeree.*

WINN. Mr Kochetov is a journalist. A Russian journalist.

SKINNER (*to* WINN). Just get that stuff out of here, will you?
(*To* KOCHETOV.) We do try to keep a fairly informal
atmosphere in here . . .

> He realises that KOCHETOV *is gazing with interest at the
> kedgeree.*

> That is pigswill. It has been duly certified as unfit for human
> consumption.

MCNAB. This is kedgeree. (*He bends and picks up the bucket of
swill.*)

SKINNER. And this is kedgeree. We like to keep a tureen of
kedgeree to hand in case of unexpected guests.

MCNAB. This is pigswill.

SKINNER. This is pigswill. Have you been offered some . . . ? *This*
is pigswill?

> He looks from swill to kedgeree in confusion.

MCNAB. You want to see it?

> He offers to tip the swill out on the floor again.

SKINNER. No, thank you! Just put it back on the sideboard,
McNab.

MCNAB. The swill?

SKINNER. The kedgeree, the kedgeree. (*To* KOCHETOV.) Now,

where do you want to work? I expect you'd prefer to shut yourself away in my office.

He steers KOCHETOV *firmly towards the centre door.*

TRISHA. I think all Mr Kochetov really wants to do is to sit down quietly somewhere and have a little chat with Mr Walpole.

SKINNER. Of course. If he wants to talk privately, I think he'd find my office more convenient . . . Mr Walpole?

WINN. I tried to tell you.

TRISHA. I can't believe I'm going to meet him at last! I've read everything he's written! I've read *Rogue Herries* five times! People are always talking about what a refined sensibility Henry James has. But I think Hugh Walpole is much more refined!

KOCHETOV. The only thing one can say about her literary judgement is that she has perfect eyebrows.

TRISHA (*to* SKINNER). They did tell you about the interview?

SKINNER. Interview?

WINN. You wouldn't listen.

TRISHA. Mr Kochetov is Russian. He's interviewing Hugh Walpole for the Russian newspapers.

KOCHETOV. They adore him in Russia. Or so Trisha tells me.

TRISHA. Well, *you* wouldn't know! All you're interested in is motor-cars and girls!

KOCHETOV. I know nothing, you see. She has to tell me everything.

SKINNER. You mean you don't want to go through the books?

TRISHA. Not now. I've read all his books!

KOCHETOV. Even I have read one of them.

TRISHA. No, you haven't.

KOCHETOV. On the train.

TRISHA. Half of one.

SKINNER. You want to interview Mr Walpole? All right. (*To* MCNAB.) Fetch Mr Walpole.

MCNAB. He's not there.

SKINNER. What do you mean he's not there?

MCNAB. He's gone.

SKINNER. Gone?

MCNAB. He went out of here this morning.

SKINNER. No one's left the house!

MCNAB. Before you were up.

WINN. I've been up since six!

MCNAB. He went before six.

> *Pause.*

WINN. Before six?

BLYTON. Went?

DEEPING. Walpole?

> WINN, DEEPING *and* BLYTON *stare at* MCNAB. MCNAB *picks up the bucket of swill and crosses to the righthand door.*

MCNAB. You want me to tell you where he went?

WINN (*hurriedly*). No, thank you, McNab.

> *Exit* MCNAB, *right.*

SKINNER (*to* WINN, *realising*). You mean . . .?

WINN. Yes!

SKINNER. You don't mean . . .?

DEEPING (*sombrely*). I think we do.

> *Pause.*

TRISHA. I don't understand.

WINN. Telegram. I've just remembered. He had a telegram.

DEEPING. Of course! He had a telegram!

SKINNER (*reinforcing them as best he can*). Telegram.

WINN. Father ill.

BLYTON. Mother dying.

DEEPING. Come at once.

SKINNER. In the middle of the night.

WINN. I'd forgotten that.

DEEPING. We'd all forgotten.

SKINNER. It went out of our heads.

BLYTON. Now we've remembered.

SKINNER. It's come back to us.

TRISHA. What's happening? I don't understand! What's going on?

WINN. Nothing.

SKINNER. Nothing!

KOCHETOV. Look at her.

TRISHA (*to* SKINNER). What are you trying to hide from me?

KOCHETOV. Trisha! My dear Trisha! Let me tell you something. You are the perfect Government guide. (*To the others.*) Everything she tells me I believe! The only trouble is, I think she believes it *herself.*

TRISHA. What have I said wrong now?

KOCHETOV. Well, my darling, it's only too clear what has happened to poor old Hugh Walpole. They have taken him out and shot him.

TRISHA. Mr Kochetov, please don't say things like that.

KOCHETOV (*to the others*). Am I right?

WINN. Certainly not.

SKINNER. Absolutely not.

DEEPING. Where did you get such an idea from?

SKINNER. Ridiculous idea.

BLYTON. We don't know what you're talking about.

SKINNER. Yes, what are you talking about?

KOCHETOV (*to* TRISHA). You see? They've shot him. This is going to make the most wonderful article!

TRISHA. I know you only do it to tease me.

KOCHETOV. Yes, because you're so beautiful when you're angry. Your cheeks glow, your eyes flash . . .

TRISHA. No one in this country is taken outside and shot.

KOCHETOV. You mean they don't even trouble to take them outside now?

TRISHA. I've already explained to you, several times — the rights of the individual here are most strictly safeguarded.

KOCHETOV. Look at her! Look at her! I'm so good for her complexion! But, Trisha, my darling, have a care. Because if you go on asking where Mr Walpole is they will take *you* outside and shoot you, and that would ruin your looks.

TRISHA (*to* SKINNER). Is there a telephone here?

SKINNER. In my office.

TRISHA. I shall place a trunk call through to London direct and get all this sorted out. (*To* KOCHETOV.) Hugh Walpole has not been shot, and I am going to find him for you if I have to go to John O'Groats to do it. And I do *not* believe everything I say! I mean, I don't say everything I believe. I mean . . . Oh! Where am I going?

SKINNER. Through here. Straight across the corridor. I shall have to charge you for the call, of course, to keep my books straight.

Exit TRISHA, *centre*.

KOCHETOV. Her first job since she left school. And everywhere we go, it's a disaster. We have lunch at the Ritz — and we wait one hour and forty minutes to be served. We visit a new sanatorium — and the doorhandle comes off in her hand. Now she takes me to see her favourite writer, and he has just disappeared in the middle of the night. Poor Trisha!

WINN. Yes, but look on the positive side. Think of all the writers who *haven't* disappeared in the middle of the night! Why don't you interview Warwick Deeping instead? His novels are very widely read in this country.

DEEPING. Or Godfrey Winn, for that matter. An astonishingly adaptable writer.

WINN. Yes, or Enid Blyton.

DEEPING. Enid is quite well known for her curiously obscure erotic verse.

WINN. They all come to Balmoral, you know! H.G. Wells — Bernard Shaw. You never know who's going to walk through that door next.

Enter MCNAB, right. He is carrying the mop and the champagne bucket, empty, but not wearing the apron. He crosses towards the lefthand door. KOCHETOV watches him.

Well, they tend to come more in summer, people like Wells and Shaw. This is really a summer place, of course. You might look out of this window and see footmen hurrying across the lawn with trays of ices. You might see the band of the Coldstream Guards playing on the terrace. In summer.

MCNAB (*to SKINNER, on the point of going out left*). All right?

SKINNER. Yes, yes, yes . . . Where's your apron? I don't know what our visitor must be thinking. (*To KOCHETOV.*) The butler — and half the time he comes waltzing through here without his green baize apron!

Exit MCNAB left.

KOCHETOV. I must find my little girl guide. You know, I think this is going to be really rather a prize-winning article. I can't help wondering, though, what will happen to all the people who feature in it. (*Laughs.*) Will they arrest the director of the sanatorium, do you suppose? Will they shoot the manager of the Ritz? Am I leaving a trail of official corpses all the way across England? A terrible responsibility we journalists bear!

Exit KOCHETOV, centre.

DEEPING. Poor old Walpole.

WINN. I suppose it might be only ten years. He could be out again by 1947.

DEEPING. Funny they should arrest *him*.

WINN. Yes — so much for his cousin in high places.

DEEPING. After all we've endured about his influence in certain quarters.

SKINNER. I think we're in the clear, though, aren't we?

DEEPING. In the clear? In the newspapers — that's where you're going to be!

SKINNER (*uneasily*). In the newspapers?

DEEPING. In this Russian fellow's article!

WINN. It won't just be the Warden. We're all going to be in it.

DEEPING. Up to our necks. Then we're *all* going to wake up one morning and find we left during the night.

SKINNER. So what are we going to do?

DEEPING. Enid's keeping very quiet.

WINN. Have you got some ideas, Enid?

BLYTON. The room's vacant, then?

WINN. The room? What room?

BLYTON. Hugh Walpole's room. The room with the kitchen flue running through it. The warm room.

SKINNER. Never mind about the room. Let's keep our minds on one thing at a time.

WINN *moves quietly and inconspicuously towards the centre door.*

Now, we're all in this together . . . Where are you off to?

WINN. Would you excuse me? I've just got to slip upstairs.

DEEPING. Oh, no, you don't! (*To* SKINNER.) Tell him he can't do that!

BLYTON (*to* SKINNER). Stop him! Stop them both!

SKINNER. What?

BLYTON. It was my idea!

DEEPING. I am the senior writer present!

WINN. And I'm first in the queue!

Exit WINN, *centre* DEEPING *and* BLYTON *fight to be next through the door.*

BLYTON. Excuse me!

DEEPING. I beg your pardon!

BLYTON. Appalling manners!

DEEPING. Disgusting display!

Exit DEEPING, *centre.*

BLYTON (*to* SKINNER). It's not fair! It's not fair!

SKINNER. What is all this?

BLYTON. They're going to steal the room!

Exit BLYTON, *centre.*

SKINNER (*goes to follow them*). Room? What room? Never mind about the room!

Enter WALPOLE, *right. He is 53, and is wearing thick spectacles, and overcoat, hat, and galoshes. He is in a considerable state of ill humour. He bears some passing resemblance to* MCNAB, *possibly because he is played by the same actor.*

WALPOLE. It really is too bad!

SKINNER (*whirls round*). And don't *you* try slipping past, McNab, because I have eyes in the back of my . . . Walpole!

WALPOLE. I intend to lodge a formal complaint with the authorities!

SKINNER. You're here!

WALPOLE. You may well look surprised! I could have been killed out there!

SKINNER. But . . . you *escaped?*

WALPOLE. Escaped? I escaped *death*, if that's what you mean.

Enter BLYTON, *centre.*

BLYTON (*to* SKINNER). He's throwing everything out of the

room into the corridor! Hair-brushes, suits, dirty socks . . .
(*Sees* WALPOLE.) Oh, my God!

WALPOLE. Yes! Every bone in my body is jarred. I am bruised
from here to here. I may well have concussion.

Enter DEEPING, *centre*.

DEEPING (*to* SKINNER). He's thrown the man's mother out into
the corridor now! A photograph in a silver frame, and he's
tossed it aside like so much . . . Walpole!

BLYTON. They broke his bones! They hit him over the head!

WALPOLE. And how long I lay in the snow out there I know
not. I am dangerously chilled.

Enter WINN, *centre*.

WINN. I've put my cabin trunk in the room and locked the door.
So I hope there'll be no more . . . Hugh!

BLYTON. They beat him black and blue!

DEEPING. They left him in the snow!

WALPOLE. My muffler is sodden. I have melted snow running
down my neck.

WINN. But . . . they let you go?

WALPOLE. What?

WINN. They arrested you — and then they let you go again?

WALPOLE. Arrested me? What in heaven's name are you talking
about?

DEEPING. Hold on a moment. You mean . . . you *weren't*
arrested?

WALPOLE. Arrested? Me? *I'm* not the one who should be
arrested! I have been standing in a queue outside the Co-op
since six o'clock this morning. There was a rumour, according
to McNab, that a delivery of ladies' winter underwear was
expected. When it arrived, of course, it turned out to be usual
itchy rubbish they sell for men. I get back here, frozen to the
marrow, and find that certain people have turned the front
doorstep into a skating-rink!

WINN. And you slipped?

WALPOLE. I may have fractured my skull! The same story every morning since the chain disappeared from the upstairs loo. There's a perfectly good earth closet at the back of the piggeries. But, oh no — not for some people! Not in the middle of the night! Not when it's below freezing! What does it matter? they think. Anything goes these days! So it's up with the bedroom window, and devil take the hindermost! But if you can't learn self-control, you might at least look to see what's below!

Exit WALPOLE, *centre.*

DEEPING. Oh, dear.

SKINNER. Is he trying to tell us he *wasn't* arrested?

WINN. I'm afraid we all rather jumped to conclusions.

SKINNER (*brooding*). McNab, that was. McNab again.

DEEPING. Never mind about McNab.

SKINNER. Yes, but where does it leave us? That Russian thinks Walpole's been shot!

WINN. But, Warden, it's all right! Because now he can see he hasn't been!

SKINNER. That girl's out there telling London he's disappeared!

WINN. But, Warden, now she can see he hasn't disappeared!

SKINNER. You mean . . . tell them they can interview him?

DEEPING. Slowly, as if through treacle, the penny drops.

SKINNER. You mean . . . say McNab said . . .?

WINN. Say anything!

DEEPING. He's here now. That's all that matters.

SKINNER. There's a catch in this somewhere.

Exit SKINNER *centre.*

WINN. I see what you mean about Skinner. He does rather go to pieces under pressure.

BLYTON. It'll be coming through that door, won't it. Any moment now.

WINN. What will?

BLYTON. The catch. Well, what sort of interview do you think Hugh is going to give when you've finished explaining to him?

WINN. Explaining to him? Explaining what to him?

Enter WALPOLE *centre holding a framed photograph.*

WALPOLE. My mother!

WINN. What?

WALPOLE. My mother! Lying in the corridor! Suits! Collars! Tooth powder! Everywhere!

WINN. Oh my God. The room.

WALPOLE. You, is it, Winn? Have you gone quite insane?

WINN. Hugh, listen. This is going to sound rather bad, but the thing is, I thought . . . Well, we *all* thought . . . I mean, Enid suggested . . . I'll put it back.

Exit WINN, *centre.*

WALPOLE. The man has gone berserk! He must be locked up!

BLYTON. Have you looked *inside* the room yet?

WALPOLE. Inside the room?

DEEPING. Enid, don't work him up!

BLYTON. You'll find a cabin trunk in there.

WALPOLE. A cabin trunk? I don't *possess* a cabin trunk!

BLYTON. Godfrey Winn possesses a cabin trunk.

WALPOLE. But this is naked violation!

Exit WALPOLE, *centre.*

DEEPING. You shouldn't have done that, Enid. He's going to go his very bright red colour.

BLYTON (*sombrely*). He won't be able to breathe. He won't be able to speak.

DEEPING. He's already the colour of his precious ladies' underwear.

Enter SKINNER *and* KOCHETOV, *centre.*

KOCHETOV (*to* SKINNER). Privacy?

SKINNER (*genial*). We do try to protect it here.

KOCHETOV. By saying people have disappeared during the night?

SKINNER. We were pulling your leg.

KOCHETOV. And I may interview him?

SKINNER. Of course.

KOCHETOV *looks at* BLYTON.

BLYTON (*shrugs*). Why not? It's a free country.

DEEPING. I'll fetch him in, shall I?

Exit DEEPING, *centre.*

KOCHETOV. Heartbreaking. It was going to be such a wonderful article.

SKINNER. I'm sorry to disappoint you.

KOCHETOV. Oh well. It will make Trisha happy. And if Trisha is happy, perhaps our journey back to London will be fruitful.

Exit KOCHETOV, *centre.*

SKINNER (*genial*). The night train from Aberdeen! That's the life, Blyton! I think if I could choose where I wanted to live I should make my home in a first-class sleeper. All yesterday's troubles miles behind, all tomorrow's miles ahead. Just a little warm room speeding through the night. Nothing in the whole wide world but the bedside light shining on the papers in your despatch box. And in the morning, a limousine waiting — everyone smiling, everyone pleased to see you. Well, it will come again, Blyton, it will come again.

Enter MCNAB, *left, wearing an apron and carrying the mop and champagne bucket of swill. He crosses slowly to the righthand door behind* SKINNER*'s back.*

I'm not as big a fool as some of you think. I don't say much. I keep quiet. I bide my time. I wait until I can reach out and catch the wrongdoer red-handed, in the very act of removing yet another champagne bucket. Don't rush away, McNab. Let me tell you some sad news. That is the oldest trick in the business. Wheelbarrow loads of old straw. They keep searching the straw. And what are you stealing? You're stealing wheelbarrows. I've seen it before, McNab — I've seen it all before. You thought; the poor fool's going to keep checking the contents of the bucket. I thought; how much rope shall I give him to hang himself? Do you know what I did this morning, McNab? I stuck a tuppeny stamp on the bottom of the bucket. So that when I pick up *this* bucket . . .

Lifts the bucket above his head.

SKINNER. . . . and discover to my surprise there is *no* tuppeny stamp on the bottom, then I have proof positive . . .

Looks at the bottom of the bucket. Silence. Then he hands the bucket back to MCNAB.

The pigs?

MCNAB. The pigs.

SKINNER. Off you go, then, McNab.

Exit MCNAB, *right.*

SKINNER *stands lost in thought.*

He's stealing something, though. I know that. It couldn't be tuppenny stamps?

Enter WINN, *centre, in a great state of agitation.*

WINN. Warden! Warden! Hugh Walpole is running amok! I *tried* to explain. I *said* I'd move everything out. But as soon as he saw my stuff he just lost control. He's throwing everything out into the corridor! There's four hundred pages of manuscript scattered all over the main stairs!

SKINNER. You haven't upset him? He's supposed to be giving an interview!

WINN. Upset *him?* He's upset *me!*

SKINNER. Writers! You can't take your eyes off them for a moment.

Enter DEEPING, *centre. He is enjoying himself.*

DEEPING. Very foolish to leave him up there on his own, you know, Winn.

WINN. Why? What's he doing now?

DEEPING. Listen.

They listen. There is the noise of a large, heavy object falling down a flight of stairs.

WINN. What in heaven's name . . .?

DEEPING. Your cabin trunk.

WINN. My cabin trunk?

The noise of the object falling down another flight of stairs.

DEEPING. He's bringing it downstairs for you.

WINN. Bringing it downstairs?

DEEPING. Ready for your departure.

Enter WALPOLE, *centre. Panting and gasping, beside himself with rage, he is dragging the cabin trunk. It is too heavy for him. He has a terrible struggle to get it through the door.*

WALPOLE. Never heard of such behaviour . . .!

WINN (*to* SKINNER). Look at him! Look! Look!

SKINNER. Calm down, Walpole.

WALPOLE (*drags trunk to middle of room*). Come back . . . soaked to the skin . . . whole morning utterly wasted . . .

WINN. Stop him! Stop him!

SKINNER (*to* WALPOLE). Now stop all this. You've got to be interviewed!

WALPOLE (*oblivious*). And what do I find? I find this little jackanapes . . .!

WINN. You've got to control him!

SKINNER (*to* WINN). Oh shut up! (*To* WALPOLE.) Control

yourself, Walpole!

WALPOLE. Now my heart's racing. Blood's pounding in my ears
. . . I won't remain in the same house! Either *he* goes, or *I* . . .

Dies.

SKINNER. That's better. Now listen, Walpole. This is going to
be just another ordinary, everyday literary interview. I don't
want you to go using this as an occasion for airing personal
grievances. All right, you may have grievances.

WALPOLE *slips out of sight behind the trunk.*

Fair enough — we all have grievances. We'll go into those at the
proper time . . . Where is he?

DEEPING. I think he's ill.

BLYTON. I think he's dead.

SKINNER. Oh, for goodness sake. Come on, Walpole, pull
yourself together. We've no time for this kind of thing now.
(*To* WINN *and* DEEPING.) Get him up. He can't sprawl about
the floor like that.

WINN *and* DEEPING *pull* WALPOLE *to his feet.*

Come on, Walpole! Work to be done!

They sit him in a chair, then stand back to look at him.

DEEPING. He doesn't look too good, you know.

WINN. I don't think he's really breathing.

SKINNER. He'll be all right. Just needs a bit of a sitdown. Get
his breath back.

WALPOLE *slowly keels forward.*

BLYTON. He's dead.

SKINNER. Of course he's not dead!

Sits WALPOLE *up again.*

DEEPING. It was heaving that trunk about that did it.

WINN. He always had a weak heart, I know that.

SKINNER. How are you feeling? A bit better?

WALPOLE *keels slowly forward again.*

BLYTON. He's dead.

SKINNER (*sits WALPOLE up again and holds him*). Well, we can't cancel the interview now.

DEEPING. He can't do an interview in this condition!

SKINNER. He's got to! He can't expect us to make more excuses at this stage! What would it look like? Be reasonable.

DEEPING. Well, if that Russian comes in and finds him like this . . . .

Enter KOCHETOV, centre.

KOCHETOV. Mr Walpole!

They turn automatically to face KOCHETOV. SKINNER lets go of WALPOLE, who begins to keel forward.

Please — don't get up!

SKINNER pulls WALPOLE back.

And don't say a word! Wait till my little girl from the Board of Trade comes in. She's just telling London we've found you.

Crosses to centre door, and calls.

WALPOLE *keels over.*

Trisha! Come on! He's here!

SKINNER pulls WALPOLE up. KOCHETOV turns back to him.

It's ridiculous! I thought you were dead!

WINN (*nervously*). No, no!

KOCHETOV (*turns to him*). I beg your pardon?

WALPOLE *keels over.*

WINN. No, no, no, no, no!

SKINNER pulls WALPOLE up, and holds him.

KOCHETOV. No, obviously not.

Turns back to WALPOLE, glancing all the time at the centre door.

KOCHETOV. If I might ask one thing of you. Trisha is very young, but she's very serious about it all, so — please — when she comes in, try not to smile.

Enter TRISHA, *centre.*

TRISHA. Is he really here?

KOCHETOV. He's really here! Mr Walpole, this is Trisha. Your greatest fan!

TRISHA (*shyly*). Hello.

She looks at the floor. Silence. KOCHETOV *watches her, amused.*

KOCHETOV (*to* TRISHA). Speak, then. Say something.

TRISHA. I don't know what to say.

KOCHETOV. Tell him you like his books.

Pause.

TRISHA. I can't say that.

KOCHETOV. Why ever not?

TRISHA. It just sounds silly.

KOCHETOV. Five hundred miles we have travelled for this moment. And not a word comes out!

TRISHA. Please just everyone go on with the conversation. Just forget about me.

KOCHETOV (*still looking at* TRISHA). She started reading your books when she was fifteen years old.

TRISHA. Mr Kochetov, please!

KOCHETOV. My love, *one* of us has to say something. She has three great heroes. Isn't that right? Tchaikovsky, Shelley, and Hugh Walpole.

TRISHA. I'll certainly never tell *you* anything again!

KOCHETOV. She's in love with all three of you. But you're a very lucky man, Mr Walpole, Because Tchaikovsky and Shelley — they're dead.

TRISHA. I hate you!

Exit TRISHA, *centre in tears.*

KOCHETOV. What have I done? But really, one can't help wanting to take a little bite out of her sometimes. Twenty years old, and she writes poetry still! I'll get her back, don't worry.

Exit KOCHETOV, *left.*

SKINNER (*panics*). Get him out of here!

WINN. But the interview . . .?

SKINNER. Out! Out! Out!

Seizes WALPOLE, *drags him out of his chair, and falls under the weight with* WALPOLE *on top of him.*

Off! Off! Off! Get him off! Help me!

WINN *and* DEEPING *lift him off* SKINNER.

DEEPING. Where shall we put him?

SKINNER. Anywhere! Outside! Not that way!

BLYTON. They'll be back any moment.

SKINNER. Just get rid of him! Behind the sofa! In the box!

Indicates the cabin trunk.

DEEPING. In the box, right.

Drops his half of WALPOLE *and tries to open the trunk.* WINN *drops the other half and runs to defend the trunk.*

WINN. No, no! Not in there! That's my trunk!

SKINNER. It's locked! Where's the key?

WINN. Upstairs. You can't open it . . . Don't wrench it about like that! It's not made to be roughly handled . . .! Now look what you've done — you've broken it!

DEEPING. It's full of clobber.

SKINNER. Throw it out!

WINN. No, no! My things!

DEEPING *throws stuff out of the trunk.*

Look here, those are my tennis togs!

BLYTON (*at lefthand door*). He's coming!

*WINN abandons the defence of his property and scrambles
with* DEEPING *and* SKINNER *to pick* WALPOLE *up off the
floor. They dump him in the trunk (whence the actor playing
him makes his escape via the stage trap, or any other means
possible).*

DEEPING. Won't shut!

SKINNER. Foot!

*Points at a familiar galoshed foot which the jamming down of
the lid has left sticking out.* WINN *and* DEEPING *cram it
inside and close the lid.*

SKINNER *stands concealing the empty chair.*

Enter KOCHETOV, *centre.*

KOCHETOV. It's all right. I'm being unbelievably charming. She
just needs to calm down and dry her eyes . . . First a trunk
appears. Now a collection of old clothes.

Picks up a handful of them.

WINN. My tennis togs.

KOCHETOV. Won't the snow rather take the speed off the ball?

WINN. No, I'm just . . . sorting out my gear for next season.

KOCHETOV *tosses the tennis stuff aside and picks up another
item. It turns out to be a pair of long johns.*

KOCHETOV. I'm sorry.

*He tactfully opens the trunk, and without looking throws the
long johns into it.*

Exit KOCHETOV, *centre.*

DEEPING (*to* SKINNER). *Now* what?

SKINNER. Sit on the box!

WINN *sits.*

DEEPING. What are you going to tell them?

WINN. Tell them the truth.

DEEPING. Just suddenly . . .?

WINN. Just suddenly . . .

DEEPING. Got taken out and shot.

WINN. They can see he's not shot! They can see he just suddenly . . .

DEEPING. Dropped dead inside that box.

Pause.

SKINNER. That's where we went wrong — putting him in the box. Right. Get him out of there!

WINN. Take him out again?

SKINNER (*gestures to him to rise*). Up! Up! Up! Down!

The righthand door is opening. WINN *closes the lid and sits on it.*

Enter MCNAB, *right, without his apron, carrying the empty champagne bucket.*

DEEPING. Oh, it's you.

BLYTON. I thought it was Hugh Walpole's ghost.

MCNAB *crosses to the lefthand door with everyone staring at him. He stops, holds up the bucket and raps on its bottom to draw attention to the stamp.*

Exit MCNAB, *left.*

WINN *jumps up, and they start to lift* WALPOLE's *legs out of the trunk.*

SKINNER. Wait!

DEEPING. What?

SKINNER. McNab!

WINN. What about him?

SKINNER. Dress him up as Walpole! Say he's Walpole!

Pause.

BLYTON. Oh, *no!*

WINN. It would never work.

DEEPING. He doesn't look anything like him.

BLYTON. No, no. no!

WINN. It couldn't possibly work.

DEEPING. McNab's a Scotsman!

SKINNER (*indicates trunk*). The coat, the coat! Get his coat off! (*Calls off left.*) McNab! Come here! Where are you? McNab! (*To* BLYTON.) Keep that door shut! (*To* WINN *and* DEEPING.) Coat! Coat! Coat!

DEEPING *shrugs. They open the trunk, and begin to remove* WALPOLE'*s overcoat.*

Enter MCNAB, *left, wearing an apron, carrying the empty champagne bucket and a garden fork.*

SKINNER. Right! Sit down! I've got a job for you.

MCNAB *remains standing, looking into the trunk.*

MCNAB. What happened to *him*, then?

SKINNER. Nothing. Sit down.

MCNAB. Comes here first class. Goes home in the luggage van.

SKINNER. Sit down!

He takes the bucket and fork away from MCNAB *and puts them on the sideboard.*

MCNAB. Sit down? (*Sits, in the chair previously occupied by* WALPOLE.)

DEEPING (*hands* SKINNER *the overcoat*). Hopeless! Hopeless!

SKINNER. Shut up!

DEEPING. It won't work!

SKINNER. It's got to work.

DEEPING. It can't work!

SKINNER. This is nothing! Inspections in factories — I've had men made out of *cardboard!* Flesh and blood — this is luxury! (*To* MCNAB.) Stand up!

MCNAB *stands up.* SKINNER *and* WINN *dress him in the overcoat.*

Arms, arms, arms!

BLYTON. They're dressing him like a dummy!

SKINNER (*to* MCNAB). Listen, one foot wrong, and you'll be in that box along with him.

MCNAB. Hold fast now. What is all this?

WINN. You're him.

MCNAB. I'm what?

SKINNER. Don't argue, McNab. We've no time for argument.

WINN. You're Mr Walpole.

MCNAB. Mr Walpole?

WINN. Just for five minutes.

MCNAB. But why . . .?

SKINNER. Because I say you are.

WINN. What about the apron?

SKINNER. Keep the coat done up.

WINN. That neck's not Walpole.

SKINNER (*to* DEEPING). Muffler! (*To* WINN.) Get that cap off his head.

WINN (*removes cap and puts it in the pocket of overcoat*). Oh dear. Hugh's bald on top.

SKINNER. Hat!

DEEPING (*brings the hat*). Look at him, though! He's nothing like him!

SKINNER. Glasses! Two arms, two legs, and a head. That's enough for me.

DEEPING (*fetches the glasses*). He won't see much through these.

SKINNER. What does he need to see?

They put the glasses on MCNAB. *He feels around blindly.*

DEEPING. He must see where he's going.

SKINNER. He's not going anywhere. (*To* MCNAB.) Don't move. Don't wave your arms about.

DEEPING. But as soon as he opens his mouth . . .!

SKINNER. Don't open your mouth.

WINN. Be rather taciturn.

SKINNER. Just grunt.

WINN (*finds a pipe in overcoat pocket*). Here, chew this.

> *Pause. They stand back and survey their handiwork doubtfully.*

BLYTON. He only wants a bonfire under him.

> *Pause.*

WINN. He'll have to say *something*, Warden. If it's an interview.

MCNAB (*encumbered with the pipe*). Interview?

DEEPING. They always ask what your message for the world is.

WINN (*to* MCNAB). Your message for the world is the dignity of man.

DEEPING. He could tell them he's against war. That always goes down well.

BLYTON. What about love? They always ask about love.

SKINNER. You're for it. For love. Against war. Now, are we ready?

DEEPING. What does he think about Einstein? Or the Gold Standard? Or the League of Nations?

WINN (*to* MCNAB). Anything else — look at us. We'll help you.

SKINNER. Right. Are they coming?

> *Pause. They all wait, looking apprehensively at* MCNAB.

WINN (*to* MCNAB). Just . . . use your imagination.

> *Pause.*

SKINNER. Boots! Get his boots off!

> WINN *and* DEEPING *fall on a foot apiece and drag his boots off.*

WINN. No socks!

SKINNER. Boots back!

> *They hurriedly replace the boots.*

> *Pause.*

> Box! Close the box!

> WINN, DEEPING, *and* BLYTON *rush to the open trunk. They push the lid down, but it springs up again.*

WINN. It won't stay shut!

SKINNER. Sit on it!

> DEEPING *sits on it.*

> *Pause.* SKINNER *looks at* MCNAB.

> It's not going to work, is it. Hopeless. Take all that stuff off. We'll just have to tell them the truth.

> *Enter* KOCHETOV *and* TRISHA, *centre.*

TRISHA. I'm sorry. I don't know *what* you must be thinking.

SKINNER. Well, let me just explain.

TRISHA. I mean, a civil servant, bursting into tears and running out of the room like that.

KOCHETOV. It was my fault.

SKINNER. In fact it was Winn's fault.

TRISHA. It was everything. It was the train journey, and the feeling of being responsible for everything.

KOCHETOV. It was the snow. It was the sheep.

TRISHA (*to* MCNAB). It was finding you weren't here.

KOCHETOV. And then suddenly finding you *were.*

SKINNER. Yes, well, anyway . . .

DEEPING. Sit down, Skinner.

SKINNER. Oh. (*Sits.*)

TRISHA (*to* MCNAB). There are so many things I want to say to you — so many things I want to ask you about.

KOCHETOV. One look at you, and it all went out of her head.

TRISHA. Well, you were sitting here looking so — I don't know — so rigid and disapproving. I thought, well, he just despises me. But now I've had a proper look at you . . . well, you do look a bit less intimidating.

KOCHETOV. Now you've got your pipe to suck you're . . . well, you're an entirely different person.

TRISHA. Yes, you're not at all as I imagined you! I imagined you as . . . I'm not sure . . . (*Sits on the floor at his feet.*) But not wearing Wellington boots, somehow. Shall I tell you how I always think of you? It's very silly, but I always think of you as a cat. Awfully delicate and fastidious and feline, with beautiful manners and silky soft paws. But with piercing eyes that see right inside me! Well, that's how you look in your photograph. I suppose it doesn't show your feet. I'm sorry. I'm just babbling on. I don't know — I'm in such a funny mood today. First I can't start and now I can't stop. (*To* KOCHETOV.) I'm sorry.

KOCHETOV. No — go ahead. Conduct the whole interview. Write the article for me.

TRISHA (*to* MCNAB). Well, I must ask you one thing. No, I mustn't. It's Mr Kochetov who's supposed to be asking the questions, and as a matter of fact I know what he's going to ask you, because he asks everyone we interview. He's going to ask you about the man in Nizhni Novgorod. (*To* KOCHETOV.) Sorry. Go on. Ask him about the man in Nizhni Novgorod.

KOCHETOV. You ask him. I'm sitting here having a holiday.

TRISHA. Don't be silly.

KOCHETOV. I'm not saying a word!

TRISHA. Well, apparently there's a man in Nizhini Novgorod who's sitting on top of a pole. Did you know there are people who sit on top of poles? This man's been up there for 83 days. (*To* KOCHETOV.) 83 days?

KOCHETOV. That was yesterday.

TRISHA. 84 days. And every morning newspaper reporters come

and stand at the bottom of the pole and ask the man what he thinks about war, and that kind of thing. And when Mr Kochetov was there, in Nizhni Novgorod, he asked him what the world looked like from the top of a pole, and the man replied . . .

KOCHETOV. 'Surprisingly large to be kept down by such a thin pole.'

TRISHA. And then Mr Kochetov asks you to say what the world looks like to you, in some brief and witty phrase like that. Well, I must stop talking, and let him ask you the question, but there's one thing I must just ask you first. Why is Isabel so strangely drawn to Moffatt's?

KOCHETOV. What?

TRISHA (*to* KOCHETOV). In Mr Walpole's novel, *Mr Perrin and Mr Traill,* which you haven't read. (*To* MCNAB.) She hates Moffatt's. So why does she keep coming back, again and again?

MCNAB *looks to* WINN *for help;* WINN *looks at* DEEPING, *who turns to* BLYTON. *She shrugs.* TRISHA *looks from one to the other.*

I'm sorry. Is that a very foolish question? (*To* MCNAB.) I'm sure everybody else knows. But please just tell me.

WINN. I know! Why don't we all have a drink?

DEEPING. A drink! What a good idea!

BLYTON. It's at least half-an-hour since breakfast.

WINN. A drink, Mr Kochetov?

KOCHETOV. If you like. (*To* MCNAB.) All right, let's get this question out of the way, and then we can do the interview. Tell her what Isabel is up to.

DEEPING. Just a moment. There's nothing to drink.

WINN. There's whisky.

BLYTON. He keeps it in his safe.

WINN. For special occasions.

DEEPING. Shall I do the honours, then?

DEEPING *gets up from the trunk to cross to* SKINNER. *The lid opens.* BLYTON *gives a wild inarticulate cry.* WINN *hurls himself across to the trunk and sits on it.*

KOCHETOV *and* TRISHA *turn to look at* BLYTON.

KOCHETOV. I beg your pardon?

BLYTON. Did I speak?

DEEPING (*holding out his hand to* SKINNER). I should think this is a special occasion, isn't it?

SKINNER *gives him a key.*

Exit DEEPING *centre.*

KOCHETOV. All right. Isabel. Set her mind at rest about Isabel.

WINN. I happen to know he's got rather strong views about war.

BLYTON. I want to hear him talking about love.

KOCHETOV. We shall come to war. We shall come to love. First, Isabel.

TRISHA. I'm sorry. I just wondered what the mysterious hold was that Moffatt's had over her.

She waits. MCNAB *at last takes the pipe out of his mouth to reply.*

WINN. Or you could ask him if he's got a message for the world.

BLYTON. Or if he ever worries about who he really is.

TRISHA. Everyone keeps interrupting! No one's giving him a chance to speak!

KOCHETOV. Yes. Quiet, please, everyone. All right, this mysterious hold.

WINN. I think I should just explain . . .

KOCHETOV. Uh!

WINN. That he's a man of . . .

KOCHETOV. Please!

Silence.

WINN. Very few words.

KOCHETOV. Then let us give him a chance to utter them. Mr Walpole . . .

MCNAB *removes his spectacles and rubs his eyes.*

SKINNER. What are you doing? (*To* KOCHETOV.) I beg your pardon. He has been strongly advised to keep his spectacles on at all times.

BLYTON. To reduce the chances of a sudden heart attack.

MCNAB *replaces his spectacles.*

WINN. They do take a close interest here in our welfare.

TRISHA. Please!

KOCHETOV. Let the man speak!

MCNAB *takes the pipe out of his mouth.*

Enter DEEPING, *centre, carrying a tray with whisky, soda and glasses.*

DEEPING. With soda or without soda?

MCNAB *puts the pipe back.*

TRISHA. He was just going to speak.

WINN. I'll be mother, shall I?

Gets up from the trunk and crosses to the drinks tray. The lid of the trunk rises.

SKINNER *utters a wild inarticulate cry.* KOCHETOV *and* TRISHA *turn to look at him as* DEEPING, *holding the soda syphon, hurls himself at the trunk.*

SKINNER *continues the cry as a cough.*

KOCHETOV *and* TRISHA *turn to look at* DEEPING, *who is sprawled across the trunk with the soda syphon spraying.*

DEEPING. Soda, anyone?

KOCHETOV. All right — who wants soda? I don't want soda. Anyone want soda? No one wants soda.

TRISHA. I want soda.

KOCHETOV. She wants soda.

KOCHETOV takes her glass to DEEPING for a shot of soda.

Now. Has everyone got a drink? Is everyone happy? No one wants to pass round the cigars, or run outside to wash their hands? All right. That's wonderful. We shall drink one toast together, and then we shall have absolute silence for Mr Walpole, while he explains to us all about the mysterious Isabel. So, ladies and gentlemen, may I ask you all to be upstanding . . .?

Everyone gets to his feet except DEEPING, who is sitting on the trunk. KOCHETOV waits, glass raised, looking at DEEPING. DEEPING exhibits symptoms of stress. Then BLYTON jumps on to the trunk with raised glass.

BLYTON. Isabel!

DEEPING gets to his feet.

OMNES. Isabel!

They drink the toast and sit down — DEEPING and WINN on the trunk. KOCHETOV and MCNAB, still standing, take their drinks at one gulp.

KOCHETOV. Oh, but look at *him!* He drinks like a Russian.

TRISHA. Now *you're* interrupting.

KOCHETOV. No, but this is a man after my own heart. Pour him another one. Pour me another one. We shall drink a toast together.

WINN pours some more whisky for the two of them.

SKINNER. Thank you. I think that bottle would be happier with me.

Takes the bottle. WINN sits down on the trunk.

KOCHETOV. To freedom of speech.

MCNAB and KOCHETOV drain their glasses.

And now, not another word from anyone. Mr Walpole . . .

KOCHETOV sits down. A pause, then MCNAB leans forward a little in his chair.

TRISHA. I think he really is going to speak!

BLYTON. And we all want to hear what on earth he's going to say.

MCNAB. This fellow of yours . . . This fellow on the top of the pole . . . Eighty-four days he's been up there? My word, he must be bursting! Eighty-four minutes, this lot, and it's up with the bedroom windy!

TRISHA. I don't understand . . .

KOCHETOV. Don't you, my love? I think perhaps I'm beginning to . . .

He gets out a notebook and pencil and begins to write.

MCNAB. There's all of you below, looking up at him? Is that it?

Gets to his feet and looks down at KOCHETOV and TRISHA.

And there's him up above . . .

He turns his chair round, and climbs on to it, as into a pulpit. SKINNER hovers anxiously.

. . . and he's been storing it up and storing it up, and now he looks down and sees you at his feet, and what does he say? I'll tell you what he says.

He snatches the bottle of whisky from SKINNER's hand, and holds it high above his head, tilted to pour. He puts his foot up on the back of the chair, and his bare knee emerges from beneath his coat.

He says . . .

SKINNER (*screams*). Pull your skirt down!

Curtain.

ACT TWO

The same, with no lapse of time.

SKINNER. Pull your skirt down!

MCNAB (*outraged*). My skirt? What do you mean, my skirt?

SKINNER. I mean, pull your trousers down!

MCNAB. Skirt, is it? (*Attempting to demonstrate to* TRISHA *and* KOCHETOV.) There's no skirt under here!

SKINNER (*trying to hold* MCNAB's *coat down*). Whatever will our visitors think?

WINN. They're short trousers.

DEEPING. His trousers are away for repair.

WINN. He's a Scoutmaster.

BLYTON. He is having treatment for this.

MCNAB *hauls up his overcoat to demonstrate.*

MCNAB. It's the kilt!

SKINNER. It's not a kilt!

MCNAB. I'm a Scotsman!

SKINNER. He's not a Scotsman!

WINN. He is a bit Scotch.

DEEPING. More Scotch than most readers realise.

MCNAB. I'm a Scotsman!

SKINNER (*washes his hands of it*). All right — he's a Scotsman!

Pause. SKINNER *goes and sits down, defeated.*

KOCHETOV (*to* TRISHA, *amused*). So — you weren't expecting a Scotsman?

TRISHA (*disconcerted*). He's not the sort of person I was expecting at all! (*To* MCNAB.) I thought from your books you'd be less . . . I don't know . . . (*To* KOCHETOV.) But didn't you?

KOCHETOV (*gravely*). Much less.

WINN. He is, he is.

TRISHA. You mean, less . . . ? (*She waves her hands, trying to capture the elusive quality she expected.*)

WINN. Oh, altogether less.

TRISHA. No, I mean I thought you'd be somehow more . . .

WINN. He is, in some ways.

BLYTON. Far, far more.

TRISHA. No, I mean more . . .

WINN. More fastidious.

TRISHA. Not exactly.

DEEPING. More spinsterly.

TRISHA. Well . . .

BLYTON. More feline.

MCNAB. Feline? Like a cat playing with a mouse? I can be feline.

KOCHETOV. You like watching people tie themselves into worse and worse knots? I understand that.

TRISHA. No, I know what I mean. I was expecting you to be much more Hugh Walpole-ish.

KOCHETOV (*to* DEEPING). Do you find him Hugh Walpole-ish enough?

DEEPING. Oh, he *can* be Hugh Walpole-ish, believe me!

BLYTON. My God, can he be Hugh Walpole-ish!

TRISHA. I don't think you're Hugh Walpole-ish at all!

KOCHETOV. I'm not sure what literary epithet springs to mind.

Rabelaisian, perhaps?

WINN. Well . . .

SKINNER. According to my records he is Episcopalian.

BLYTON. You should have seen him with the pilchards.

DEEPING. Oh, the pilchards, yes! He wasn't very Rabelaisian with the pilchards.

TRISHA. The pilchards?

MCNAB. Oh, don't talk to me about the pilchards!

KOCHETOV. And at once, of course, we talk to you about the pilchards.

MCNAB. Sunday dinner, it was. I've got them a tin of pilchards, and don't ask me where, because tins of pilchards don't grow on trees, believe me. So there all this lot sit, wolfing down their pilchards — except him.

TRISHA. Except whom?

WINN. (*indicates* MCNAB). Him.

MCNAB. Me?

WINN. You, Hugh.

MCNAB. What?

WINN. Hugh, you just sat there, Hugh. If you remember, Hugh.

SKINNER. Buck your ideas up, McNab . . . McWalpole . . .

MCNAB. Oh, yes. Right. Me it was that was sitting there. Right. So I just sat there, not eating, saying nothing, with a terrible pained expression on his face. On my face. So I said to him, 'What's the trouble, Mr Walpole?' I said to *me*, 'What's the trouble?' *He* said to me, 'What's the trouble?' He, the butler, said to me, Mr Walpole, 'What's the trouble?' And you know what I said? I said, 'I may be reduced to eating bread-and-butter without butter, and eggs and bacon without bacon or eggs, but I'll not eat pilchards without a fish-fork.'

DEEPING. You were always very punctilious about the silverware.

KOCHETOV. The perfect gentleman.

WINN. Exactly.

MCNAB. And the tea. He was forever on at me about the tea. I was forever on at him about the tea. 'McNab,' I'd say, 'how many times must I tell you? Tea in the teapot first. Milk in the teapot afterwards. And McNab, don't pick up the sugar with your fingers, or we'll have nothing but a teapotful of germs.'

TRISHA. McNab? Who's McNab?

MCNAB. Oh, he's the butler. 'McNab,' I'm always saying to him, 'if you're the butler, then bustle about and buttle.'

DEEPING. 'McNab,' you'd say, 'don't stand there holding out your greasy hand for the meal vouchers. Offer a tray.'

WINN. 'If you won't put on gloves to serve the residents, McNab, at least take off the boots you've been wearing to serve the pigs.'

MCNAB. I came in yesterday in a terrible state. You should have seen my face as I walked through the door. It was a study.

Crosses to righthand door to demonstrate.

'It really is too bad. I came hideously close to doing myself a mischief on the doorstep. But let people beware, McNab. I am not entirely without cousins in certain quarters.' Oh, I'm quite a character, I can tell you. I'm forever trying to get my hands on ladies' underwear. 'McNab,' I say, 'have you heard any whisper of knickers in the village? There's sixpence in it for you, McNab. That rubbish they sell for men — I can't wear it, McNab. It's too tickly for a man of sedentary disposition.' (*Sits beside* KOCHETOV.) And the bathroom.

KOCHETOV. Tell us about the bathroom.

MCNAB. Every bath night the same. I come slopping down here in my carpet slippers, and it's: 'McNab, here's sixpence for you. Be a good lad and ventilate the bathroom for me. There's somebody else's steam in there.' Carpet slippers — that's the life. Some days I don't believe I get my feet out of those carpet slippers from morning till night. Except when I'm up there working, as they call it. I take my feet out of the slippers, and I put them against the wall, just on the warm patch where the kitchen flue comes through. I sit like that for hours together, and the dear knows what I'm thinking. Am I thinking up a few fine fancy notions to put in books? Or am I trying to remember from the old days whether you eat a grapefruit with a teaspoon or an eggspoon? I'll give you a word of advice, mister, and I'll give it you for nothing. When you get home, you buy yourself a good, hardwearing pair of carpet slippers, and you put up your plate as writer.

KOCHETOV. Today, I notice, you're wearing boots.

MCNAB. Today we've got company.

SKINNER. I hope our visitors are not taking all this too seriously.

KOCHETOV. I'm taking it very seriously. Almost as seriously as the rest of you.

WINN, DEEPING, and BLYTON all hurriedly convert their anxious expressions into smiles.

WINN. No, but he's a terrible tease, is Hugh. I'm sure that's not what he really feels about the writer's life.

KOCHETOV. Is it?

MCNAB. No, I'm pulling their legs. No, there's an awful lot of brain-fag attached to it. And then there's the strain on the eyes. And the spelling of some of those words is no joke. But, it's not without its compensations.

Holds out his glass to SKINNER, who is forced to refill it.

And see the rest of them are all right, will you. Keep them going with all those semi-colons and such.

SKINNER fills the other glasses.

No, looking back, over the years, taking the rough with the smooth, it's not a bad life. So here's to literature!

KOCHETOV. To literature!

TRISHA. Yes, to literature!

WINN
DEEPING } Literature!

SKINNER. Well, all good things must come to an end. So if

you've asked all your questions . . .

TRISHA. Oh, I don't think we have, have we?

KOCHETOV. On the contrary. We have hardly started.

MCNAB. No, I could tell you a thing or two about writers and what they get up to, never you fear. All that stuff about her heart beating wildly, and him pressing his burning lips against hers — I could tell you where they get that from, and it's not all out of books. Oh, my word, literature! Here's to it!

KOCHETOV. Literature — and life!

TRISHA. Life!

BLYTON. Life!

WINN
DEEPING } Literature.

SKINNER. And there we really must stop. I'm afraid Mr Walpole is a very busy man.

MCNAB. Don't worry about me, Mr Skinner. I've all the time in the world.

SKINNER (*genial*). Nose back to the grindstone, Walpole! Your readers are waiting!

MCNAB. Let them wait, Mr Skinner. Let everyone wait for once in a while.

SKINNER. (*to* KOCHETOV, *apologetically*). Writers! Half a chance, and they sit down and drink the day away. Come on, Walpole.

MCNAB. You want us all to get up and go back to work?

SKINNER. Yes. Up you get. (*To* KOCHETOV.) It's for their own good, I'm afraid.

MCNAB rises.

MCNAB. (*to* DEEPING, WINN *and* BLYTON). Right, then. Up we all get.

WINN. Oh . . .

Looks anxiously at SKINNER. DEEPING *looks at him sardonically. They remain sitting on the trunk.*

BLYTON. Perhaps we ought to sit and drink a little more of the day away first.

KOCHETOV. They can't bear to miss what's going to happen next.

SKINNER (*surrenders*). We're going to be here forever at this rate.

MCNAB *sits*.

TRISHA. Now you've taken off your glasses, I know where I've seen you before.

KOCHETOV. Here, when we arrived. With the pigfood.

MCNAB. Oh, the specs. Well, it's no use. I can't see a damn thing through them. They give you all these bits and pieces and say, 'Put them on.' And for all they care the floor can come up and hit you between the eyes.

TRISHA. And the apron.

MCNAB. Oh, the old apron.

SKINNER. He was cleaning his typewriter.

WINN. We were talking about how fastidious he is.

DEEPING. He is very fastidious about his typewriter.

TRISHA. But you had a bucket of pigswill.

DEEPING. His typewriter was in a disgusting state.

BLYTON. He drops bits of food into it as he types.

WINN. No, he was cleaning his room.

TRISHA. I see. You help with the jobs about the house?

MCNAB. You could say that.

DEEPING. We like to think of this place as a workers' co-operative.

WINN. We all share the domestic chores.

MCNAB. Oh, do we? (*To* TRISHA.) You ask him when was the last time *he* fed the pigs.

SKINNER. Well, we mustn't bore our visitors with our little

domestic arguments about who's done what.

MCNAB. Who's done what?

WINN. The usual family squabbles!

MCNAB. Who's done what? Who's done *any* what? What's *any* who done?

SKINNER. All right, the others remain seated — and you back to work . . .

MCNAB. I'll tell you who does what. I'll tell you who does *who*!

DEEPING *jumps up urgently.* KOCHETOV *smilingly makes a note.*

DEEPING (*to* KOCHETOV). A little more whisky? Oh, it's empty.

WINN (*jumps up*). I'll get another one.

The lid of the trunk comes up. WALPOLE's *legs become visible.*

SKINNER (*to* WINN). Look, I'm not standing for any more of this!

MCNAB. I should sit for it if I were you, Mr Skinner.

He nods at the trunk.

SKINNER. No, no, I'm not going to sit here and watch you open another . . .

Sees the trunk. Sits down abruptly on it. KOCHETOV *and* TRISHA *look round.*

SKINNER. . . . trunk of whisky.

WINN. Oh my God.

TRISHA. Are you all right?

MCNAB. His heart missed a beat.

DEEPING. He needs another trunk of whisky.

KOCHETOV. *Trunk* of whisky?

SKINNER. *Drunk* of whisky . . . What do I mean? Whusk of drunky.

DEEPING. Anyway, he needs one.

MCNAB. Come on, then, Mr Winn! It's the butler's day off.

DEEPING *gives* WINN *the key*.

WINN. No, all I meant was, we all make our own beds . . .

MCNAB. Bustle about and buttle, Mr Winn. That's your job for the day. Just buttle us another bottle.

Exit WINN, *centre*.

BLYTON. He'll have us all scrubbing the floors before this interview's out.

MCNAB. Don't you start. I know the kind of poems you write. 'Smouldering eyes and steaming thighs.'

BLYTON. You've been prying. You've been looking at my papers.

MCNAB. You left them on the bathroom floor.

BLYTON. And I did not write 'steaming thighs'.

MCNAB. You and that fellow that was here in November.

BLYTON. Dornford Yates? What about him?

MCNAB. In the billiard room. I saw the pair of you. Smouldering eyes, was it?

BLYTON. The expression to which I believe you're referring is 'slow-burning eyes'.

MCNAB. Slow-burning eyes in the billiard room. Steaming thighs in the gun room.

BLYTON. I have never set foot in the gun room. And I have never written any phrase remotely resembling 'steaming thighs'!

DEEPING. This is becoming intensely squalid.

BLYTON. Oh, thank you! Not as squalid as some things I could mention!

DEEPING. Oh, not that again. There is no truth in that story whatsoever. I scarcely knew the woman.

BLYTON. He scarcely knew her!

MCNAB. And he wasn't the only one who did!

SKINNER. Anyway, this sordid squabbllng can hardly be of interest to our guests.

KOCHETOV. What? A real literary quarrel in front of our eyes? We're enjoying every moment of it! Aren't we, Trisha?

TRISHA. I must say, I do find it all . . . very surprising.

KOCHETOV. So fortunate we're here. You're all going to be the most famous writers in the world.

Enter WINN, *centre, with another bottle of whisky.*

SKINNER. Whisky! Give them some more whisky! Come on, come on!

DEEPING. Yes, let's all have another glass of whisky and change the subject.

WINN *refills their glasses.*

MCNAB. Who's done what? That's a good one. Who's cooked the breakfast? Who's cleaned Mr Skinner's boots?

TRISHA. But you don't do everything yourselves? You said there was a butler.

MCNAB. Oh, there's a butler right enough.

KOCHETOV. This is the unfortunate McDonald?

MCNAB. McNab. Capital m small c capital n. John McNab. The son of John McNab of Tomintoul. And John McNab of Tomintoul was the great-great-grandson of the famous John McNab of Craigellachie.

TRISHA. He was famous, was he?

MCNAB. He was famous enough in Craigellachie.

TRISHA. And where is this McNab today?

MCNAB. Ah! Now there's the question. Where is old McNab today? What's the answer to that one, then, Mr Skinner?

SKINNER. I don't think we need go into that.

MCNAB. (*to* KOCHETOV). I'll tell you where he is. He's . . .

SKINNER. (*sharply*). McNab! (*Realises.*) I mean . . . (*Calls.*) McNab!

WINN (*calls too, to help out*). McNab!

SKINNER. McNab!

WINN (*opens left-hand door, and calls off*). McNab . . . ! No, he's not there.

MCNAB. That's right. He's not there for once, and I'll tell you why — because for once he's . . .

SKINNER (*jumps to his feet authoritatively*). Drink! Another drink!

The lid of the trunk rises. MCNAB *calmly sits on it.*

MCNAB. . . . Because for once he's having a bit of a sit-down. (*Drains his glass and holds it out.*) I won't say no, Mr Skinner, I won't say no.

SKINNER *takes the bottle and refills* MCNAB's *glass.*

Yes, poor old McNab's having a bit of a sit-down. And I'll tell you something else. It's the first bit of a sit-down he's had today. In fact it's the first bit of a sit-down he's had since Hogmanay. And the only reason he had a bit of a sit-down at Hogmanay was that he found the key to the safe, and shortly after midnight, he still not having had a chance to get his backside to a chair, the chair upped and came for *him.*

SKINNER. Yes, and where was he for the whole of the next day?

MCNAB. In bed, a sick man!

KOCHETOV. You seem to be very concerned about this McNab fellow.

MCNAB. If I don't concern myself about him, none of this lot are going to.

SKINNER (*to* KOCHETOV). Please don't worry about the butler. He's well looked-after.

MCNAB (*to* KOCHETOV). Have you ever heard of a butler who gets the lunch?

SKINNER. Plenty of butlers get the lunch.

MCNAB (*to* KOCHETOV). Who goes *out* to get the lunch?

SKINNER. Plenty of butlers go out to get the things for lunch.

MCNAB (*to* KOCHETOV). From the snares he's set the night before? Have you ever heard of a butler who had to dig the garden and mow the lawns?

SKINNER. Those lawns haven't been mown since the pigs were let out on them.

MCNAB (*to* KOCHETOV). And tend the pigs? And repair the plumbing? And catch the rats? And shoot the poachers? And darn the socks? And then sit up all night hidden behind the chimney-stack with a pair of opera-glasses waiting to see who it is who's thieving the lead off the roof? And then come down in the morning and be accused of taking the lead himself? *And* the ping-pong ball! *And* the bucket for cooling the champagne!

SKINNER. I'm sure our visitors have seen far too much of the world to pay any attention to this nonsense.

MCNAB. 'Show me the pigswill, McNab'.

WINN. He has these dark moods.

MCNAB. 'McNab, I've stuck a tuppenny stamp on your bucket.'

BLYTON. They'll never stop him now.

WINN. Though we're all very fond of him. Aren't we?

MCNAB. You're all very fond of me today. You're right there. It's not like this every day of the week, mister, I can tell you. Even Mr Skinner's got a soft spot for me today. Isn't that right, Mr Skinner? Put your hand in the fire for me today, wouldn't you, Mr Skinner?

SKINNER. If there's anything I can do to help you, then naturally . . .

MCNAB. Jump to it fast enough if I asked you to jump, wouldn't you. Mr Skinner?

SKINNER. I don't know what all this is leading up to.

MCNAB (*quietly*). Jump, Mr Skinner. Let's see you jump.

KOCHETOV (*to* TRISHA). This is what happens when you put power into the hands of the people.

MCNAB. Jump.

SKINNER. I don't know what this is.

MCNAB. Jump.

SKINNER. I'm not playing games with you.

MCNAB (*gets up*). Jump!

> *The lid begins to rise.*

> SKINNER *springs to his feet in alarm.*

MCNAB (*sits*). Sit down.

> SKINNER *sits.*

> MCNAB *suddenly half-rises again — and again* SKINNER *rises, too. He at once sits down.* MCNAB *feints rising a third time — and still* SKINNER *cannot prevent himself jerking in response.*

> MCNAB *waves his hand dismissively, suddenly melancholy.*

> Sit down, sit down. You'll break our hearts.

KOCHETOV (*to* TRISHA). You see why we prefer autocracy.

> WINN *moves to sit down on the trunk beside* MCNAB.

WINN (*to* KOCHETOV). Oh, we do an awful lot of ragging at Balmoral. Don't we, Warry? A lot of apple-pie beds. A lot of drawing-pins on chairs.

DEEPING. Oh, we pull Blyton's pigtails. We pour treacle in Winn's socks.

KOCHETOV. It reminds me of War and Peace.

WINN. Really?

KOCHETOV. Prose fiction sustained to incredible lengths.

MCNAB (*gets up from the trunk and moves elsewhere*). Now, you asked how the world appeared to me.

WINN. Oh, no, I don't think so, Hugh. I don't think anyone asked you anything.

MCNAB. They asked me to describe the world as I would see it . . .

WINN. That was hours ago! That's all over now.

MCNAB. . . . As I would see it if I were sitting on the top of a pole.

BLYTON. He's going to go on all night.

MCNAB. Now, I'll be quite frank with you. To my eyes the picture is very black. Very black indeed. I look down from the top of my pole and what do I see? I see mistrust and suspicion between man and man. I see false accusation mounted upon a high horse, and slander raging. I name no names, but the people down there know who I'm looking at.

BLYTON. This is worse than his knees.

MCNAB. I see the drinking-cup chained to the fountain, and the stamp stuck to the bucket.

WINN, DEEPING, *and* BLYTON *are sunk in embarrassment.* SKINNER *gazes at* MCNAB *with defeated malevolence.*

I see lust in the billiard room and foreign silk undergarments in the gun room, and potatoes in the shops at ninepence a pound. And I stand up here on the top of my pole looking down at the world, and I hoist up my kilt, and I . . .

KOCHETOV (*smoothly, holding out his glass*). . . . pour us all another glass of whisky.

MCNAB *pours.*

Well, you did your best.

WINN. We did our best.

DEEPING. And we all got a glass of whisky out of it.

KOCHETOV. And it didn't work. The person I feel sorriest for is poor Trisha. Look at her! She's heartbroken!

TRISHA (*tries to smile*). No, no . . .

KOCHETOV. Five hundred miles we've come. The longest

journey she's ever made in her life. The first time she's ever been in a sleeping car. And all just to meet the great man, the famous writer. What did she expect to find?

TRISHA. I don't know what I expected to find.

KOCHETOV. But something. You hoped for something. A few words of wisdom.

TRISHA. No, not words of wisdom.

KOCHETOV. A little chat about books.

TRISHA. No, not books. I couldn't have talked about books.

KOCHETOV. Something in his face, then. Some special look that showed the pain and struggle inside. Something in his eyes. A little light from the fire within. A little warmth from the fire.

TRISHA. I can't remember now.

KOCHETOV. And what happens? First of all they won't let us see him. Then they won't let him speak. Then they make him talk a lot of nonsense about fish-knives. And in the end they can hide it no longer. A green apron — rubber boots — a passionate interest in the price of potatoes. Fish-knives! — The man's a peasant!

TRISHA. You think that's wonderful, don't you.

KOCHETOV. The most wonderful thing I've ever seen.

SKINNER. Heartbreaking, isn't it. You do your best, you make plans, you try to see your way through. And what happens? People let you down. You've got all the ideas — but you can't get the quality of people you need to carry them out. There just aren't the people.

KOCHETOV. My sweetheart, I'll tell you something about writers.

SKINNER. I could tell you a thing or two about people.

KOCHETOV. Writers are terrible people.

TRISHA. Some writers are, I'm sure.

KOCHETOV. All writers.

BLYTON. Some writers are terrible writers.

MCNAB. Some people are terrible people.

SKINNER. All people are terrible people.

KOCHETOV. Shall I tell you what writers talk about? One thing.
Themselves. Oh, they tell you they hate war, of course. But is
it war they care about? Not at all. What they care about is how
they hate it.

TRISHA. You're just completely cynical.

KOCHETOV. Utterly cynical! Until today. Until I met Mr
Walpole. Because, really, it's amazing. What Mr Walpole wants
to talk about is not himself at all! It's another human being!
What Hugh Walpole feels most strongly about is not Hugh
Walpole — it's John McNab! An ordinary servant. A common
butler. And yet, when Mr Walpole speaks about John McNab
he becomes eloquent, he becomes passionate. He feels
passionate resentment for McNab's wrongs. He feels passionate
pride in McNab's ancestry. This — for me — is what the
imaginative writer is seeking to do: to enter into the heart and
mind of another. And when Walpole talks about McNab he
becomes McNab! He *is* McNab!

TRISHA. I see what you mean. I suppose that is rather surprising.

MCNAB. The boots, was it, that gave it away?

KOCHETOV. Boots! Imagine! A writer in boots!

MCNAB. The thing about the boots is, they tried taking them off,
but there was no socks.

KOCHETOV. No socks! My God! A writer with no socks! And
you're ashamed of him! You even make him ashamed of
himself! You don't deserve him!

SKINNER. Look, if I could just explain. McNab said that Walpole
had . . .

WINN (*to* SKINNER). Have some more whisky.

SKINNER. I just want to explain . . .

DEEPING. Don't explain anything.

SKINNER. Yes, but it was all because McNab said . . .

DEEPING. Shut up!

SKINNER. What?

DEEPING. Listen to what he's saying, for heaven's sake!

WINN (*to* KOCHETOV). Please go on. A writer with no socks . . .

KOCHETOV. I must confess, I came to this country without faith. I came to mock. And I was wrong. I find that some things here really have changed. There are pigs in the palace gardens. A simple peasant can become a writer. I find here the possibility that society may after all be changed. That men may after all be transformed. Mr Walpole, I'm going to be very Russian for a moment. I hope you won't be embarrassed. I'm going to kiss you.

Kisses MCNAB *on both cheeks.*

MCNAB. Oh, my word! And I haven't shaved this morning!

TRISHA. Mr Kochetov — you've been converted!

KOCHETOV. Absurd! I'm the classic case! Came to mock and stayed to pray! And I can't tell you how ridiculously happy it makes me feel. As if some ancient heavy weight had been lifted off my heart.

TRISHA. Oh, Mr Kochetov! You're a different man!

She kisses him.

KOCHETOV. Volodya — call me Volodya.

TRISHA. Volodya! I thought you'd never see it!

KOCHETOV. I fought against it, Trisha! With all my force I struggled not to give in!

TRISHA. Volodya, I knew all the time you could do it if you tried.

KOCHETOV. It's Mr Walpole who did it. He's the one you should kiss.

TRISHA. Mr Walpole! I realise now I didn't understand you at all when I read your books. Or even when you were speaking. I feel as if *my* eyes had been opened, too.

Kisses MCNAB.

MCNAB. Oh, my word, literature!

TRISHA. I'm so happy!

KOCHETOV. You're so wise!

Kisses her.

MCNAB. Is this Wednesday? Or is it closing time?

KOCHETOV. So beautiful!

Kisses MCNAB.

TRISHA. So good!

MCNAB. Well, here's one for you, love.

Kisses TRISHA.

KOCHETOV. So new and strange!

Embraces both of them together. They all laugh and kiss each other.

SKINNER (*rises*). Perhaps I should just round the occasion off with a few words . . .

KOCHETOV (*ecstatic, ignoring SKINNER, his Russian intonation becoming rather more noticeable*). This is how it must be! No grass on the lawn — no socks on the feet! Only pigs and boots and sometimes a glass of spirits. This is how it must and shall be!

SKINNER. If I might break in here . . .

MCNAB (*raises glass*). To the pigs!

KOCHETOV. The pigs!

TRISHA. The pigs!

SKINNER. The pigs.

They drink the toast.

If I might just break in here. I should like, if I might, to propose a toast to the development of peaceful cultural relations between our two peoples . . .

KOCHETOV. To Hugh Walpole!

TRISHA. Yes, to Hugh Walpole!

SKINNER. All right, then, to Hugh Walpole.

MCNAB. To Hugh Walpole, the poor old devil.

They drink the toast.

KOCHETOV (*to* SKINNER). Isn't he wonderful?

SKINNER. Wonderful. So let me just say this before our guests depart. I believe that this has proved to be a most successful venture in promoting mutual understanding between our two great nations . .

KOCHETOV. This other writer. He's another good writer. I can see it in his face. What's your name?

WINN. Winn. Godfrey Winn.

KOCHETOV. Godfrey. We drink to Godfrey.

OMNES. Godfrey!

They drink.

MCNAB. Speech!

KOCHETOV. Yes! Speech! Speech!

WINN (*rises*). Oh, Great Scott! I don't know what to say! Except to say oh my God!

Sits down rapidly, to close the rising lid.

Cheers and applause.

KOCHETOV. Wonderful! The perfect speech!

Turns to DEEPING.

And this writer here. Another fine writer.

WINN. Yes, here's to Warry!

OMNES. Warry!

They drink.

WINN. Speech!

KOCHETOV. Speech!

MCNAB. Come on, Mr Deeping!

DEEPING (*rises*). Well, that's very charming of you and I'm very

touched. Because I should just like to say one thing. Today
more than ever . . .

KOCHETOV (*jumps up*). Listen! Listen *I* make a speech!

His accent has now become quite strongly Russian.

KOCHETOV. Something I never tell before. Why did I hate
England so much? Because I am half-English! Yes! My mother
she was English. And when I am a child we are so poor, my
mother and me!

DEEPING. Because today more than ever, we authors must fight
for our rightful place . . .

KOCHETOV. Listen! Listen! So I think everything English it's
poor and it's mean. As I grow up I think, English? I'm not
English! I'm Russian! I'm like my father! But now I come to
this country — now I come to this house — it makes me think
again about my mother — and I see how hard life was for her
. . . And that's all I want to say. What do you want to say?

DEEPING. All I want to say is this . . .

KOCHETOV. All I want to say is — I'm not Russian, I'm English.

Cheers.

DEEPING. Anyway . . .

KOCHETOV. So — wait — I understand all of you so well!
Because, all of us, we have — in here — English soul!

SKINNER. Hear, hear.

KOCHETOV (*to* DEEPING). Now you make your speech.

DEEPING. Well, I only wanted to say one thing, and I've
completely forgotten what it was.

Cheers. DEEPING *sits down, grinning.* KOCHETOV *turns to*
SKINNER.

KOCHETOV. And then we have this man.

WINN. Yes, Mr Skinner! Arthur Skinner, isn't it?

KOCHETOV. Arthur Skinner. What can I say to you? You're a
terrible man, Arthur !

SKINNER. Well, it's very kind of you to say so, but — I beg your pardon?

KOCHETOV. No. I must tell you frankly, Arthur — because we are speaking sincerely to each other now — we are speaking from the soul, yes? — I must tell you that you have many faults. No, wait. *Many* faults, and your worst fault is this: you are so humble. Wait! Wait! You are ashamed that everything in this house is so poor. You are ashamed that Hugh Walpole is a simple peasant. And you try to conceal these things from me.

SKINNER. No, no, no.

KOCHETOV. You tried to decieve me.

SKINNER. No, no, no.

KOCHETOV. Sincerely, Arthur. From all your soul.

SKINNER. Well . . .

KOCHETOV. Ah! 'Well.' You see? But, Arthur, let me tell you something. This poor house is a happy house. These simple people are happy people. And who is the head of this happy place? Arthur, let me tell you a surprising thing. The head of this happy place is you! (*Raises glass.*) Arthur Skinner!

OMNES. Arthur Skinner!

They drink.

SKINNER. I think that is the most wonderful thing that anyone has ever . . . I'm sorry . . .

MCNAB. Tears! From Skinner's eyes! This is like Moses smiting the rock!

SKINNER. No one has ever . . . I'm sorry . . .

KOCHETOV. Arthur, don't misunderstand! I'm not saying so very much!

SKINNER. I know. I know. But it just happens to be more than anyone else has ever . . .

KOCHETOV. Oh, Arthur!

MCNAB. Oh, now *he's* off!

KOCHETOV. I embrace you.

Kisses SKINNER *on both cheeks.*

SKINNER (*weeps openly*). Terrible . . . terrible . . . Haven't shed tears in all these terrible years . . .

TRISHA. Oh dear! You're making me cry!

Holds SKINNER*'s hand.*

MCNAB. This is as good as a funeral.

SKINNER. If my mother could be here now to hear you say what you said just then! When I think of all the struggles we had to make ends meet!

KOCHETOV. When I think of my mother with her safety-pins . . .

SKINNER. Scrimping and saving all week to make the books balance! Everything I know I learnt from her!

KOCHETOV. My mother the English governess. My father the count. And all these years I have tried to make myself like *him!*

They weep.

WINN. There's something about Russians. It just takes one Russian and a bottle of spirits, and in five minutes everyone's weeping!

KOCHETOV. English! I am Englishman!

WINN. One Englishman and a bottle of spirits. Well, I can't help thinking of *my* mother, and all the happy times . . . Oh dear . . .

MCNAB. Go on, Mr Winn. Have a good cry. You'll feel all the better for it.

BLYTON. My God! If they could see what they looked like from here!

They all turn and see her.

DEEPING. Enid! We haven't toasted Enid!

BLYTON. Please don't worry about *me.*

WINN. We'd forgotten about you!

BLYTON. I'm quite used to being ignored.

SKINNER. Enid! Come here!

BLYTON. I've no wish to get involved in this public bathhouse of emotion.

They absorb her into the group.

KOCHETOV. You're a wonderful writer.

BLYTON. Oh, honestly . . .

WINN. No, she is, isn't she, Warry?

DEEPING. Wonderful!

KOCHETOV. And a very beautiful woman.

BLYTON. I just want to be left alone.

SKINNER. This is my house. No one's left alone in my house.

DEEPING. Let's give her a kiss.

He and KOCHETOV kiss her.

BLYTON. Oh, for God's sake . . .

SKINNER (*raises glass*). To Enid!

OMNES. Enid!

BLYTON. This is quite absurd.

KOCHETOV (*puts his arm round her*). But also quite delightful.

BLYTON. What's this thing? Oh God, it's a hand!

She laughs. They all laugh.

TRISHA. This is the best party I've been to for ages!

KOCHETOV. We cry. We laugh.

WINN. It's a Russian party.

KOCHETOV. English, English! I am Englishman!

DEEPING. Of course. It's an English party.

KOCHETOV. Soon probably we shall cry again. Because soon we shall be parted.

WINN. Never!

KOCHETOV. Who knows where fate will drive us? The earth is broad. Life is as vast and hazy as the autumn sky. Think of me sometimes!

SKINNER. I won't forget you! I can't remember your name . . .

KOCHETOV. Volodya.

SKINNER. Volodya.

KOCHETOV. Arthur . . .

SKINNER. Volodya!

KOCHETOV. Arthur . . . Arthur . . .

Feels in his pockets.

I want to give you something — something of mine — so you remember me, Arthur . . . This watch. Take this watch, Arthur.

SKINNER. Volodya, it's gold!

KOCHETOV. It's nothing.

SKINNER. It's got fourteen jewels!

KOCHETOV. It's yours. Trisha . . . Godfrey . . .

He begins to distribute the contents of his pockets to everyone.

I want you all to have something . . .

TRISHA. But these are your cigars.

KOCHETOV. Take them, take them.

WINN. But you'll need your fountain pen!

KOCHETOV. I need nothing, Godfrey.

SKINNER. Volodya — it's got a second hand!

DEEPING. I can't accept money.

BLYTON. No, no, no — not money.

KOCHETOV. Money — it's dirt.

DEEPING. But this is thirty-five pounds!

BLYTON. This is four and ninepence-halfpenny!

MCNAB. What's this? His pocket comb?

WINN. It's like Christmas!

SKINNER. Volodya — it's got luminous numbers!

But KOCHETOV is busy tearing off his jacket and tie and distributing them.

KOCHETOV. Here . . .! Here . . .! Why should I have all this? I am rich. You are poor.

TRISHA. No, no, no!

DEEPING. No more!

WINN. You must keep your trousers!

They all restrain him by force.

DEEPING. How can we ever repay you as it is?

TRISHA. I can't think of anything except this brooch.

WINN. Look, this is a clean handkerchief.

MCNAB (*gives him* WALPOLE*'s hat*). Try this hat.

BLYTON. And this scarf.

DEEPING. I want you to have this picture of my mother.

SKINNER. One and twopence — it's all I've got on me.

KOCHETOV. Oh, but this is lovely . . . this is beautiful . . . I shall keep this always.

SKINNER (*holds up his hands for silence*). Listen! I should just like to say, with all my heart . . . I don't know what I'd like to say!

BLYTON. I know! We must swear that we'll always be friends!

KOCHETOV. We swear a solemn oath!

BLYTON. We'll be a kind of gang!

TRISHA. Yes!

BLYTON. And it'll be a secret! We'll be the Secret Seven!

OMNES. The Secret Seven!

KOCHETOV. We put our hands on our souls.

WINN. Where are our souls?

KOCHETOV. Here. (*The heart.*)

SKINNER. And we swear!

BLYTON. To be friends for ever and ever and ever!

KOCHETOV. And never to deceive each other again!

BLYTON. Never!

SKINNER. Never!

KOCHETOV. And also never to forget . . .

He stops. A thought has struck him. They all stand, hand on heart.

WINN. Never to forget what, Volodya?

KOCHETOV. John McNab!

WINN. John McNab?

KOCHETOV. Your wonderful butler! He must come and swear with us! Where is he?

TRISHA. Yes! Where is he?

WINN. Oh . . .

DEEPING. Well . . .

WINN (*takes his hand away from his heart*). He's lying down.

KOCHETOV. Bring him in.

DEEPING. He's out for a walk.

KOCHETOV. Lying down? Out for a walk?

MCNAB. He doesn't know where he is, and that's the truth.

KOCHETOV. Why are you saying these things to me? We swore! Arthur, we swore!

SKINNER. We did. We swore, Godfrey! We swore, Warwick! (*Starts to laugh.*) And, Volodya, it's so ridiculous! You're never going to believe it!

KOCHETOV. What?

TRISHA. What?

SKINNER. McNab's here! Right in front of your eyes.

WINN. Arthur!

DEEPING. Moderation in all things!

BLYTON. Don't spoil everything when it's all so nice!

SKINNER. He'll understand! We don't have to have secrets any more! He's not that kind of person!

KOCHETOV. You mean . . . one of these people is . . .?

SKINNER. You're going to be so cross!

WINN. Arthur, *please* . . .!

KOCHETOV (*indicates* WINN). You're not saying *he* is . . .?

SKINNER. No!

DEEPING. He's gone mad!

KOCHETOV (*indicates* DEEPING). You mean *him?*

SKINNER. No!

KOCHETOV (*turns to* BLYTON). Not *her?*

SKINNER. No! So that only leaves . . .? Oh, Volodya, you're going to kick yourself!

KOCHETOV *and* TRISHA *slowly turn towards* MCNAB *and gaze at him.*

KOCHETOV. You're not trying to tell me . . .?

MCNAB. Oh, and it was a good coat, too.

Resignedly takes off WALPOLE's *overcoat.*

WINN. Arthur, you can't start saying that Hugh Walpole is McNab.

BLYTON. Because where would Hugh Walpole be in that case?

SKINNER. In what case?

DEEPING (*opens the trunk*). In *that* case!

KOCHETOV. You mean it's . . .?

SKINNER. Not him.

KOCHETOV. *Not* him?

TRISHA. But there's no one else in the room! Except you.

DEEPING. She's guessed it!

WINN. Brilliant!

KOCHETOV. *He's McNab?*

BLYTON. Obvious as soon as you think about it.

KOCHETOV. *You're McNab?*

SKINNER. I'm McNab.

MCNAB. He's the butler, is he? Well, I'll not be the one to argue with him.

KOCHETOV. I don't believe it.

MCNAB (*takes off the green baize apron*). Here — put on the apron. We'll soon see. Where's the cap . . .?

Gets it out of the pocket of WALPOLE'*s overcoat.*

Put this on, McNab, or you'll be catching your death out there in the piggeries . . . There he is! There's your butler!

They all gaze at SKINNER, *as he stands amongst them in flat cap and apron.*

KOCHETOV. I don't believe it. I don't believe it! *I don't believe it!*

But it is clear from his delighted tone that he does.

MCNAB *refills his own glass.*

MCNAB. John McNab!

Everyone snatches up a glass to toast SKINNER.

OMNES. John McNab!

MCNAB. May he increase and multiply!

They drink the toast. KOCHETOV *embraces* SKINNER.

KOCHETOV. But really, it's amazing! I was completely deceived! Weren't you, Trisha? I believed absolutely and entirely that you were Arthur Skinner! So you're John McNab.

SKINNER, *still in a state of shock after his error, does his best to smile and nod.*

The perfect butler. The man who does everything.

SKINNER *smiles and nods.*

Even makes a fool of visiting journalists. Oh, John, John, John! May I call you John?

SKINNER *smiles and nods.*

Of course, I really knew it all the time. You were making this man so exaggerated! The books — the kedgeree — the pig food. All the time I just wanted to laugh!

SKINNER. Yes, well, all right, it may seem funny to you. But *someone's* got to worry about the books. *Someone's* got to sort out the kedgeree from the pigswill.

KOCHETOV (*to the others*). Listen to him! He understands this man's type exactly!

SKINNER. You don't think he *wants* to be that type, do you? He hates it! He'd rather be one of this lot, and sit around writing books all day. He'd rather be McNab, even!

KOCHETOV. He envies you?

SKINNER. What? Me? (*Sees the green baize apron he is wearing.*) Yes! Me! He'd rather be me!

MCNAB. That's a new one.

SKINNER. He would! He would! Of course he would! No responsibilities. No worries. Nothing to do but slollop around the house all day with a bucket of pigswill. There's even something about the way I hold the bucket that gets on Skinner's nerves.

KOCHETOV. Why? How do you hold it?

SKINNER. Where is it?

MCNAB *fetches the champagne bucket and fork from the sideboard and hands them to* SKINNER.

Nothing to do but play with buckets and spades and make poor Skinner's life a misery. It's as good as being back at school!

MCNAB. Off you go then, McNab, and muck out the piggeries.

SKINNER. I come in that door . . . (*Imitates* MCNAB.) Never think of putting the bucket down to close it. Oh no. Always put my leg up behind me, like a dog at a lamp-post, and kick it with my filthy boot. Then off I go, swinging the bucket about, swaggering around as if I owned the place. I've got a way of moving my shoulders somehow — it's a calculated insult.

DEEPING, WINN, *and* BLYTON *laugh and applaud.*

MCNAB. What's this?

WINN. This is you!

KOCHETOV. This is *him?* (*Indicates* MCNAB.)

WINN . I mean, it's *him.* (*Indicates* SKINNER.)

DEEPING . He's got himself exactly.

MCNAB (*amused in spite of himself*). He never prances around like that.

WINN
DEEPING } He does! He does!
BLYTON

SKINNER. Every syllable I utter is a studied mockery. (*Imitates* MCNAB.) Fair enough, Mr Skinner. It's only a bucket of kedgeree, Mr Skinner. And it's yes, Mr Skinner, and no, Mr Skinner, and three buckets full, Mr Skinner, and never taking a blind bit of notice all the same.

MCNAB (*delighted*). Oh, but he's got the trick of it now, hasn't he.

KOCHETOV. And you're a Scotsman all the time!

SKINNER. Oh, by God, am I a Scotsman!

KOCHETOV. I knew that English accent wasn't real!

SKINNER. Oh, it's whishty-tushty, Mr Skinner. It's Dundee and Dundoon. It's crallochs and bollochs and wee cowerin' beasties.

MCNAB. What language is this?

SKINNER. I'm a Scotsman, right enough. As pig-headed as granite. As lofty as a mountain. As prickly as that pair of antlers. But not above snitching up anything that's left around. Oh no!

He slyly finishes up a glass of whisky in passing.

Not too proud to poke my wee snoutie into what dusnae concern me.

Slyly opens in passing the file that contains DEEPING's work.

MCNAB (*delighted*). Oh, but isn't he the fellow!

SKINNER. Oh, I'm the fellow today! When I've got the old accent on! When I've got the old green baize apron round me! There's no holding me now!

Crosses towards righthand door.

Oh, it's a sly wee cowerin' creature I am! And all the time, right under poor wee Skinner's nose, it's . . .

He stops dead. His accent returns abruptly to English as he realises.

Green baize aprons!

KOCHETOV. What? What?

SKINNER. Every time I go out I've got it on. Every time I come back I haven't.

He turns accusingly upon MCNAB.

Green baize aprons! That's what I'm stealing!

MCNAB. Oh, there's no fooling him today!

DEEPING. Of course!

WINN. Of course!

BLYTON. But that's beautiful!

KOCHETOV. You steal, do you, McNab?

SKINNER (*looking at the apron in amazement*). Two dozen, there were. And out they went, right in front of Skinner's eyes!

KOCHETOV (*to* TRISHA). What a character!

SKINNER. That's it! That's his life! Aprons and lavatory chains. Buckets and ping-pong balls. And there it goes . . .

He follows the imaginary progress of the aprons from lefthand door to righthand.

Out of the front door and away! And listen! Listen!

He jumps on to the trunk.

I just want to say that this is the happiest day of my life! Two
hours ago we were all so worried! What were we worried about?

Three dull thuds, off. All of them except KOCHETOV *and*
TRISHA *freeze.*

KOCHETOV. What? What?

TRISHA. Someone at the door . . .

BLYTON (*sombrely*). That's what we were worried about.

KOCHETOV. Someone at the door?

MCNAB. The Inspector.

KOCHETOV. What inspector?

SKINNER. The Government Inspector.

Three more dull thuds, off.

KOCHETOV. The Government Inspector? He comes here? But
this is wonderful! He sees this happy house — he gives everyone
a medal! Let him in!

SKINNER (*dubiously*). Let him in!

KOCHETOV. Don't worry! Leave it to me! I tell him everything!
How happy we are! The Secret Seven! Everything!

BLYTON (*moved*). Oh, Volodya! We could be married! I could
write children's books! I've always wanted to write for
children!

KOCHETOV (*to* SKINNER). Let him in!

DEEPING, WINN,
BLYTON, MCNAB, } (*to* SKINNER, *happily*). Let him in!
TRISHA

SKINNER *is just about to get off the trunk.*

KOCHETOV. Wait!

He quickly picks up the empty whisky bottles.

Even in paradise . . .

SKINNER *jumps down from the trunk and goes out, right. The others all turn in the same direction as* KOCHETOV *opens the trunk.*

. . . dead men to hide!

He puts the bottles inside the trunk, closes the lid and sits on it, then realises what he has seen, just as the others realise what he has said and turn back to look at him.

Curtain.

Wild Honey

(from the untitled play
by Anton Chekhov)

About *Wild Honey*

In 1920, sixteen years after Chekhov's death, a new and unknown play by him came to light. The bulky manuscript, in Chekhov's own hand, was found inside a safe-deposit in a Moscow bank. The circumstances of the discovery are somewhat cloudy. But then there is an element of mystery about the play itself. The title-page of the manuscript was missing, and with it all record of the play's identity and origins. Since it was published by the Soviet Central State Literary Archive in 1923 it has become known under a variety of appellations. In England it is usually called by the name of its hero, Platonov; or rather, as English-speakers insist on pronouncing it, Plate On/Off. From the handwriting and the frequent provincial usages it was plainly written at the very beginning of Chekhov's career. In fact it is agreed by all authorities to be his first extant play. The puzzle is to know whether it is also the first full-length play that he ever wrote; and the question is not entirely academic.

It is a remarkable and tantalising work. Commentators seem to have been more struck by its youthful shortcomings than by its surprising strengths. Its defects are obvious enough. Its length, for a start; if it were staged uncut it would run, by my estimate, for something like six hours. In fact it is altogether too much. It has too many characters, too many disparate themes and aims, and too much action. It is trying to be simultaneously a sexual comedy, a moral tract, a melodrama, a state-of-Russia play, and a tragedy. The traces of Chekhov's early theatre-going as a schoolboy in Taganrog (often in disguise, to elude the school inspector – it was a forbidden vice) are too baldly obvious. Platonov himself is that archetype of nineteenth-century Russian literature, the 'superfluous man'. He is also Hamlet, the hero crippled by conscience and indecision; and Chatsky (in Griboyedov's *Woe from Wit*), the hero incapacitated by chronic honesty. The play is also marred by a certain coarseness, particularly in the drawing of some of the minor characters; perhaps most particularly in the characterisation of Vengerovich, 'a wealthy Jew' (though his predictable vulgarity is somewhat counterbalanced

by a streak of outspoken idealism in his son). Worse, for the
workability of the play, is a rambling diffuseness of action and
dialogue. Worse still, at any rate for the adaptor who is trying to
find a practical solution to all these problems, is a defect that
foreshadows one of the great glories of the later plays – a fundamental ambiguity of tone between comic and tragic, which will eventually be resolved into a characteristic Chekhovian mode, but which
appears here mostly as an indeterminate wavering. All in all, it has
been generally dismissed as unstageable. Ronald Hingley, in his
biography, describes the play as a botched experiment which it is
not surprising that Chekhov should have wished to bury in decent
oblivion. What interests the commentators most is the way in which
the later plays are here prefigured. Platonov is a sketch for Ivanov;
Anna Petrovna, the widowed local landowner, foreshadows Ran-
yevskaya. There is the great theme of the lost estate, and the
dispossession of the rural landowners by the new mercantile bour-
geoisie, that will recur in *The Cherry Orchard*. There is the unhappy
wife attempting to poison herself, as in *Three Sisters*. There is the
drunken doctor, and the vain longing of idle people to lose
themselves in work, and so on.

All this is true. More striking by far, however, to someone
engaged in the actual practice of playwriting, are the play's precocious and inimitable virtues. Platonov himself, for a start. He may
be a mixture of Hamlet and Chatsky and others; but overwhelm-
ingly, wonderfully, appallingly he is Platonov. He is not really like
anyone else at all; he is not even remotely like his author. He is like
himself, and – even more to the point – he just *is*. So is Anna
Petrovna. She is a most surprising character to find in a nineteenth-
century play. There are plenty of heroines of the time who inspire
erotic feeling in men (and who usually end up dead or disfigured for
their pains). There are a few, like Katerina Ismailovna in Leskov's
A Lady Macbeth of the Mtsensk District, who are driven by some dark
appetite of their own, and who pursue it to crime and degradation.
But where else is there one who is permitted to express such shining
physical desire, and to remain – though punished, it is true, by the
loss of her estate – essentially unhumiliated? And where else would
such a powerful charge of feeling have led, by an only too human
process of contrariness and confusion, to the seduction of the wrong
woman? David Magarshack, in *Chekhov the Dramatist*, sees Anna

Petrovna as a figure out of a medieval morality play, the personifi-
cation of lust. She is nothing of the kind. She is a living, breathing,
changeable human being who has a warm friendship for Platonov
as well as desire. She repeatedly surprises – in the sudden impatience
provoked by Platonov's vacillation, for example, and the sudden
mean contempt with which she turns not only upon Sofya, when
she discovers her to be her successful rival, but upon Sofya's
wretched husband for failing to be man enough to control his wife;
and perhaps most of all in the despair she reveals to Platonov in
their last great scene together.

In this play for the first time we see Chekhov demonstrating his
uncanny ability to enter the lives of people both unlike himself and
outside his own experience. He makes Platonov 27, but the desperation that the reappearance of Sofya releases in him is the desperation
of middle age, when we realise that our youth and promise have
gone, and that we shall do no better in life. He does not specify
Anna Petrovna's age; she is simply 'a young widow'. But she, too,
is driven by the same fear that life is passing her by. It is difficult to
understand how Chekhov could have known at the age he was then
what it was like inside the hearts and minds of people who see their
lives already beginning to slip from their grasp.

But what age *was* he exactly? This is where we come to the
mystery. The only known account of the play's origin comes from
Chekhov's younger brother Mikhail. He referred several times, in
articles and memoirs written in the years after Chekhov's death, to
an 'unwieldy' play which he later specifically identified with the one
found in the safe-deposit. He says that his brother wrote it 'in the
year after his arrival in Moscow', and 'in his second year at
university' – both of which phrases fix the year as 1881, when
Chekhov was 21, and studying medicine at Moscow University.
(Chekhov's sister, in a letter written in the 1920s, refers to the play
as having been written in his first year at university, which is not
significantly different). Mikhail says that Chekhov 'dreamed of
having [it] produced at the Maly Theatre in Moscow', and that he
showed it to a well-known actress, M. N. Yermolova. In fact
Mikhail says that he copied the play out for Chekhov, who took it
round to Yermolova in person, in the hope that she would put it on
for her benefit performance. And indeed on the first page of the
manuscript from the safe-deposit (which is presumably the draft

from which Mikhail worked when he copied it out) is a partly erased note in pencil, addressed to Marya Nikolayevna Yermolova, saying: 'I am sending you . . . Mar Nik. Have no fear. Half of it is cut. In many places . . . still needs . . . Yours respectfully, A. Chekhov.' The actress was apparently not impressed. 'I do not know what answer Yermolova gave my brother,' wrote Mikhail later, 'but my efforts to make a legible copy of the drama went completely for nothing; the play was returned and was torn up by its author into little pieces.'

Now, this is puzzling enough. Chekhov, to judge by his other works, was not a precocious writer. At the age of twenty-one he had only just started out on his career as a humorous journalist, and the sketches and spoofs that he was producing then are short, facetious, and two-dimensional. They are often quite stylishly flippant, but they are within the range of a humourously-inclined medical student. The sheer size of the play would be surprising enough in this context. Donald Rayfield, in *Chekhov: the Evolution of his Art*, advances a plausible textual reason for dating the play two years later (a bizarre reference to Sacher-Masoch, whose works Rayfield believes Chekhov came across only when he was preparing his dissertation in 1883). But even then Chekhov had only just begun to write real stories. It is difficult to believe that he could have written some of the scenes in the play at that stage of his career. One might be tempted to suspect a forgery – except that it is even more difficult to believe that anyone else wrote them, at any stage in any career.

But this is only the beginning of the puzzle. Because two years before he entered university, when he was eighteen and still at school in Taganrog, Chekhov had already written a full-length drama. It was called *Bezotsovshchina*, and it was read both by his elder brother Alexander, who found in it two scenes of genius, but who dismissed the whole as unforgivable, and by Mikhail, who says he kept a copy of it until his brother arrived in Moscow to start university, when he asked for it back and tore it up into little pieces. This was the last anyone ever saw of it. Or was it? A play without a title, and a title without a play . . . Some scholars have always maintained that the two are in fact one.

On the face of it this is beyond belief. If it is difficult to imagine how Chekhov could have written the play when he was a medical student of 21, it is clearly even more difficult to imagine how he could have done it when he was a schoolboy of eighteen. Besides, if Mikhail was familiar with the first play, why should he say (as he does) that the play he copied out for Yermolova to read (and of which he lists details that plainly identify it with the one from the safe-deposit) was another one? It is possible to imagine that only one text was torn up into little pieces, and that Mikhail has attached one single recollection to two different occasions. It is very difficult to believe, though, that he would have failed to remark upon the fact if the play he had copied out was the same as the one he had seen before – or even noticeably similar to it.

Still, this was a quarter of a century and more after the events, and memory can be deceptive. It may be significant that in the final edition of his memoirs, in 1933, Mikhail expunged all reference to the destruction of either manuscript. And in the authoritative 30-volume *Complete Collected Works and Letters* of Chekhov, of which publication in Moscow is now complete, opinion has hardened in favour of the one-play theory. M. P. Gromov, in his exhaustive introduction to the play in this edition, bases his conclusions on the evidence of the handwriting and language; on the fact that none of the historical events referred to in the text occurred later than 1878; on the unlikelihood of Chekhov having in the course of four increasingly busy years written two major plays; on the provenance of the setting and some of the characters' names from the Taganrog area – there was for instance a General Platonov living next door to the school; and on the appropriateness of *Bezotzovshchina* as a title.

I am not competent to comment on the evidence of the handwriting and language, and respect the intensive research on which Gromov has drawn. All the same, I am not sure that I find his arguments convincing enough to close the case. There is some evidence that he overlooks. He notes the date when Sacher-Masoch's book was translated into Russian (1877), but does not consider Rayfield's argument that Chekhov came across it only in 1883. Nor does he consider the many snatches of medical Latin in the text, or the plausibility of the symptoms in Platonov's attack of DTs, all of which suggests the medical student rather than the schoolboy.

Then again, *Bezotsovshchina*, which means the general condition of fatherlessness, seems to me to have no particular applicability to the play. This is why the question of the play's identity has some practical importance; if its title really is *Bezotsovshchina* then this plainly affects our reading of the text. Gromov argues that 'a desperate quarrel is occurring in the play between fathers and children . . . The children are insecure and unhappy because they do not have fathers whom they can respect.' In the original text, it is true, Platonov speaks bitterly about his memories of his drunken father, and this may reflect the feelings that Chekhov had about his own father's bullying mediocrity. But it has no real bearing upon the action of the play, and the other examples that Gromov offers of a 'quarrel' between the generations seem to me either insignificant or misconstrued, and in any case irrelevant to the action. No doubt everyone in the play would behave better if he had been better brought up; but then so would most of the characters in most of the world's plays.

Any reader with an interest in this, or in any of the other academic questions posed by the play, will have to consult the original text, which can be found in Volume 11 of the complete edition referred to above, or in Volume 12 of the more easily obtainable 20-volume edition by Yegolin and Tikhonov, published in 1948. There is also an English translation of the complete text by Ronald Hingley in Volume 2 of the Oxford Chekhov. The version that follows was commissioned by the National Theatre (at the suggestion of Christopher Morahan, who was the moving force behind this enterprise, and who first persuaded me to read the original). It is not intended as an academic contribution or as a pious tribute, but as a text for production. It is extensively reworked, and I have not been influenced by Gromov's reading. There is no more reference to fatherlessness in what follows than there is to plates being turned on and off.

It is not, of course, the first time that this 'unstageable' play has been staged. It was done in England as *Platonov* at the Royal Court in 1960, with Rex Harrison playing the name part, in a fine translation by Dmitri Makaroff (who was once, briefly, one of my instructors in Russian). I follow with hesitation in the steps of one of my own teachers. But Makaroff's translation was simply a condensation of the original, and it seemed to me that it needed a more radical approach than this. Chekhov's text is more like a rough draft than a finished play. It may never have been intended as anything else. If Mikhail is right, Chekhov tore up the fair copy. The manuscript from the safe-deposit is quite heavily corrected already, but the pencilled note to Yermolova suggests that there were more corrections to come. Not that mere corrections would have been enough. Any translator of the late Chekhov plays becomes aware how tightly and elegantly organised they are – how each apparently casual and autonomous word is in fact advancing the business of the play. The more one works on these plays, the more exactly one wishes to recreate each line in English. But the more closely one looks at the text we are considering here, the more one's fingers itch to reshape it.

In fact the only way to proceed, it seemed to me, was to regard the play, if not the characters, as fatherless, and to adopt it – to treat it as if it were the rough draft of one of my own plays, and to do the best I could with it, whatever that involved. I have not sought to make it more like any of Chekhov's other plays. What I have tried to do is to recognise the story and characters that are beginning to emerge, and to give them more definite dramatic form. To this end I have felt free to reorganize the chronology of the play; to shift material from one place to another and one character to another; to write new lines and to rewrite old ones. I have cut out entire subplots. I have reduced the number of characters from twenty to sixteen, and brought on a couple more – two of the peasants who shoot Osip. I have tried to resolve the tone of the play by reducing the melodrama and the editorialising, and by moving from lighter comedy at the beginning, through farce, to the darker and more painful comedy of the final scenes. I should perhaps stress that the farcical element is not something that I have imposed upon the play. I have refocused it, but it was there in the original. So was the pervasive erotic atmosphere. So was the feminism. The emancipation of women was a topic of the time – Sofya refers to it in her first scene with Platonov. But the painful directness with which Anna Petrovna finally talks about her fate as an educated woman with nothing to do is something alive and felt – and it is there in the original, not added by me with hindsight as a nod to modern sensibilities.

Then there was the question of a title. The play has sometimes been called *Without Fathers*, from *Bezotsovshchina*, but I have explained my reasons for rejecting this. I am not enamoured of *Platonov* as a title, even if a national campaign could be launched to pronounce it correctly. It has also been called *That Worthless Fellow Platonov*; *Ce fou de Platonov*; and *Don Juan, in the Russian Manner*. They all suggest that the play centres exclusively around the one character, which is plainly not how Chekhov thought about it, or he would scarcely have offered it in the first place to an actress. The best title to date seems to me to be Alex Szogyi's *A Country Scandal*. But Chekhov himself has provided an even better one in the text. The play covers the period of the Voynitzevs' honeymoon (and its catastrophic end). Anna Petrovna refers to it in a phrase that seems to include all the various sexual intrigues – 'a month of wild honey' (in the original, 'a month smeared with wild honey'). This seems to me to evoke precisely both the wayward sweetness of forbidden sexual attraction, and the intense feeling of summer that pervades the play.

It is a presumptuous enterprise to rewrite someone else's work. I realise that by the very act of giving these characters and their story more definite form I have deprived them of the 'indefiniteness', the *neopredelyonnost*, that Glagolyev in the original finds so pervasive in Russian society at the time, and of which he suggests Platonov as a hero; the very quality, so difficult to pin down precisely, that to a foreigner seems one of the most characteristically Russian at all times.

I was encouraged in my presumption, though, by a letter from Chekhov to his brother Alexander in 1882, urging him to approach the translations he was then doing with more freedom. 'Either don't translate rubbish, or do and polish it up as you go along. You can even cut and expand. The authors won't be offended, and you will acquire a reputation as a good translator.' The original in question here, of course, is far from being rubbish, and any virtues in what follows must be credited towards Chekhov's account, not mine.

One final puzzle – the circumstances of the play's discovery. This is a minor footnote to literary history. It has no bearing on our understanding of the play, but it does perhaps tell us a little more about Russian 'indefiniteness', and its survival in Soviet form.

In his otherwise scrupulously thorough introduction to the text in the new 30-volume Chekhov, Gromov becomes curiously evasive on the subject of the actual discovery. He merely quotes, without explanation, an account by N. F. Belchikov. Perhaps Nikolai Fyodorovich Belchikov, who died only recently, needs no introduction to Soviet readers. He was in fact the scholar who introduced and annotated the first edition of the play in 1923, after the fortunate discovery was made. He was thirty at the time, and he subsequently went on to a long and successful career as a Soviet literary specialist, joining the Party in 1948, at the height of Zhdanov's campaign against the arts, and ending up, in his late eighties, as head of the editorial board producing this same collected Chekhov in which Gromov is writing. Gromov quotes him thus: 'As N. F. Belchikov recounts, in the Moscow bank of the Russo-Azov Company were located the personal safes of its depositors. Here were preserved letters, documents, papers, little items of monetary or personal value, etc. Here among them was the safe of M. P. Chekhova. In it was discovered the manuscript of the play . . .'

Gromov does not say *where* Belchikov 'recounts' all this – an odd omission in such a scholarly edition. Perhaps it was over a glass of tea in the editorial offices. It was certainly not in Belchikov's own introduction to the first edition, where he says merely that the manuscript was among the Chekhov papers that 'were accessioned to the Central State Literary Archive in 1920' – a remarkably self-effacing formulation, because it is plain from Gromov's article that Belchikov was actually present when the great discovery was made. He says: 'N. F. Belchikov recalled, also lying in the same safe, an ancient stitched blue bead reticule that had possibly belonged to Y. Y. Chekhova [Chekhov's mother].' In fact there is an odd air about the whole account, as quoted by Gromov – a *neopredelyonnost* that seems characteristic of certain Soviet accounts of awkward events. It is a series of impersonal constructions that beg all the obvious questions about who opened the safe and why.

Now, a lot of human discovery is only relative. Columbus's discovery of America was no discovery to the Indians who lived there already. This discovery of the play, similarly, was scarcely a discovery to M. P. Chekhova, who had put the manuscript into her safe-deposit for the same reason that people usually put things into safe-deposits – precisely in order to stop them being 'discovered'. M. P. Chekhova was Chekhov's devoted sister Masha, who had inherited his house in Yalta, and all the papers inside it. From his death up to the time of the Revolution she had been hard at work sorting and publishing this material. In 1914, as Gromov himself mentions, she told the correspondent of the *Moscow Gazette* in Yalta: 'A long play without a title, written in the eighties, was recently found by me while sorting my brother's papers.'

So the discovery had already been discovered six years earlier. In a letter from Masha to Maxim Gorky, written in 1918[1] she explains that she has moved all her brother's papers to Moscow for safekeeping – some of them to her flat in Dolgorukovskaya Street, 'the more precious' into a safe-deposit. Gromov does not mention this letter, written because Masha was desperately anxious about the fate of her brother's papers in Moscow during the period of the Revolution (she was unable to leave Yalta then because of her mother's illness) and wanted Gorky's help in having a guard put on both flat and safe-deposit until her arrival. But Gorky never received the letter, and in a note she appended later Masha recorded: 'And in the event AP's literary and other valuables were removed from the safe in my absence.'

Nor, curiously, does Gromov mention either of the other letters written by Masha that make clear her feelings about the 'discovery'. In 1921, after being cut off from Moscow for three years by the Civil War, she wrote to Meyerhold asking for his help in getting protection for her brother's papers; she had now heard that her flat in Dolgorukovskaya Street had been 'wrecked'. And in a letter to Nemirovich-Danchenko at the Moscow Arts Theatre, written a year or more later (the date is uncertain), she was still hoping that her brother's manuscripts, 'seized from me out of the safe-deposit, will in time be returned to me by the State Literary Archive.'

There is no reference, either to the terrible journey that Masha undertook in 1921, as soon as it became possible to travel to Moscow, to find out what had happened to the papers. The Civil War had only just ended in the Crimea, and conditions were chaotic. The only place she could find in the overcrowded train was up in the luggage-rack, and she would have been put off *en route* as a class enemy if she had not happened to notice a boy reading one of Chekhov's stories in the compartment, and been able to identify herself as the writer's sister. She was 58 years old at the time. The journey took three weeks.[2]

There may of course have been good reason why corners were cut, which Gromov felt his editor would be too modest to want publicised. All those indefinite impersonal constuctions may conceal only the most diligent attempts to contact Masha in the war zone, and the most high-minded impatience to extend our knowledge of Chekhov's work. Belchikov's career would no doubt have prospered even without this windfall. In any case, what does it matter?

Masha's safe-deposit was a very small egg among all the eggs that were broken to make that enormous omelette. She survived. In fact she was appointed official guardian of her brother's old house in Yalta, and lived to be 94. At the end of her life she wrote gratefully about how the new Soviet government had come to her aid in 1920.[3] Perhaps there was a little tactful *neopredelyonnost* here, too. It hadn't seemed quite like that at the time, to judge by her letters, when the flat in Moscow was wrecked; when she got back from sorting that out only to find that the house in Yalta had been shot up by 'hooligan-bandits' in her absence, and she wrote to Nemirovich-Danchenko: 'At night I am alone in the whole house, I scarcely sleep, of course, I'm afraid and I don't know how I shall go on living. The prospect is a gloomy one – hunger, robbery, and the lack of any means of existence . . . ! Please don't forget about me. Bear in mind that I am very afraid and that I am suffering. If there should happen to be any money to spare, please send me some – against royalties. I implore you!'; nor when she added a wistful note about Nemirovich's life in the relative cleanliness of the Moscow Arts Theatre, where 'it smells of old times'; nor when she wrote to him again, some time between 1922 and 1924, complaining about the seizure of her brother's manuscripts from the safe-deposit, saying that 'there is among them much that is still unpublished, even a play written by him when he was a first-year student, all his letters to me, and up to some hundred photographs. A lot has disappeared, of course, such as relics, for example – I don't even want to remember it . . . I ought to come to Moscow myself and see to a great many things, but I am living in the most unfavourable conditions. My situation is undefined, unexplained, hopeless, and lonely. Many promises are made, but so far nothing has been done.'

Old and irrelevant pain. But perhaps worth recovering from the haze of the indefinite for one moment in all its sharpness.

1. This and all the other letters of Masha's quoted here can be found in Chekhova, Maria Pavlovna: *Khozyayka chekhovskogo doma*. Moscow 1965.
2. S. G. Bragin, *op cit*, Introduction.
3. Chekhova M. P. & Chekhov M. P.: *Dom-muzey A. P. Chekhova v Yalte*. Moscow 1963.

The Pronunciation of the Names

The following is an approximate practical guide. In general, all stressed a's are pronounced as in 'far' (the sound is indicated below by 'aa') and all stressed o's as in 'more' (they are written below as 'aw'). All unstressed a's and o's are thrown away and slurred. The u's are pronounced as in 'crude'; they are shown below as 'oo'.

Anna Petrovna Voynitzeva – *Aan*na Petraw*v*na Vie-*neetz*eva (as in 'vie' meaning 'contend')

Sergey Pavlovich Voynitzev – Ser*gay Paav*lovich Vie-*neetz*ev

Sofya Yegorovna Voynitzeva – *Saw*fya Ye*gaw*rovna Vie-*neetz*eva

Yakov – *Yaa*kov

Vasily – Va*seely*

Colonel Ivan Ivanovich Triletzky – Ee*vaan* Ee*vaan*ovich Tree*letz*ky.

Doctor Nikolai Ivanovich Triletzky (Kolya) – Niko*lie* (as in 'lie' meaning 'untruth') Ee*vaan*ovich Tree*letz*ky (*Kawl*ya)

Alexandra Ivanovna Triletzkaya (Sasha, Sashenka) – Alek*sand*ra Ee*vaan*ovna Tree*letz*kaya *(Saash*a, *Saash*enka)

Mikhail Vasilyevich Platonov (Misha, Mishenka) – Meekha-*eel* Va*seely*evich Pla*tawn*ov (*Meesh*a, *Meesh*enka)

Porfiry Semyonovich Glagolyev – Por*feery* Sem*yawn*ovich Gla*gawl*yev

Gerasim Kuzmich Petrin (Gerasya) – Ge*raas*eem Kooz*meech* Petrin (Ge*raas*ya)

Osip – *Aws*seep

Marko – *Maar*ko

Vova (the Platonovs' son) – *Vawv*a

Wild Honey was first presented at the National Theatre, in the Lyttleton, on 19 July 1984, with the following cast:

DR TRILETZKY, *the local doctor*	Karl Johnson
YAKOV, *a servant in the Voynitzev household*	Peter Dineen
ANNA PETROVNA, *the late General Voynitzev's widow*	Charlotte Cornwell
PORFIRY SEMYONOVICH GLAGOLYEV, *a local landowner*	Basil Henson
SERGEY, *Anna Petrovna's stepson*	Nicholas Jones
COLONEL TRILETZKY, *a retired artillery officer and father of Dr Triletzky and Sasha*	Brewster Mason
SOFYA, *Sergey's wife*	Elizabeth Garvie
VASILY, *another servant*	Peter Gordon
MARKO, *process server to the local Justice of the Peace*	Anthony Douse
MARYA YEFIMOVNA GREKOVA, *a chemistry student*	Abigail McKern
PLATONOV, *the local schoolmaster*	Ian McKellen
SASHA, *his wife*	Heather Tobias
GERASIM KUZMICH PETRIN, *a wealthy merchant*	Gertan Klauber
OSIP, *a horsethief*	Roger Lloyd Pack
PEASANTS	Lewis George
	Matthew Green

Directed by Christopher Morahan
Settings by John Gunter
Costumes by Deirdre Clancy
Music by Dominic Muldowney
Lighting by Robert Bryan

The action takes place on the Voynitzev family estate, in one of the southern provinces of Russia.

It was first presented at the Ahmanson Theatre, Los Angeles, on 9 October 1986, and then at the Virginia Theatre, New York, on 18 December 1986, by Duncan C. Weldon, Jerome Minskoff, Robert Fryer, Karl Allison, Douglas Urbanski, Jujamcyn Theatres/Richard G. Wolff, and Albert and Anita Waxman, in association with the National Theatre of Great Britain, and with the following cast:

DR TRILETZKY	Sullivan Brown
YAKOV	Timothy Landfield
MAIDS	Vivienne Avramoff
	Kitty Crooks
ANNA PETROVNA	Kathryn Walker
PORFIRY SEMYONOVICH GLAGOLYEV	Jonathan Moore
SERGEY	Frank Maraden
COLONEL TRILETZKY	Franklin Cover
SOFYA	Kim Cattrall
VASILY	Ron Johnston
MARKO	George Hall
MARYA YEFIMOVNA GREKOVA	J. Smith-Cameron
PLATONOV	Ian McKellen
SASHA	Kate Burton
GERASIM KUZMICH PETRIN	William Duff-Griffin
OSIP	Stephen Mendillo
PEASANT	William Cain

Directed by Christopher Morahan
Settings by John Gunter
Costumes by Deirdre Clancy
Lighting by Martin Aronstein
Music by Dominic Muldowney

The text in this edition incorporates the cuts and changes that were made for this production.

ACT ONE

Scene One

The verandah of the Voynitzevs' country house. It looks out on to a sunlit garden, with the tall trees of the forest beyond, bisected by a grassy walk.

The whoosh of a rocket taking off. The lights come up to reveal YAKOV *in the garden with a large box of assorted fireworks in his arms. Beside him stands* DR TRILETZKY, *a match in his hand. They are gazing up into the sky –* DR TRILETZKY *with delight,* YAKOV *with apprehension. There is a smell of sulphur in the air. The rocket bursts, off.*

DR TRILETZKY. Look at it! It's like someone bursting out laughing!

The stick falls into the garden.

Let's set two off together!

YAKOV *backs away on to the verandah in alarm, as* DR TRILETZKY *begins to light the touchpapers of the other rockets sticking up from the box.*

Let's set four off! Let's send the whole lot up!

Enter ANNA PETROVNA *in alarm.*

ANNA PETROVNA. Doctor!

YAKOV *turns to face* ANNA PETROVNA, *still holding the box of fireworks.*

DR TRILETZKY. Fireworks!

ANNA PETROVNA (*to* YAKOV). Outside!

YAKOV. Outside . . . (*He puts the fireworks down and flees.*)

ANNA PETROVNA. Yakov! Come back! Take the fireworks!

YAKOV *picks them up uncertainly.*

Now outside! Quick! Run!

Exit YAKOV hurriedly with the box.

(*To* DR TRILETZKY.) For heaven's sake. The whole house will be in flames!

The sound of a series of rockets departing, off.

ANNA PETROVNA. Doctor, really! They're for later! When it gets dark!

DR TRILETZKY. Anna Petrovna! (*He takes her hand.*) It's all your fault! (*He kisses her hand.*)

ANNA PETROVNA. My fault?

Enter YAKOV, with the blackened box of fireworks, and a blackened face.

(*To* YAKOV.) Take them away! Put them with the others behind the old summerhouse! I told you before.

Exit YAKOV through the garden.

My fault?

DR TRILETZKY. Of course! You're back! So we're all quite light-headed. You don't know what it's been like here in the country without you. I can't imagine how we've all survived the winter. Was it wonderful in town? Did you go to the theatre? Did you have dinner in restaurants? Did you miss us all? Are you pleased to be back? Or are you bored already? If you think this place is dull when you're here you should be here when you're *not* here. We all live under dust-covers, like the furniture. But now you're back, and the covers are off, and it's the first perfect day of summer, and when are we going to eat?

ANNA PETROVNA. Not for ages yet. Cook's got drunk to celebrate our arrival . . . Are you feeling my pulse, doctor? Or are you taking a little bite to keep you going until lunchtime?

DR TRILETZKY. I was just thinking. You arrived last night?

ANNA PETROVNA. On the evening train.

DR TRILETZKY. Where did you get the fireworks, then?

ANNA PETROVNA. Your father sent them. He came over first thing this morning.

DR TRILETZKY. He's shameless! He could have waited until lunch, like the rest of us. He is coming to lunch?

ANNA PETROVNA. Of course. We must have the colonel.

DR TRILETZKY. And Porfiry Semyonovich is here already. I met him in the garden with your stepson.

ANNA PETROVNA. Poor Sergey! But I endured him for an hour or more first.

DR TRILETZKY. So you'll have us all at your feet again. Just like last summer.

GLAGOLYEV *appears in the garden, making frequent halts to lean on his stick and pontificate to* VOYNITZEV, *who listens with perfect deference.*

ANNA PETROVNA. Here comes Porfiry Semyonovich now.

DR TRILETZKY. He was telling Sergey about the decline in modern manners when I met them.

ANNA PETROVNA. What a cruel stepmother I am!

GLAGOLYEV (*to* VOYNITZEV). No, we had real respect for them, you see.

VOYNITZEV. Like the knights of old.

GLAGOLYEV. We looked up to them.

VOYNITZEV. You put them on a pedestal.

GLAGOLYEV. We put them on a pedestal.

DR TRILETZKY. I think they've got on to the subject of women.

GLAGOLYEV. We loved women, certainly. But we loved them in the way that the knights of old loved them.

VOYNITZEV. You had respect for them.

GLAGOLYEV. We had respect for them.

DR TRILETZKY. Your stepson has become the most agreeable of men.

ANNA PETROVNA. Poor Sergey!

DR TRILETZKY. He goes away an artist and poet. He comes back with his beard shaved off – and underneath he's not an artist and poet at all! He's a very agreeable young man like everybody else.

ANNA PETROVNA. He doesn't need an artistic nature now. He has a wife instead.

GLAGOLYEV (to VOYNITZEV). So you see, we poor old setting stars have the advantage of you young rising stars!

VOYNITZEV. You knew the world when the world was young.

DR TRILETZKY. All your old admirers! However will you bear it? Where's Platonov? You'll never put up with us all without Platonov here to amuse you.

ANNA PETROVNA. I've sent across for him twice already.

GLAGOLYEV *and* VOYNITZEV *approach the verandah.*

GLAGOLYEV (to VOYNITZEV). No, we believed in women, we worshipped the ground they walked on, because we saw in woman the better part of man . . .

DR TRILETZKY. I'll tell Vasily to run over there again.

Exit DR TRILETZKY.

GLAGOLYEV *and* VOYNITZEV *come in from the garden.*

GLAGOLYEV. Anna Petrovna! We were just talking about the fair sex, as chance would have it.

ANNA PETROVNA. You have always given the subject a great deal of time and attention.

GLAGOLYEV. I was saying to your stepson that woman is the better part of man. Or so we believed in my day. So your late husband believed, I know that, God rest his soul. (*To*

VOYNITZEV.) Oh yes, your father was like me, God give him peace – one of the old school, the General . . . So hot! I must sit down, I'm quite done up . . .

COLONEL TRILETZKY *appears in the garden, leaning on a stick like* GLAGOLYEV.

VOYNITZEV. And here's the colonel.

GLAGOLYEV. The colonel, was it, who sent those fireworks? Dangerous things, fireworks. I'm no great lover of fireworks.

COLONEL TRILETZKY *comes in from the garden.*

COLONEL TRILETZKY (*to* ANNA PETROVNA). Your Majesty!

ANNA PETROVNA. Colonel!

COLONEL TRILETZKY. A twenty-one gun salute to the queen of the district! (*He raises the stick into his shoulder.*) Bang bang bang! Bang bang . . .!

VOYNITZEV. Colonel! Still ready with a salvo?

COLONEL TRILETZKY. Sergey Pavlovich!

VOYNITZEV. You're well, are you?

COLONEL TRILETZKY. I'm always well. The good Lord endures me with remarkable patience. Porfiry Semyonovich!

GLAGOLYEV (*disgusted*). Fireworks!

COLONEL TRILETZKY (*to* ANNA PETROVNA). Arrived, have they?

ANNA PETROVNA. So kind of you. Something for us all to look forward to.

COLONEL TRILETZKY. Only supporting fire I can provide these days.

GLAGOLYEV. He'll blow you all up if you're not careful.

COLONEL TRILETZKY. A twenty-one rocket salute! (*He raises the stick to his shoulder.*)

Enter DR TRILETZKY.

DR TRILETZKY. Don't shoot! It's your long-lost son!

COLONEL TRILETZKY. Kolya!

DR TRILETZKY. And in the nick of time, by the look of it.

COLONEL TRILETZKY (*lowers his stick, and embraces* DR TRILETZKY *with emotion*). My dear boy!

DR TRILETZKY. Father!

COLONEL TRILETZKY. Haven't seen you for . . . what . . .?

DR TRILETZKY. It must be nearly two weeks now, Father.

COLONEL TRILETZKY. Have to come to Anna Petrovna's to see my own son! Keep meaning to call on you. Never manage it. Too busy!

DR TRILETZKY (*to* ANNA PETROVNA). Summer again, and your little court is assembling for the season.

ANNA PETROVNA. It's not me you've all come to see this time. It's my new daughter-in-law.

DR TRILETZKY (*to* VOYNITZEV). Yes! Where is she?

COLONEL TRILETZKY. Of course! He's got married! There's my memory for you!

ANNA PETROVNA (*to* VOYNITZEV). Everyone's longing to meet her.

COLONEL TRILETZKY. But what a funny fellow! Gets married, and never says a word about it! Talks about nothing but guns! Well, life and happiness to you, Sergey Pavlovich! Life and happiness! Is she beautiful?

ANNA PETROVNA. Enchanting!

COLONEL TRILETZKY. Two queens on the board against us! We're done for!

DR TRILETZKY. Fetch her out, then! It's not fair to keep us all in suspense.

ANNA PETROVNA. Especially Porfiry Semyonovich. He's such a great lover of women.

GLAGOLYEV. I certainly prefer them to sporting guns and fireworks.

VOYNITZEV. I think she's walking under the trees. I'll see if I can find her.

VOYNITZEV *goes out into the garden.*

COLONEL TRILETZKY (*takes* ANNA PETROVNA's *hand*). This is the girl for me, though!

ANNA PETROVNA (*to* DR TRILETZKY). Your father's going to take me quail-shooting.

GLAGOLYEV. If you are interested in birds, I could show you several quite rare species on my estate.

DR TRILETZKY (*to* ANNA PETROVNA). They're fighting over you!

ANNA PETROVNA (*a hand on both their arms*). We'll all come and see your birds. We'll bring the colonel's new twelve-bore.

COLONEL TRILETZKY. God strike me down, but this is the girl for me! The emancipation of women in person, this one! Get a sniff of her shoulder! Powder! A warrior-chief, if ever I saw one! Put a pair of epaulettes on her and she'd outgeneral the lot of us!

GLAGOLYEV. Have you been drinking already, colonel?

COLONEL TRILETZKY. Of course I have! Started at eight o'clock this morning! Came over here – found everyone asleep apart from the empress herself. Couldn't have been more delighted to see me, so we split a bottle of Madeira.

ANNA PETROVNA. You didn't have to tell everyone!

GLAGOLYEV. When you come to visit me we shall sample a glass of my housekeeper's whortleberry liqueur.

Enter VOYNITZEV *and* SOFYA *through the garden.*

DR TRILETZKY. And here she is!

VOYNITZEV *stops to present* SOFYA *with a flower. They laugh together.*

COLONEL TRILETZKY. Oh, but she's an absolute bullseye!

ANNA PETROVNA. I told you!

GLAGOLYEV. Charming couple.

DR TRILETZKY. The ideal stepson.

ANNA PETROVNA. And the ideal wife for him.

VOYNITZEV *and* SOFYA *come in from the garden.*

SOFYA. Oh, Anna Petrovna, I've never seen such a beautiful garden! I'm quite dizzy with sunlight and the scent of flowers! And I've been walking in the forest. It's so cool under the trees, and there's a kind of faint sound in the air all the time, as if the forest were sighing to itself with pure happiness. I can't imagine living in such a place.

ANNA PETROVNA. Well, now you do, my dear.

SOFYA. Do I really?

VOYNITZEV. It's all yours.

SOFYA. It's like a dream! I'm afraid I shall reach out to touch it and everything will vanish.

COLONEL TRILETZKY. Aren't you going to introduce us?

ANNA PETROVNA. Oh, yes. Now, Sofya, these are your new neighbours. The colonel . . .

COLONEL TRILETZKY. Triletzky, Ivan Ivanovich.

ANNA PETROVNA. Who will take you duck-shooting at dawn . . .

COLONEL TRILETZKY. Snipe! That mighty swamp on Porfiry Semyonovich's estate must be full of them! A great polar expedition! We'll all go!

ANNA PETROVNA. Sofya Yegorovna. And this is the colonel's
son . . .

DR TRILETZKY. Nikolai Ivanovich.

ANNA PETROVNA. He's the local doctor, who will nurse you
back to health again afterwards. And this is Porfiry
Semyonovich, the owner of the mighty swamp. He is . . . what
are you, Porfiry Semyonovich? He is a great lover of women.

SOFYA. Really?

GLAGOLYEV. I make the claim in all humility.

SOFYA. And Platonov. Isn't he here?

VOYNITZEV. Yes – Sofya knows Platonov!

SOFYA. Only slightly.

VOYNITZEV. But isn't that extraordinary?

SOFYA. I don't suppose he'll know me.

DR TRILETZKY. Of course he will! Platonov knows everything.

COLONEL TRILETZKY. He certainly knows all the pretty
women!

GLAGOLYEV. Really, colonel! We're talking about a serious
scholar!

COLONEL TRILETZKY. Our local Socrates!

ANNA PETROVNA (*to* DR TRILETZKY). Where is he?

DR TRILETZKY. I sent Vasily running.

SOFYA. He was a student when I met him. I was only a
schoolgirl. He won't remember me.

VOYNITZEV. We'll see! We won't introduce you. We'll find out
what kind of scholar he really is!

SOFYA. Oh, but it's so lovely here!

Enter VASILY.

DR TRILETZKY. The perfect picture of country life! We're only missing one thing . . .

ANNA PETROVNA. Yes, is he coming, Vasily?

VASILY. Directly, he says, Anna Petrovna, but Anna Petrovna, it's Marko.

ANNA PETROVNA. Marko?

VASILY. From the magistrate, Anna Petrovna.

ANNA PETROVNA. Marko the process-server?

DR TRILETZKY. What, with a summons?

VASILY. Big envelope, it is.

VOYNITZEV (*to* ANNA PETROVNA). He's done it! He's taken us to court!

SOFYA. Who? Platonov?

ANNA PETROVNA. No. No one.

DR TRILETZKY. Someone who lent money to the old general.

VOYNITZEV. He's suing us for it! We've lost the estate!

ANNA PETROVNA. Don't be ridiculous. It's all some silly mistake. (*To* VASILY.) Send the man in.

VASILY. This way . . .

Enter MARKO, *an old man with a neat, soldierly bearing. He has an envelope in his hands, and more envelopes in a satchel round his neck.*

DR TRILETZKY (*to* SOFYA). The old general was sick.

MARKO. Anna Petrovna Voynitzeva?

COLONEL TRILETZKY (*to* SOFYA). He signed anything they put in front of him.

ANNA PETROVNA. Give it to me, then.

MARKO hands her the envelope.

I'll open it later.

VOYNITZEV (*to* MARKO). Yes, you come bursting in here, badgering my stepmother in front of her guests . . .

MARKO. Sergey Pavlovich Voynitzev?

VOYNITZEV. Yes?

MARKO hands him another envelope. He gazes at it in astonishment.

DR TRILETZKY. Sergey! What have you been up to?

MARKO. Dr Nikolai Ivanovich Triletzky?

DR TRILETZKY. Me?

MARKO hands him an envelope. He gazes at it in astonishment in his turn.

ANNA PETROVNA. You, too?

GLAGOLYEV. My dear Anna Petrovna, if you will allow me to be of assistance . . .

MARKO. Porfiry Semyonovich Glagolyev?

GLAGOLYEV. I beg your pardon?

ANNA PETROVNA. Not you!

MARKO hands him an envelope. He gazes at it, flabbergasted. They all look at each other's envelopes.

What, have we all got one, then?

COLONEL TRILETZKY. Not me! Wouldn't do it to an old soldier! Old soldier yourself, aren't you?

MARKO. Artillery, sir.

COLONEL TRILETZKY. Thought so! Corporal Marko, wasn't it?

MARKO. That's it, sir. And you're Colonel Triletzky?

COLONEL TRILETZKY. That's right!

MARKO. Colonel Ivan Ivanovich Triletzky?

COLONEL TRILETZKY. Exactly!

MARKO *hands him an envelope.*

Not a man left standing!

ANNA PETROVNA. Look at Sofya staring.

SOFYA. No, no!

ANNA PETROVNA. I suppose we'd better open them.

They open them.

GREKOVA *appears in the garden. She stops, awkward and flustered, to dab a handkerchief to her face.*

DR TRILETZKY *is the only one to notice her.*

DR TRILETZKY (*goes to meet her*). Marya Yefimovna!

ANNA PETROVNA (*reads*). 'His Imperial Majesty's Justice of the Peace . . .'

VOYNITZEV (*reads*). '. . . will be at home on Sunday June the fifteenth . . .'

GLAGOLYEV (*reads*). '. . . on the occasion of his son's christening . . .'

ANNA PETROVNA. It's not a summons!

MARKO. No, ma'am.

COLONEL TRILETZKY. It's an invitation!

MARKO. Yes, sir.

DR TRILETZKY (*brings* GREKOVA *into the room*). It's Marya Yefimovna . . .

The others look up from their letters, and burst out laughing with relief. GREKOVA takes one horrified look at them, and flees back into the garden.

ANNA PETROVNA. Oh dear. What an unfortunate moment to choose!

COLONEL TRILETZKY. Poor girl! Comes seven miles on a hot

afternoon, and what happens? Gets her head blown off! Same thing every time she comes here. Walks in – head blown off.

VOYNITZEV. It's usually Platonov who does it.

ANNA PETROVNA. He's not even here, and already she's hiding under the trees again. It's just like last year.

COLONEL TRILETZKY. Never get her back now.

DR TRILETZKY (*looking at his letter*). A christening . . . I suppose I should try . . .

SOFYA. I'll go. I know what it's like, coming into a room full of people.

SOFYA goes out into the garden, followed by VOYNITZEV.

GLAGOLYEV. Charming young woman!

ANNA PETROVNA. Go and help her, Porfiry Semyonovich.

COLONEL TRILETZKY. We'll all go and help her! (*To* MARKO.) And we'll all come to the christening on Sunday! The siege of Sevastopol?

MARKO. And Balaclava, sir.

COLONEL TRILETZKY. See it in your eyes. (*He gives him a coin.*)

MARKO. Thank you, sir.

GLAGOLYEV and COLONEL TRILETZKY go into the garden.

DR TRILETZKY. I'd better go and talk to her.

ANNA PETROVNA. I think you'd better stay and talk to me. (*To* VASILY.) Take him out to the kitchen and give him something to drink. Fancy telling us he was bringing a summons!

Exeunt VASILY and MARKO.

So! It wasn't me you came to see at all, and it wasn't Sofya! It was your Marya Yefimovna.

DR TRILETZKY. Anna Petrovna, I was sure she wouldn't come! I thought she'd refused to set foot in the same house as Platonov again, after all that business last summer.

ANNA PETROVNA. I like her! I love her sharp little nose. Is she still studying chemistry?

DR TRILETZKY. She reads books, too.

They watch her from the verandah. COLONEL TRILETZKY *and* GLAGOLYEV *approach her, but are taken discreetly aside by* VOYNITZEV, *leaving* SOFYA *to stroll with her under the trees.*

ANNA PETROVNA. Are you serious about her?

DR TRILETZKY. Platonov thinks she's a fool. That's what the trouble was last summer. He's got it into that unkempt head of his that he has some kind of mission in life to rebuke fools.

ANNA PETROVNA. I know what a fool *you* are. Plenty of brains in that head of yours, but they're not always much in evidence. *Are* you serious?

DR TRILETZKY. I call on her nearly every day. I make conversation, I endure the boredom, I put her poor mother to some expense in coffee, and there we are. I talk about what interests me; she talks about what interests her. Then she takes hold of me by the lapels, and brushes the dust off my collar. I always seem to be covered in dust. But quite what draws me back each time, whether it's love or whether it's boredom, I don't really know.

Pause.

All I know is that I miss her quite painfully after lunch sometimes.

ANNA PETROVNA. So it's love, then. And here he is.

PLATONOV *and* SASHA *appear in the garden.*

VOYNITZEV. Platonov!

COLONEL TRILETZKY. Mishenka! My dear fellow!

PLATONOV. Sergey Pavlovich!

Joyful kisses and handclasps are exchanged.

VOYNITZEV. You've put on weight!

PLATONOV. You've taken off your beard.

VOYNITZEV (*to* SASHA). Alexandra Ivanovna!

PLATONOV (*shakes hands with* GLAGOLYEV). Porfiry
   Semyonovich.

GLAGOLYEV. We've been talking about you, Platonov.

COLONEL TRILETZKY. Late on parade again!

PLATONOV. Colonel!

COLONEL TRILETZKY. Keeping Her Majesty waiting!

ANNA PETROVNA (*to* DR TRILETZKY). Now we shall be all
   right.

   VOYNITZEV, COLONEL TRILETZKY *and* GLAGOLYEV
   escort PLATONOV *and* SASHA *on to the verandah in triumph.*

PLATONOV. At last – we're away from home! Anna
   Petrovna . . .!

VOYNITZEV. Here he is!

COLONEL TRILETZKY. This is the man!

PLATONOV. Say hello to everyone, Sasha . . . Anna Petrovna!
   (*He takes both her hands and kisses them.*)

ANNA PETROVNA. Cruel man! How could you make us wait
   so long? You must have known how impatient I should be.
   Alexandra Ivanovna! My dear! (*She kisses* SASHA.)

PLATONOV. Out of our house at last! Glory be to God! We
   haven't seen high ceilings for six whole months! We haven't seen
   people! We've been hibernating in our lair like two old bears,
   and we've only crawled forth into the world today!

VOYNITZEV. And Alexandra Ivanovna! Are you well?

PLATONOV. She's fine, she's fine. And her ladyship's household
   physician is in attendance, I see. (*He embraces* DR TRILETZKY.)

Radiant with health, by the look of it. Drenched in perfume, by the smell of it. And that haircut must have cost you a ruble or two.

DR TRILETZKY. You should be pleased to have a well turned-out brother-in-law.

ANNA PETROVNA. But how are you both? Sit down! Tell us everything! We'll all sit down.

PLATONOV (to VOYNITZEV, *laughing*). Is this really you? Heavens above! Where's the beard and the long hair?

SASHA. Sergey Pavlovich, I must just say one thing . . .

PLATONOV. Sasha, my love, will you never stop talking?

SASHA (to VOYNITZEV). Congratulations.

PLATONOV. Oh, yes! Of course!

SASHA. May I wish you every possible happiness?

PLATONOV. You've got yourself married! My warmest congratulations, too! (*He bows.*) Love and harmony all your days! Who is the lady?

VOYNITZEV. You'll see.

PLATONOV. I must confess I never expected it of you. Rather an about-face for a man of your views.

VOYNITZEV. Well, you know me. Didn't think twice! Fell in love – married her!

PLATONOV. We've had the falling in love part every winter. It's the getting married that's such a novel departure. Have you found a job?

VOYNITZEV. I've been offered a job in a high school of sorts, and I don't know what to do. It's not what I should have chosen.

PLATONOV. You'll take it, though?

VOYNITZEV. I really don't know. Probably not.

PLATONOV. So you'll be letting more time slip by. Three years now, isn't it, since you left university? You need someone to give you a bit of a kick. I must have a word with your wife. Three good years wasted! Isn't that right?

DR TRILETZKY. He hasn't been in the house five minutes, and already he's flaying us all!

GLAGOLYEV. Well, it's rare enough these days – someone with clear moral standards.

COLONEL TRILETZKY. My own son-in-law – the village Savonarola!

ANNA PETROVNA (*to* PLATONOV). Yes, go on! How have we got through the winter without your moral refreshment?

PLATONOV. It's too hot today to be serious. And it's far too pleasant sitting here again to be indignant at the evils of the world . . . I can see Sasha positively sniffing the air.

SASHA. Yes, I was. (*He laughs.*)

PLATONOV. You know what it smells of here? Human flesh! And what a delightful smell it is! I feel as if we hadn't seen each other for a hundred years. The winter went on and on forever! And there's my old armchair! Recognise it, Sasha? Six months ago I was never out of it. Sat there day and night talking to Anna Petrovna about the nature of the world, and losing all the housekeeping at cards.

ANNA PETROVNA. I've been so longing to see you again! I was quite out of patience . . . And you're well?

PLATONOV. Very well . . . But I must tell you one piece of news: you have grown just a shade more beautiful than before.

ANNA PETROVNA. And you've both put on weight! Such lucky people! So how have things been?

PLATONOV. Terrible, as usual. Never saw the sky for the whole six months. Ate, drank, slept. And read schoolboy adventure stories aloud to my wife. Terrible!

ANNA PETROVNA (*to* SASHA). Was it?

SASHA. I thought it was lovely.

PLATONOV. Sasha, it was appalling!

SASHA. It was a little bit dull, naturally.

PLATONOV. It wasn't a little bit dull, my love – it was extremely dull. (*To* ANNA PETROVNA.) I was pining for you!

SASHA. You got back yesterday?

ANNA PETROVNA. On the evening train.

PLATONOV. I saw lights here at eleven, but I thought you would be tired out.

ANNA PETROVNA. You should have come in! We sat up talking until two.

PLATONOV. So hot today. And so oppressive.

GLAGOLYEV. I think we may have a storm.

PLATONOV. I'm already starting to pine for the cold again.

COLONEL TRILETZKY. Sashenka, Sashenka! (*He puts a hand on* SASHA's *arm.*)

DR TRILETZKY. I thought you were asleep.

COLONEL TRILETZKY. My daughter . . . my son-in-law . . . my son . . . All the great stars of the Colonel Triletzky constellation!

DR TRILETZKY. If we're not careful, he's going to be weeping at the sight of us all. Aren't you, Father?

COLONEL TRILETZKY. Weep? Why should I want to weep?

DR TRILETZKY. Because you always do! Look at us all! What a family! And think of your grandson!

COLONEL TRILETZKY (*to* SASHA). Yes, how is the little fellow? Come and see him one of these days.

SASHA. He's well. He sends you his love.

COLONEL TRILETZKY. Really? Amazing child he is! Knows how to send his love to people now, does he?

VOYNITZEV. I think she means metaphorically speaking, colonel.

PLATONOV. He's not one yet, Father–in–law!

DR TRILETZKY. No, he's always talking about you! He waves his little arms and he pipes: 'Grandpapa! Grandpapa! Where's my grandpapa?'

PLATONOV. He's eleven months old!

DR TRILETZKY. 'I want to pull my grandpapa's moustache!'

COLONEL TRILETZKY. Good for him! (*He takes out his handkerchief.*) But you're not going to get me crying about it!

DR TRILETZKY. I don't see tears, do I, colonel?

PLATONOV. Stop it now, Kolya.

DR TRILETZKY. All right, so how about Anna Petrovna feeding us instead?

ANNA PETROVNA. You'll have to wait, doctor, like everybody else.

DR TRILETZKY. She doesn't realise how hungry we are. It's all on the table in there! Caviar, salmon, smoked sturgeon. A great seven–storey pie . . .

ANNA PETROVNA. How do you know what there is?

DR TRILETZKY. I went and looked! Aren't you hungry, Porfiry Semyonovich? Be absolutely frank, now!

SASHA (*to* DR TRILETZKY). You're not all that hungry – you just want to make trouble. You can't bear to see people sitting there in peace.

DR TRILETZKY. I can't bear to see people dying of hunger, Fat Lady.

PLATONOV. Another flash of quicksilver medical wit.

ANNA PETROVNA. What a bore the man is! All right, impudence, you wait here and I'll find you something to eat.

Exit ANNA PETROVNA.

PLATONOV. Though it wouldn't come amiss, now you mention it. I'm rather hungry myself.

SOFYA *and* GREKOVA *appear in the garden*.

VOYNITZEV. Here are the ladies, anyway. Now we'll put our great scholar to the test!

PLATONOV. Who is it?

VOYNITZEV. Aha!

COLONEL TRILETZKY. She's coaxed our little bolter back, by the look of it. (*To* PLATONOV.) Took one look at us before and fled!

PLATONOV. Who are we talking about?

DR TRILETZKY. Oh, yes, and now you're here!

COLONEL TRILETZKY. Come in and go straight out again, I should think!

GLAGOLYEV. May I suggest we pay her no attention?

VOYNITZEV. Just concentrate on the other one, Platonov, and tell us who she is.

SOFYA *ushers* GREKOVA *in from the garden*.

PLATONOV. Oh, it's the beetle-juice girl!

GREKOVA *stops in her tracks*.

PLATONOV *pays no attention to* SOFYA, *who watches the scene gravely*.

DR TRILETZKY (*reproachfully*). Misha!

GREKOVA (*coldly*). Mikhail Vasilyevich.

PLATONOV (*takes her hand*). Marya Yefimovna! My compliments!

VOYNITZEV. And here is someone else who is longing to meet you, Platonov . . .

PLATONOV. One moment. It's such a pleasure to meet Marya Yefimovna again. (*He tries to kiss her hand.*)

GREKOVA (*pulls her hand back*). I don't want my hand kissed. Thank you.

PLATONOV. I'm not worthy to kiss your hand, even?

GREKOVA. I've no idea whether you're worthy or not. I just know you don't mean it.

PLATONOV. Don't mean it? What makes you think that?

GREKOVA. You know I don't like it. That's the only reason you do it. It's always the same – you only like doing things that I don't like you doing.

DR TRILETZKY. Leave her alone, Misha.

PLATONOV. All in good time. (*To* GREKOVA.) How are you progressing with your beetle-juice?

GREKOVA. Beetle-juice? What is this about beetle-juice?

PLATONOV. Someone told me you were trying to make ether out of crushed beetles. Pushing forward the boundaries of science. Admirable!

GREKOVA. You must always make a joke of everything, mustn't you.

DR TRILETZKY. Always! Of everything!

PLATONOV. I make the doctor my model.

VOYNITZEV. Platonov . . .

PLATONOV. But what a charming pink your cheeks are! You're feeling the heat, I can see.

GREKOVA. Why do you keep saying these things to me?

PLATONOV. I'm merely trying to hold a conversation with you.

I haven't talked to you for six months or more. Why are you getting so cross about it?

GREKOVA. The sight of me seems to have some strange effect on you. I don't know how I've managed to upset you so. I stay out of your way as far as I possibly can. If Dr Triletzky hadn't promised me faithfully that you wouldn't be here I shouldn't have come.

DR TRILETZKY. I said I didn't know whether he'd be here or not.

GREKOVA (*to* DR TRILETZKY). You should be ashamed of yourself!

PLATONOV (*to* DR TRILETZKY). Absolutely! Deceiving her like that! (*To* GREKOVA.) Now you're going to cry, aren't you. All right – have a little cry, then. It can sometimes be a great relief.

Exit GREKOVA *in tears.*

DR TRILETZKY (*to* PLATONOV). You're such an idiot! One more little incident of that sort and we'll never be friends again!

PLATONOV. What's it to do with you?

DR TRILETZKY. Well, let's suppose – just for the sake of argument – that I happened to be in love with her!

PLATONOV. Then you'd be grateful to me for the chance to run after her and wipe away her tears.

DR TRILETZKY. I sometimes wonder if you're responsible for your actions!

Exit DR TRILETZKY *after* GREKOVA.

SASHA (*reproachfully*). Misha! Please!

GLAGOLYEV. There was a time when we treated women with respect!

COLONEL TRILETZKY. We get her back in, and – bang! – there's her head on the floor all over again!

PLATONOV. Yes. Stupid of me. Stupidity begets stupidity.

SOFYA. And you never could bear stupidity.

PLATONOV (*turns to her*). I'm sorry . . .

SOFYA. I didn't think you were even going to notice me.

PLATONOV. I don't believe we've met.

SOFYA. You don't recognise me, then?

VOYNITZEV (*to* PLATONOV). Careful! This is a serious examination!

COLONEL TRILETZKY. Future career depends on it!

VOYNITZEV. No? Well, then, may I introduce my wife? Sofya Yegorovna.

PLATONOV. Sofya Yegorovna . . . Your wife?

SOFYA. Have I changed so much?

PLATONOV. No, but . . . here! And you're married? (*To* VOYNITZEV.) This is the lady? Why didn't you say?

VOYNITZEV. A little surprise.

SOFYA. Have you forgotten, Platonov?

VOYNITZEV. A little reminder of your student days.

SOFYA. I was hardly out of school.

VOYNITZEV. And this is his wife, Alexandra Ivanovna.

SOFYA (*to* SASHA). I'm very pleased to meet you.

VOYNITZEV. The colonel's daughter. And the sister of the wittiest man in the world. Apart from Platonov himself.

SOFYA (*to* PLATONOV). So we're both married?

PLATONOV. I wonder you recognised me. The last five years have ravaged me like rats at a cheese. My life has not turned out as you might have supposed.

VOYNITZEV. She thought you were the second Byron!

COLONEL TRILETZKY. We all thought he was another Newton!

SOFYA. And in fact you're the village schoolmaster?

PLATONOV. Yes.

SOFYA. The village schoolmaster. I find that difficult to believe. Why haven't you . . . done better?

PLATONOV. Why haven't I done better?

VOYNITZEV (*to* PLATONOV). Now *you're* being called to account!

COLONEL TRILETZKY. This makes a change!

PLATONOV. Why haven't I done better? What can I say?

SOFYA. You finished university, at any rate?

VOYNITZEV. No, he gave it up.

COLONEL TRILETZKY. He knew it all. Nothing more they could teach him.

PLATONOV. I got married.

SOFYA. I see. Still, that doesn't stop you leading a decent life, does it?

PLATONOV. A decent life?

COLONEL TRILETZKY. The boot's on the other foot now, and no mistake!

SOFYA. Perhaps I shouldn't have put it like that. But giving up university doesn't stop you doing something worthwhile, does it? It doesn't stop you fighting for political freedom or the emancipation of women? It doesn't stop you serving a cause?

PLATONOV. Oh, dear. What can I say to that?

GLAGOLYEV. I think our Savonarola has met his match!

COLONEL TRILETZKY. Come on, Misha! Return her fire!

PLATONOV. No, she's right. There's nothing to stop me. The

question is whether there was every anything there to be stopped. I wasn't put into this world to do things; I was put here to prevent others from doing them.

PETRIN *appears in the garden.*

To lie here like some great flat stone and trip them up. To make them stub their toes against me.

SOFYA. And shall you lie in the same place for the rest of your life?

PLATONOV (*indicates* PETRIN). Who's going to hinder people like him, for instance, if I don't do it? Look at him! Anna Petrovna hasn't been back for a day, and already he's round here dunning her.

VOYNITZEV. Platonov – please! Don't start, I beg of you. We went through all this last summer.

PETRIN *comes on to the verandah.*

Gerasim Kuzmich!

They shake hands.

PLATONOV. You were deep in thought out there. What were you contemplating? Life and death? Or bills and promissory notes?

VOYNITZEV (*to* PETRIN). And this is my wife. Sofya Yegorovna.

PETRIN (*to* PLATONOV). Don't talk to me about bills. (*He shakes hands with* SOFYA.) How do you do? (*To* PLATONOV.) Don't talk to me about promissory notes! (*To* VOYNITZEV.) Yes, of course. Congratulations! (*To* PLATONOV.) They're nothing but dreams and delusions, my friend! They say: 'You possess money!' But when you reach out your hand for the money you possess, you find you possess nothing.

PLATONOV (*to* SOFYA). The old general didn't know what he was doing at the end of his life.

PETRIN. Yes, and who was there to help him?

PLATONOV. He didn't know what he was signing.

PETRIN. Who sat with him to the last and closed his eyes?

PLATONOV (to SOFYA). You wonder at me. And rightly so. But there's a whole world for you to wonder at here! A whole new world of fools and knaves.

VOYNITZEV. Now, Platonov . . .

PLATONOV. Sixty taverns, this fine gentleman owns.

PETRIN. Sixty-three.

PLATONOV. I beg your pardon.

PETRIN. And I should think you've drunk in all of them, haven't you?

PLATONOV. A public benefactor. Someone we all touch our caps to.

PETRIN. I am also a member of a learned profession. I am a qualified lawyer! Did you know that? On top of which I'm in the seventh grade of the civil service. And I have lived a little longer than you!

VOYNITZEV. Please!

GLAGOLYEV. No, but it's true! Some of us have lived a little longer than others!

PLATONOV. Wonderful. And what does that prove?

PETRIN. When you get to my age you'll find out!

GLAGOLYEV (to PLATONOV). You never knew the past, you see.

PETRIN. To survive your life – that takes some doing!

GLAGOLYEV (agreeing). We knew how to enjoy our life!

PETRIN. But there's a price to be paid!

PLATONOV (to SOFYA). Look at him, though! They all bend the knee before this jumped-up nobody. And why? Because they're all up to their ears in debt to him!

VOYNITZEV. Now that's enough, Platonov! It's very awkward for the hosts when guests fall out.

PLATONOV (*to* SOFYA). Are you embarrassed by our rural entertainments?

SOFYA. I find it all very illuminating.

VOYNITZEV (*to* PLATONOV). Sometimes you go too far, though.

PETRIN. What have I ever done to him?

PLATONOV. But that's the worst thing of all – that even those with some pretension to honour will say nothing! They all maintain this silence, this deathly silence!

COLONEL TRILETZKY *snores in his sleep.*

SASHA (*shakes him*). Wake up, Papa! You can't go to sleep here!

COLONEL TRILETZKY. Lunch?

PLATONOV. No. Go back to sleep again.

SASHA. Misha!

OSIP *appears in the garden, waiting awkwardly.*

PLATONOV. I prefer the company of good honest criminals. (*He calls.*) Osip!

VOYNITZEV. Oh, no!

GLAGOLYEV. Not him again!

PETRIN. What's he going to do – invite him in?

PLATONOV. Come in, Osip.

OSIP *comes on to the verandah, very out of place. He is concealing something under his shirt.*

PLATONOV (*to* SOFYA). May I introduce my friend Osip?

VOYNITZEV (*resignedly*). Wipe your boots then, Osip.

PLATONOV. Osip is our local horsethief.

VOYNITZEV. What are you doing here, Osip?

OSIP. Waiting for the mistress. Say welcome home, like.

VOYNITZEV. Very thoughtful of you, Osip. (*To* SOFYA.) All part of your introduction to local society, I suppose.

COLONEL TRILETZKY. Lives rough, this one.

GLAGOLYEV. In the forest.

PETRIN. Like a wild animal.

PLATONOV. Our local burglar. And murderer. Aren't you, Osip?

OSIP (*to* VOYNITZEV). Came to say congratulations, hope you'll be very happy, sir.

VOYNITZEV. Thank you, Osip.

PLATONOV. Look at that grin! There's a ton of iron in that face!

VOYNITZEV. So what have you been stealing off us this winter, Osip?

OSIP. Haven't been stealing nothing, sir.

VOYNITZEV. No?

OSIP. No, sir. Been away, sir.

VOYNITZEV. Where have you been, Osip?

OSIP. Been in prison, sir.

PLATONOV. Why have you been in prison?

OSIP. Because it's cold in the forest in winter.

PETRIN. Prison! Why have they never packed you off to Siberia for good and all? Look, he's got something hidden under his shirt even now!

VOYNITZEV. What is it, Osip?

OSIP. Nothing, sir.

PLATONOV. Nothing, he says! And nothing is what we do about

it! That's why he doesn't go to Siberia! We all know he's a thief
– but we all know he's a murderer, too, so no one's got the
courage to look inside his shirt. And that's all that stops the rest
of them here from going to Siberia! They're all standing here
with a bulging wad of nothing stuffed away in their shirts, and
no one's got the courage to challenge them!

VOYNITZEV. Platonov, really!

GLAGOLYEV. He's gone too far this time! There is a limit to
everything, and he has gone beyond it!

PLATONOV. Sixty-three taverns, this man owns! (*To* OSIP.) I
don't suppose you've got sixty-three kopecks. You're only a
beginner at thieving!

PETRIN. Are you seriously comparing me with a common
horsethief?

PLATONOV. Certainly not! I wouldn't insult horsethieves!

Uproar, through which COLONEL TRILETZKY *sleeps.*

VOYNITZEV. Please! Please!

PETRIN (*pointing at* PLATONOV). Either he goes or I go!

VOYNITZEV (*to* OSIP). *You* go! You're the cause of all this!

PLATONOV (*pointing at* OSIP). If he goes, I go!

SASHA (*to* PLATONOV). For the love of God! You're shaming
me in front of everyone!

Enter ANNA PETROVNA.

ANNA PETROVNA. Stop it! Stop it! It's getting like last year all
over again! I won't have it! Platonov, we were all perfectly
happy until you arrived!

PLATONOV (*offended*). Oh, you're on their side, are you? You
don't want me here, either? In that case I'll go!

PLATONOV *goes out into the garden.*

SASHA (*to* ANNA PETROVNA). I'm so sorry!

ANNA PETROVNA (*to* SASHA). Don't be silly. He'll calm down in a moment. Osip, what are you doing here?

OSIP. Nothing. Say welcome home, like. Brought you a little baby owl. (*He produces it from inside his shirt.*)

ANNA PETROVNA. Oh, how sweet. Take it round to the stables and find a box for it. Then go to the kitchen door and they'll give you something to eat.

OSIP *goes out into the garden.*

In fact we can all eat. Lunch is served!

SASHA (*to* ANNA PETROVNA). Please forgive him!

ANNA PETROVNA. There's nothing to forgive! It's all over. It's all forgotten.

GLAGOLYEV. We all know what Platonov's like.

VOYNITZEV (*to* SOFYA). Yes, there's your Platonov for you, my love!

SOFYA. I'm afraid I upset him. I shouldn't have spoken so frankly.

GLAGOLYEV. No, no, the man's a crank. (*To* SASHA.) Saving your presence. (*To* SOFYA.) There's no telling what will make him fly up next.

PETRIN. It's like having a performing bear in the house. Will he perform, or will he maul you?

ANNA PETROVNA. Gerasim Kuzmich, I haven't said hello to you.

PETRIN. Anna Petrovna! Could I have a word with you?

ANNA PETROVNA. You'll stay to lunch?

PETRIN. Yes, but if I could just have one word first . . .

ANNA PETROVNA. Where's our performing bear hiding himself now? (*To the others.*) Do go on in to lunch!

ANNA PETROVNA *goes towards the garden, followed by* PETRIN.

PETRIN. If you could just give me some hope . . .

ANNA PETROVNA. After lunch! There's always more hope after lunch.

ANNA PETROVNA *goes out into the garden.*

SASHA (*despairingly*). Father! Please!

COLONEL TRILETZKY (*wakes with a start*). Haven't had lunch, have we?

VOYNITZEV. Come on, Colonel . . .

VOYNITZEV *helps* COLONEL TRILETZKY *out.*
GLAGOLYEV *begins to usher* SOFYA *and* SASHA *out after him.*

SASHA. I'm sorry. I'm sorry.

GLAGOLYEV. No, no! What should we do without the colonel and his family to entertain us?

Exeunt SOFYA *and* SASHA. GLAGOLYEV *is detained by* PETRIN.

PETRIN. Just tell me. Did you?

GLAGOLYEV. Did I what?

PETRIN. Did you ask her?

GLAGOLYEV. Not yet.

PETRIN. My dear fellow! What are you waiting for? The colonel will get in ahead of you!

GLAGOLYEV. The colonel? The colonel hasn't got two kopecks for a candle!

PETRIN. He's got kopecks enough to buy skyrockets for her! Behind the old summerhouse – Yakov showed me. Might say more to a woman than flowers! You do want to marry her?

GLAGOLYEV. I'm not averse to the idea.

PETRIN. Well, then.

GLAGOLYEV. But will *she* want to marry *me*? That could be the difficulty, you see.

PETRIN. Of course she will!

GLAGOLYEV. Will she? Which of us knows the secrets of another's heart?

PETRIN. Lovely woman – handsome man. You're made for each other! Shall I ask her for you?

GLAGOLYEV. I can do my own courting, thank you! What's it to do with you?

PETRIN. A man needs a wife, Porfiry Semyonovich! An estate needs a man! And debts need someone to pay them! I don't want to take her to court and force her to sell up! I'm a reasonable man, Porfiry Semyonovich! All I want is my money!

ANNA PETROVNA *appears in the garden, her arm in* PLATONOV's.

Here she is, Porfiry Semyonvich! Ask her now!

GLAGOLYEV (*hesitates*). I can't do it on an empty stomach. Lunch first!

PETRIN. Your happiness – that's all I want! Your happiness and my money.

Exeunt GLAGOLYEV *and* PETRIN *in the direction of lunch.*

Enter ANNA PETROVNA *and* PLATONOV *from the garden.*

ANNA PETROVNA. But I *can't* get rid of them, you see. Nor can you, for all your eloquence. I depend upon them! It's like a very complicated position on a chess board. If I didn't make Porfiry Semyonovich just a little bit jealous of the colonel . . . if I didn't make the colonel just a little bit jealous of the doctor . . . if I wasn't protected from the doctor by poor little Grekova – if our good tavern-keeper didn't believe he'd get his money from our great lover of women . . . if you weren't here to lighten my heart . . . why, then the queen would fall. I should lose the estate, Platonov! I should lose everything. Then what would you do? Any of you? The lion must roar – of course he must – but a

little more softly, Platonov, or he'll roar the whole house down.
Yes? Now you wait here. I'm going to send Marya Yefimovna
out to you. I found *her* in tears, Platonov! So you're going to
give her your paw and apologise.

Enter VOYNITZEV.

VOYNITZEV. Come on! They're all waiting to drink our health!

ANNA PETROVNA. He's got something else to do first. (*To*
PLATONOV.) Now, wait! Don't you dare come into lunch
until you've done as I told you!

Exit ANNA PETROVNA.

VOYNITZEV. What's all this?

PLATONOV. I'm offering my paw to get my lunch . . . Sergey,
you're a lucky man. She's a lovely woman, your Sofya. Are you
happy?

VOYNITZEV. I don't know . . .

PLATONOV. You don't know?

VOYNITZEV. Are you and Sasha happy?

PLATONOV. We're a family! We've made a nest! One of these
days you'll understand what that means. Take Sasha away from
me and I think I should be finished. Utterly destroyed. We're the
perfect couple – she's a fool and I'm a rogue. *Aren't* you happy?

VOYNITZEV. I suppose we are. I suppose this is what being
happy is.

Enter DR TRILETZKY, *eating, glass in one hand, bottle in the other.*

PLATONOV (*to* DR TRILETZKY). You've been stuffing
yourself already, then. Have you forgiven me?

DR TRILETZKY. What for? Come on! We've got to drink to the
great homecoming. (*He puts his arm round* PLATONOV.) Drink,
drink, drink!

PLATONOV. Have you seen your patients today?

DR TRILETZKY (*moves away from him*). Misha, once and for all, if you're going to lecture me, let's make a regular arrangement. Private moral coaching, an hour a day, four to five, and I'll pay you a ruble a time!

VOYNITZEV (*puts his arm round both of them*). Come on, my friends, let's go and drink together! Then fate can do its worst. To hell with moneylenders, to hell with creditors! Just so long as all the people I love in this world are alive and well. You're all I have!

DR TRILETZKY. We're all we all have!

Enter GREKOVA. *She stops at the sight of them.*

PLATONOV. Come on! I'm going to drink to everything, with everything there is to drink! I haven't been drunk for a long, long time, and I'm going to get drunk today!

They start to go, but stop at the sight of GREKOVA.

Marya Yefimovna! I apologise. I publicly beg your forgiveness. I burn with shame. Give me your hand . . . I go down on one knee and publicly kiss your hand!

GREKOVA *snatches her hand back.*

And now she's going to start snivelling again!

Exit GREKOVA *in tears.*

Come back here, Beetle-juice!

Exit PLATONOV *after her.*

DR TRILETZKY. Misha, I implore you!

VOYNITZEV. Can you *never* be serious?

Exeuent DR TRILETZKY *and* VOYNITZEV *after him.*

Curtain, as a cheerful dance is struck up offstage.

Scene Two

The garden. As in the previous scene, less the verandah. The music continues offstage. Enter SASHA, *carrying something under a napkin.*

SASHA (*calls, softly*). Where are you? Are you there?

   OSIP *emerges, from the trees.* SASHA *takes the napkin off what she is holding; it is a plate of food.*

OSIP. We're both of us thieves, then. (*He takes the plate, sits down, and eats hungrily with his fingers.*)

SASHA. Take your cap off. It's a sin to eat with your head covered. And you say a little grace, now!

   OSIP *removes his cap, and continues to eat. There is the distant whistle of a train.*

   There – that's the evening train. It'll be dark soon. And they still haven't finished lunch! Eating, drinking. Singing, dancing. Then eating and drinking again. My head's ringing . . . And they couldn't find a few scraps in the kitchen for you . . .? Well, God be with them . . . As soon as it's dark we'll be having the fireworks. I haven't seen fireworks since I was a girl. Not since people gave parties for all the officers, when my father had his regiment . . .

   Another train whistle, a little nearer, and then for a moment the faint sound of the locomotive.

   There it goes. Over the crossing. Past our little house . . .

   Pause. OSIP *hands the plate back to* SASHA *and wipes his mouth.*

OSIP. I kissed her once.

SASHA. Anna Petrovna? You kissed her? (*She sits beside him.*)

OSIP. Hot summer's day. Like today. In the forest here. I'm going along this track and I look round and there she is, she's standing in a little stream and she's holding her dress up with one hand and she's scooping up water in a dock leaf with the other. She scoops. She drinks. Scoops. Drinks. Scoops again, and pours it over her head. It's one of those days when you can feel the air heavy on you, and you can't hear nothing but the buzzing of the flies . . . She pays no heed to me. Just another peasant, she thinks. So I go down to the edge of the stream, right close up to her, as close as I am to you now, and I just look at her. Like this, like I'm looking at you. And she stands there in the water in front of me, with her skirts up in her hand, and she bends, she scoops, she pours. And the water runs over her hair, over her face and her neck, then down over her dress, and all she says is: 'What are you staring at, idiot? Haven't you ever seen a human being before?' And she scoops and she pours, and I just stand gazing. Then suddenly she turns and gives me a sharp look. 'Oh,' she says, 'you've taken a fancy to me, have you?' And I say: 'I reckon I could kiss you and die.' So that made her laugh. 'All right,' she says, 'you can kiss me if you like.' Well, I felt as if I'd been thrown into a furnace. I went up to her – into the stream, boots and all, I didn't think twice – and I took her by the shoulder, very lightly, and kissed her right here, on her cheek, and here on her neck, as hard as ever I could.

SASHA. So what did she do then?

OSIP. 'Now, then,' she says, 'be off with you! And you wash a little more often,' she says, 'and you do something about your nails!' And off I went.

SASHA. She's a bold one, all right.

OSIP. After that you'd have thought I'd gone mad. Couldn't eat. Couldn't sleep. Everywhere I went I could see her in front of me. Shut my eyes – there she was again. I must have looked right soft. I wanted to go round and shoot the poor old general! And then when she was widowed I started doing all kinds of little things for her. Shot partridges for her – caught quails – painted that old summerhouse of hers all different colours. Took her a live wolf once. She's only to say and I'd do it. Tell me to eat myself and I'd eat myself . . .

ANNA PETROVNA *appears among the trees in the background. She moves irresolutely first in this direction and then in that, looking for someone.*

SASHA. There she is . . . She'll see you.

OSIP. Why should I care?

SASHA. It's true, though. When you're soft on someone there's nothing to be done with you. When I first loved Platonov and still didn't know that he loved me I went through terrible torments. Wandered about the forest like a lost soul?

OSIP. And now what does he do? He dangles round her ladyship! Not much heart, that husband of yours. Got the brains, though, and he's got the words. He could have the whole female race after him if he wanted.

SASHA. That's enough now. I don't like that kind of talk.

VOYNITZEV (*calls, off*). Sofya! Sofya!

DR TRILETZKY (*calls, off*). Misha! Where are you?

ANNA PETROVNA *vanishes.*

SASHA. Now they're all coming out. They'll find you, for sure. Anyway, it's no good sitting here moping after her. That won't get you anywhere.

OSIP. Why should he want more women after him, though? He's got the best of them already.

OSIP *melts away beneath the trees as* VOYNITZEV *enters.*

SASHA. Is it time for the fireworks?

VOYNITZEV. Yes, but I've lost Sofya.

SASHA. I'll fetch Platonov. You won't start without us, will you?

VOYNITZEV. I thought she was in the garden.

Enter DR TRILETZKY, *noticeably drunk.*

Have you seen Sofya?

DR TRILETZKY. No. Looking for Misha.

VOYNITZEV (*calls*). Sofya . . .!

Exit VOYNITZEV.

DR TRILETZKY (*calls*) Misha! (*To* SASHA.) I've got a ruble for him! Have a ruble, Sasha . . . (*He sees the empty plate in her hand.*) Poor Sasha! Eating out here on your own! Have two rubles, Sasha! Have three!

SASHA (*brushes the money aside*). Oh, no! Are you as drunk as that?

DR TRILETZKY. I'm not drunk, Sasha! It's Gerasim Kuzmich who's drunk! Gave me all his money to look after! 'If I don't give this to you', he said, 'I know I'll only go and give it to someone else.' (*He sniffs the money.*) Peasant money . . . Here – four rubles for my lovely sister. And if you think I'm drunk you want to see Father!

SASHA. What have I done to deserve this? Where is he?

DR TRILETZKY. Behind the sofa.

SASHA. No use expecting any help from you, I suppose. Where's Misha?

DR TRILETZKY. I can't find him!

SASHA. Well, find him! I'll find Father.

Exit SASHA.

DR TRILETZKY (*calls*). Misha! Misha!

Exit DR TRILETZKY.

Enter SOFYA *from under the trees. She sits down on one of the garden seats.*

VOYNITZEV (*calls off*). Sofya! Where are you?

DR TRILETZKY (*calls off*). A reward of one ruble for anyone who finds Platonov!

Enter PLATONOV *from the same direction as* SOFYA.

PLATONOV. I follow you into the living-room – you go back into the dining-room. I go into the dining-room – you go into the garden. I come into the garden – you run back towards the house.

SOFYA. You keep talking about the past. What does it matter? A student loved a schoolgirl; a schoolgirl loved a student. It's an old story! Old and trite! Too old and trite for it to mean much to us now.

PLATONOV. Then what are you so frightened of?

SOFYA. I'm not frightened of anything!

PLATONOV. Is every man you meet really such a threat to your Sergey? If I've talked to you too much this evening, if I've wearied you with my attentions, then it's because you're an intelligent and sympathetic woman. What do you think? That I want to take you away from your husband? That I'm in love with you? That you've somehow made a conquest of the local intellectual? Tamed the village eccentric? How wonderful! What bliss! What a nice box of chocolates for our little egotist!

SOFYA. You've gone mad.

PLATONOV. Run away, then! Run back to him! No one's forcing you to stay here!

Pause.

So hot, even now . . . I shouldn't have drunk so much . . .

Pause.

Why haven't I done better? The first thing you asked me! Not 'Are you well?' or 'Are you happy?' Not at all! 'Why haven't you done better?'

SOFYA. I'm sorry.

PLATONOV. No, you're right. Why haven't I? Teeming evil all around me, fouling the earth, swallowing up my brothers in Christ, while I sit here with folded hands. I shall be the same when I'm forty, the same when I'm fifty. I shan't change now. Not until I decline into shuffling old age, and stupefied indifference to everything outside my own body. A wasted life! Then death. And when I think of that death I'm terrified.

Pause.

Why haven't I done better? I might ask the same of you. What's happened to that pure heart you used to have? Where's the old sincerity, the truthfulness, the boldness? You ask me why I haven't done better; do you ever ask your husband?

SOFYA *gets to her feet.*

PLATONOV *makes her sit down again.*

One last word, and then I'll let you go. You were so splendid once! No, let me finish . . . You were good. You had greatness in you. (*He takes her hand.*) What in all the wide world made you marry that man?

SOFYA. Sergey? He's a fine man!

PLATONOV. He's a moral pygmy!

SOFYA. He's my husband!

PLATONOV. He's bogged down in debt – he's helpless with doing nothing!

SOFYA. Lower your voice, will you! There are people about!

PLATONOV. I don't care! Let them all hear! (*Quietly.*) I'm sorry if I spoke sharply. I loved you, though. Loved you more than all the world. This hair. These hands. This face . . . And what can you do here? You'll only go deeper and deeper into the mire. Why do we never lead the life we have it in us to lead? If I had the strength I should uproot us from this mudhole – uproot us both! We'd leave! Tonight! Take the night train and never return!

SOFYA. What are you saying?

PLATONOV. You know what I'm saying . . .

Enter PETRIN *and* GLAGOLYEV, *both a little bit drunk.*

PETRIN (*to* GLAGOLYEV). Put a ruble in front of me and I'll steal it!

SOFYA *flees into the depths of the garden.*

PLATONOV. Sofya! (*He runs after her.*)

PETRIN. I should, Porfiry! I'd steal it! I honestly should! If I thought I could get away with it! Put a ruble in front of *you* and you'd steal it!

GLAGOLYEV. I shouldn't, Gerasya! I shouldn't, you know!

PETRIN. Show me an honest man, Porfiry, and I'll show you a fool!

GLAGOLYEV. I'm a fool, Gerasya!

PETRIN (*sadly*). Yes. You're a fool. And it's no good just sitting in there and staring at her! What kind of way is that to win a woman? You were just sitting there like a mushroom!

GLAGOLYEV. I'll win her, Gerasya, never you fear! I'll marry her yet!

PETRIN. Yes, but when, Porfiry, when? Who knows how long we've got, at our age? Ask her tonight, Porfiry! It's a beautiful summer's night. And she's in love! Didn't you see her laughing at lunch? Didn't you see the wild look in her eye? Here she comes. Look at her! Look at her!

Enter ANNA PETROVNA *and* GREKOVA, *in the depths of the garden.*

She's followed you out here.

GLAGOLYEV. She's got Marya Yefimovna with her.

ANNA PETROVNA (*calls*). Doctor! Doctor?

PETRIN. She's trying to get rid of her. She wants to be alone.

DR TRILETZKY (*calls, off*). Misha! Where are you, Misha?

ANNA PETROVNA urges GREKOVA *off in the direction of the voice.*

PETRIN. You see? She's waiting for you! Quick! Before the colonel comes out! One more glass to get his courage up and he'll go into battle! You'll never have another chance like this!

ANNA PETROVNA, now that GREKOVA *is out of sight, goes off purposefully in another direction.*

After her, then, Porfiry! Steal that ruble!

Exit GLAGOLYEV *uncertainly after* ANNA PETROVNA.

Enter VOYNITZEV.

VOYNITZEV. I've lost Sofya. I can't understand it . . . (*He looks off in the direction taken by* ANNA PETROVNA.) That isn't her, is it?

PETRIN. No, no! That way, that way!

He points VOYNITZEV *in some other direction, then goes off anxiously after* GLAGOLYEV. *Enter* GREKOVA.

GREKOVA (*to* VOYNITZEV). Platonov?

VOYNITZEV. Sofya?

GREKOVA. I'm sorry.

VOYNITZEV. I beg your pardon.

Exit GREKOVA, *in some confusion.*

Enter SOFYA, *in some agitation.*

SOFYA. Sergey!

VOYNITZEV. Sofya! I thought I'd lost you forever! Where have you been?

SOFYA. Let's go away from here!

VOYNITZEV. Away?

SOFYA. Anywhere! Abroad!

VOYNITZEV. If you like.

SOFYA. Now!

VOYNITZEV. Now?

SOFYA. Tonight.

VOYNITZEV. Sofya!

SOFYA. Please, Sergey!

VOYNITZEV. But . . . but . . . what about the fireworks?

SOFYA. No – no fireworks!

VOYNITZEV. Sofya, my love, I know how dull it is for you here . . .

SOFYA. There's a train. There's a night train.

VOYNITZEV. My love, we're not *that* boring! Not all of us, anyway. I'm sure it would help if you talked to Platonov.

SOFYA. Platonov?

Enter PLATONOV at the sound of his name. He stops at the sight of VOYNITZEV, and stands at the edge of the trees, unnoticed, watching them.

VOYNITZEV. I know you're disappointed in him, I saw you avoiding him all afternoon. And he has become a bit of a bear, I admit. But he's not like the others. He's someone I love. He's someone you'll love, too, when you know him a little better. Come on, let's find him!

SOFYA. Sergey, please listen . . .

VOYNITZEV. No, no – you listen to Platonov. I know he'll persuade you to stay! At least until we've had the fireworks!

Exeunt VOYNITZEV and SOFYA.

PLATONOV goes to follow them.

Enter ANNA PETROVNA.

ANNA PETROVNA. And here he is. Our philosopher. Shunning us all. Pacing the garden and thinking his own thoughts. But what a perfect summer's night! Cool air at last. And the first star . . . What a pity ladies aren't supposed to sleep outside under the open sky. When I was a little girl I always slept in the garden in summer.

Pause.

You've got a new tie.

PLATONOV. Yes.

ANNA PETROVNA. I'm in such an odd mood today . . . I feel
pleased with everything . . . Say something, Platonov!

PLATONOV. What do you want me to say?

ANNA PETROVNA. I want to hear the sound of your voice. I
want to hear it saying – I don't know – something new,
something sharp, something sweet. Because you're being
terribly clever today, and you're looking terribly handsome, and
I'm more in love with you than ever. And you're being so nice!
You're causing scarcely any trouble at all!

PLATONOV. I've never seen you looking more lovely.

ANNA PETROVNA. Are we friends, Platonov?

PLATONOV. Of course. If we're not friends, who is?

ANNA PETROVNA. Real friends? Great friends?

PLATONOV. What is this? We're friends, we're friends! You're
behaving like a schoolgirl!

ANNA PETROVNA. So, we're friends. But you know, do you,
my dear sir, that from friendship between a man and a woman
it's only a short step to love?

PLATONOV. Is it indeed? You and I shall not be taking that one
step to perdition, however short it may be.

ANNA PETROVNA. So you see love as perdition, do you? I see
it as something noble. Why should we be ashamed of it? Why
shouldn't we take that one short step?

PLATONOV (*stares at her*). Let's go inside and dance, shall we?

ANNA PETROVNA. You can't dance! I think it's time you and I
had a little talk. I don't quite know where to begin, though.
You're such a difficult man! Now try to listen for once, and not
to philosophise . . . (*She sits.*) Sit down . . . Look, he's quite
embarrassed! It's all right, my dear – your wife can't hear us!

PLATONOV. Perhaps I should say something first.

ANNA PETROVNA. Perhaps you should.

PLATONOV. It's not worth it. I promise you, Anna Petrovna –
it's simply not worth it.

ANNA PETROVNA. Isn't it? Now you listen to me. Sit down
. . . Sit down!

He sits beside her.

Look, if you were free, I shouldn't think twice – I'd make myself
your wife. I'd bestow my rank and station on you. But as it
is . . .

Pause.

Am I to take your silence as a sign of agreement?

Pause.

I think in the circumstances it is a little ungentlemanly of you not
to say *something*.

PLATONOV (*leaps to his feet*). Let's forget this conversation! Let's
pretend it never took place!

ANNA PETROVNA. You are a clown, Misha.

PLATONOV. I respect you! And I respect in myself the respect I
have for you! I'm not against harmless diversion . . .

ANNA PETROVNA. I know, Platonov.

PLATONOV. But not with a beautiful, intelligent, untrammelled
woman like you! What – a month or two of foolishness, and
then to go our ways in shame? I couldn't do it!

ANNA PETROVNA. I wasn't talking about foolishness. I was
talking about love.

PLATONOV. And do you think I don't love you? I love you for
your goodness, for your generous heart. I love you desperately –
I love you to distraction! I'll lay down my life for you, if that's
what you want! Does every love have to be reduced to the same
common denominator? I love you as a woman, yes, but I also
love you as a person. On top of which, my dear, I am just a tiny
bit married.

ANNA PETROVNA (*rises*). You've also had just a tiny bit too much to drink, and you're being just a tiny bit hypocritical. Go on, then. When your head's clear we'll have another talk.

PLATONOV. No, the trouble is, I can't hide my true feelings from you. (*Quietly and intimately*.) If only it were a game, my precious, I should long since have been your lover.

Exit PLATONOV.

ANNA PETROVNA (*to herself*). Intolerable man! (*She calls*.) Come back here! Misha! Misha . . .

She is about to run after him when GLAGOLYEV *enters suddenly from among the trees.*

GLAGOLYEV. Anna Petrovna!

ANNA PETROVNA. Oh! You quite startled me!

GLAGOLYEV. Anna Petrovna, you know, I believe, in what high regard I hold your sex. I have more than once been accused of romanticism, but for me a world without women would be akin to a paradise without angels. And yet such is the world, during the winter months at any rate, in which I myself live. Anna Petrovna . . .

COLONEL TRILETZKY (*calls, off*). Anna Petrovna!

ANNA PETROVNA. I'm afraid we've been spotted by the artillery.

GLAGOLYEV (*turns to look at* COLONEL TRILETZKY). Yes, I'll come straight to the point, then. (*Exit* ANNA PETROVNA.) Anna Petrovna, will you be the angel in my paradise?

COLONEL TRILETZKY (*off*). You're getting my feet all muddled up! Perfectly all right on my own!

GLAGOLYEV (*becomes aware that* ANNA PETROVNA *has departed*.) Anna Petrovna!

Enter PETRIN *from behind the trees.*

PETRIN. That way!

Exit GLAGOLYEV *after* ANNA PETROVNA, *and* PETRIN *after* GLAGOLYEV.

Enter COLONEL TRILETZKY, *drunk, attended by* DR TRILETZKY *and* SASHA. DR TRILETZKY, *who is wearing the officer's peaked cap in which his father arrived, is amused by the colonel's condition.*

COLONEL TRILETZKY. Don't push me! Don't push me! (*He discovers he is not being pushed.*) Oh, you're there.

SASHA. If you've no fear before God you might at least have some shame in front of other people! Everyone staring at you! Everyone laughing at you! (*To* DR TRILETZKY.) It's nothing to laugh about!

DR TRILETZKY. Where's Misha, though?

COLONEL TRILETZKY. Where's Anna Petrovna?

SASHA. Vanished at the sight of you, of course.

COLONEL TRILETZKY. Something I wanted to ask her.

DR TRILETZKY. He's forgotten what it was!

SASHA. It's not funny, Kolya!

COLONEL TRILETZKY. What was I saying?

DR TRILETZKY. You could have been a general.

SASHA. Don't encourage him!

COLONEL TRILETZKY. Yes! Another five years or so, and I could have been a general! If I'd been five years older when I reached retiring age . . . No, if I'd been five years younger when I was born . . . What do I mean?

SASHA. Come on – home. You shouldn't be allowed inside a decent house. You're an old man! You should be setting the others an example!

COLONEL TRILETZKY. You're just like your mother! Do you know that? Day and night she used to go on. This isn't right, that isn't right . . . Just like your poor old dear departed mother, my pet! Same eyes, same hair. Same way of waddling like a goose . . . (*He kisses her.*) God, how I loved her!

SASHA. That's enough, now. Come on!

COLONEL TRILETZKY. I will, my love. Whatever you say. I haven't always been a good man, Sasha. But I loved your mother. And I never took money from anyone.

DR TRILETZKY. Have another ruble. (*He gives him one.*)

COLONEL TRILETZKY (*takes the money*). All I had to do was to dip my hand in with the rest of them and I could have been rich and famous . . . I could have been a general!

SASHA. Kolya, give him his hat back before he catches cold. Tell Misha I've gone, when you find him.

DR TRILETZKY. What about the fireworks?

SASHA. I'll just have to wait for another time.

COLONEL TRILETZKY. Right, then, quick march . . . ! I'll tell you what. I'll carry you.

SASHA. Don't be silly.

COLONEL TRILETZKY. I'll carry you! Always used to carry your mother. Couldn't walk straight myself – still pick her up and carry her! Come on!

SASHA. Certainly not. Put your cap on properly. (*She straightens his cap for him.*) Smarten you up a bit.

COLONEL TRILETZKY. We rolled all the way down a hill together once. Never said a word about it, poor love. Just laughed, bless her.

Exit COLONEL TRILETZKY, *supported by* SASHA. *Enter* VOYNITZEV.

VOYNITZEV. Where's Platonov? I can't find him anywhere.

DR TRILETZKY. Nor can I. Have another ruble instead. Is it the fireworks?

VOYNITZEV. There won't be any fireworks if I can't find Platonov.

DR TRILETZKY. Won't be any . . . ? (*He calls.*) Misha!

VOYNITZEV (*calls*). Misha!

DR TRILETZKY (*calls*). Misha!

Exeunt VOYNITZEV *and* DR TRILETZKY.

Enter PLATONOV *and* SOFYA.

PLATONOV. Going?

SOFYA. Tonight.

PLATONOV. Forever?

SOFYA. Forever.

PLATONOV. What did you tell Sergey?

SOFYA. Nothing.

PLATONOV. What did he say?

SOFYA. He told me to talk to you.

PLATONOV. To *me*?

SOFYA. He said you'd persuade me to stay.

Pause. They look at each other.

PLATONOV. Go.

SOFYA. Go?

PLATONOV. Tonight. At once. You're right – it's the only way. Otherwise I can't answer for the consequences.

Pause. They stand looking at each other.

Enter GREKOVA.

GREKOVA. Platonov . . .

She stops at the sight of SOFYA. *But* SOFYA *suddenly turns and flees.*

I'm sorry. But I can't bear this any longer. You seem to be following me! Everywhere I go – there you are! *Are* you following me?

PLATONOV. Beetle-juice! Come here, you lovely creature!

GREKOVA. What? (*She crosses to him nervously.*)

PLATONOV. You weird and wonderful woman! (*He kisses her.*)

GREKOVA. Why are you kissing me?

PLATONOV. I've got to kiss someone!

GREKOVA. Do you . . . do you love me, then?

PLATONOV. Why, do you love me, you foolish headstrong woman?

GREKOVA. I don't know. That depends on whether you . . .

He kisses her.

You shouldn't do that if you don't.

He kisses her.

Do you love me?

PLATONOV. Not at all, my precious! That's why I'm kissing you!

She bursts into tears, flees, and runs into DR TRILETZKY.

DR TRILETZKY. And here he is! The man everyone wants to see!

GREKOVA. *I* never want to see him again! And if you have any respect for me at all – if you have any respect for yourself – you'll never see him again, either.

DR TRILETZKY. But he's my brother-in-law!

GREKOVA. Yes, everything's a joke to you, too, isn't it. Well, you joke away together, then. That's all you can ever do!

DR TRILETZKY. Have a ruble.

GREKOVA *turns to flee, with a cry of pain, but is stopped by* VOYNITZEV *as he enters.*

VOYNITZEV. Fireworks!

GREKOVA. What?

VOYNITZEV. Don't run away! (*To* PLATONOV.) We're
staying! I don't know what you said, but you persuaded her! I
told her you were the most eloquent man in the world! I won't
forget this, Misha. Come on! I'm going to light the fireworks!

GREKOVA (*to* DR TRILETZKY). I'm going to watch the
fireworks, I don't care about you.

Exit VOYNITZEV *and* GREKOVA *after him.*

Enter ANNA PETROVNA.

DR TRILETZKY (*excited*). Fireworks! Fireworks!

Exit DR TRILETZKY.

PLATONOV (*to* ANNA PETROVNA). My God! What have I
done?

ANNA PETROVNA. Sasha's gone. She'll miss the fireworks.

PLATONOV (*takes* ANNA PETROVNA's *hands in his*). What's
going to be come of us all?

ANNA PETROVNA. You seem just a tiny bit less married.

PLATONOV. How are we going to survive our lives?

ANNA PETROVNA. First of all by enjoying the fireworks.

ANNA PETROVNA *begins to lead* PLATONOV *off after the
others.*

Enter GLAGOLYEV.

GLAGOLYEV. Anna Petrovna!

She turns back to him.

Let me say at once that I should renounce the usual rights of a
husband . . .

ANNA PETROVNA. And let me say one word to you, my
friend.

GLAGOLYEV. Yes?

ANNA PETROVNA. Fireworks!

Exit ANNA PETROVNA *after* PLATONOV.

Enter PETRIN.

PETRIN. What did she say? What did she say?

GLAGOLYEV. She said fireworks.

Exit GLAGOLYEV *after* ANNA PETROVNA, *and* PETRIN *after* GLAGOLYEV.

Enter SOFYA.

SOFYA (*to herself*). Is it ruin, or is it happiness? Is it the beginning of a new life, or is it the end of everything?

Enter COLONEL TRILETZKY.

COLONEL TRILETZKY. It's the fireworks!

Exeunt COLONEL TRILETZKY *and* SOFYA *after the others.*

Enter OSIP *from under the trees.*

VOYNITZEV (*off*). Look out, everyone! We're starting!

OSIP whips out a long-bladed hunting knife; and at the same moment there is the whoosh of a rocket taking off. OSIP stands gazing upwards, knife raised, as the coloured stars burst in the sky. There is a collective sigh of satisfaction from the spectators, off. The stars fade. OSIP brings the knife down into the back of one of the garden chairs.

Curtain.

ACT TWO

Scene One

A clearing in the forest. Right – the local schoolhouse. In the background – the same tall trees as in the previous act. Here, though, they are bisected not by a grassy garden walk, but by a railway line, which comes straight down to the front of the stage, where it passes between the wooden baulks of a rough level crossing.

Before the curtain rises there is the sound of a goods train, clanking and whistling as it passes through the auditorium. The curtain goes up to reveal the red tail light of the train at the front of the stage, moving away from us, then disappearing among the smoke left by the locomotive.

PLATONOV emerges from the smoke, stepping over the rail on to the track, and walking dejectedly towards us. When the smoke finally clears it reveals a brilliant moonlit night, as bright as day.

PLATONOV (*calls, gloomily*). Sasha . . . ! Sasha . . .!

A window in the schoolhouse opens, and SASHA looks out, in her nightgown.

SASHA. Misha?

PLATONOV. Sasha . . .

SASHA. Sh! You'll wake the baby.

PLATONOV. Sasha . . .

SASHA. Are you drunk?

PLATONOV. Sasha, do you love me?

SASHA. Wait. I'll come out.

The window closes. PLATONOV sinks gloomily down on to the step of the schoolhouse verandah. The door opens, and SASHA comes out.

SASHA. What's the time? Was that the goods or the passenger?
  Are the fireworks over?

PLATONOV. Do you, Sasha?

SASHA. You are a bit drunk. Aren't you, Misha?

PLATONOV. Do you love me?

SASHA. Misha! It took me hours to get him to sleep!

PLATONOV. Do you, though? I want to know.

SASHA. Of course I love you.

PLATONOV. Why?

SASHA. Why?

PLATONOV. Name one single good thing in me that you love
  me for! Name one good quality that could possibly make you
  love me!

SASHA. You're in a funny mood, aren't you, Misha? Obviously I
  love you! You're my husband!

PLATONOV. That's the only reason you love me, because I'm
  your husband?

SASHA. Misha, sometimes I don't understand you at all.

PLATONOV. Don't you? (*He laughs.*) No, you're a fool, aren't
  you. A complete fool. You should have been a fly. In the land of
  the flies, with your brains, you'd have been the cleverest fly of
  all. (*He kisses her brow.*) Where should we be if you understood
  me, if you realised how little there was to love in me?

SASHA. What happened? Didn't you enjoy the fireworks?

PLATONOV. Fireworks, fireworks . . . I ran away, Sasha!

SASHA. From the fireworks?

PLATONOV. From myself! Fled, in shame and terror! Came
  running all the way back to you!

SASHA (*laughs*). You're the fool, Misha!

PLATONOV. And I'm not drunk. I'm not drunk now. I certainly wasn't drunk then.

SASHA. When?

PLATONOV. When I told her she'd married a moral pygmy.

SASHA. Told who? Told Sofya Yegorovna?

PLATONOV. My tongue ran away with me! I behaved like a schoolboy! Postured, strutted, showed off . . .

SASHA. She's beautiful.

PLATONOV. Why did I say all those things? I didn't believe them! *She* believed them, though!

SASHA. I don't think I've ever seen anyone as beautiful as that.

PLATONOV. Anna Petrovna got a proposal of marriage.

SASHA. From Porfiry Semyonovich? What did she say?

PLATONOV. Nothing. He had a heart attack.

SASHA. Oh no! Is he all right?

PLATONOV. Your brother bled him.

SASHA. They want my brother in the village. It's the storekeeper – he's very poorly. Had Kolya sobered up at all?

PLATONOV. I grandly mock people like Porfiry Semyonovich and Gerasim Kuzmich. But who's going to mock me? When are they going to start? It's ridiculous! I don't take bribes, I don't steal, I don't beat my wife, I think high-minded thoughts – and still I'm a scoundrel, a ridiculous scoundrel!

SASHA. Misha, you're talking nonsense. It's time you were in bed.

PLATONOV. Oh, my precious! My lovely silly little noodle! I shouldn't think of you as a wife – I should put you in a glass case with a label on you. How did you and I ever manage to bring a baby into the world? You shouldn't be bearing children, my love; you should still be making little men out of dough. (*He tries to kiss her.*)

SASHA (*refuses to be kissed*). Get away from me! Why did you marry me, if I was such a fool? I didn't force you to! You should have got yourself a clever one, if that's what you wanted! I'm going back to bed.

Exit SASHA into the house.

PLATONOV (*laughs*). Oh, and she can manage to lose her temper sometimes! But this is a great discovery! She's learning how to lose her little temper!

He begins to follow her into the house.

All hurt and cross, are we . . .?

Enter ANNA PETROVNA from the shadows of the forest. She is wearing a riding habit and carrying a whip.

ANNA PETROVNA. Platonov!

PLATONOV *stops and turns.*

I knew you wouldn't be asleep. How can anyone sleep on a night like this? God made the winter for sleeping! Come here, Platonov.

PLATONOV (*reluctantly crosses to her*). What are you doing here?

ANNA PETROVNA. Taking a little walk in the moonlight. (*She leads him gently by the arm away from the house.*) What are *you* doing here? You disappeared without so much as a word of goodbye. You didn't think that I should let you get away with such discourtesy?

PLATONOV. I apologise.

ANNA PETROVNA. But what big eyes he has, out here in the moonlight! Don't be frightened – I'm not going to eat you.

PLATONOV. I see you are set upon some foolishness.

ANNA PETROVNA. Foolishness comes with age, Platonov.

PLATONOV. And age excuses it. But you're not old. You're as young as the summer itself. You have your life in front of you.

ANNA PETROVNA. I don't want my life in front of me – I want

it now! Because, yes, I am young! It's terrible how young I am! I can feel it stirring in me like the night air among the trees.

PLATONOV. Anna Petrovna, I beg you to think what you're doing.

ANNA PETROVNA. I have thought.

PLATONOV. All your intelligence, all your beauty, all your youth – and you have to come to me! You come bent on conquest, on storming a stronghold. But no great conquest will you have. I know I took a high tone with you before. But I realise, when I look back on my behaviour tonight, that I had no right to such a tone.

ANNA PETROVNA. Self-abasement is a form of pride. But what are we to do, Misha? We've got to finish the thing one way or another.

PLATONOV. Finish it? We haven't started it!

ANNA PETROVNA. How can you say that? How can you lie to me, on such a night as this, beneath such a sky? Tell your lies in the autumn, if you must, in the gloom and the mud, but not now, not here. You're being watched! Look up, you absurd man! A thousand eyes, all shining with indignation! You must be good and true, just as all this is good and true. Don't break this silence with your little words!

She takes his hands, and they sit down on the timbers of the crossing, facing each other.

There's no man in the world I could ever love as I love you. There's no woman in the world you could ever love as you love me. Let's take that love; and all the rest, that so torments you – we'll leave that to others to worry about.

PLATONOV (*kisses her hands*). Odysseus was worth the sirens' song, but I'm no Odysseus, you lovely siren of the forest. If only I could give you happiness! But I can't, and I shan't. I shall do what I've done to every woman who has thrown herself at me; I shall make you unhappy!

ANNA PETROVNA. Are you really such a terrible Don Juan? You look so handsome in the moonlight!

PLATONOV. I know myself! The only stories that end happily are the ones that don't have me in them.

ANNA PETROVNA. Such a solemn face! It's a woman who's come to call, not a wild animal! All right – if you really hate it all so much I'll go away again. Is that what you want? I'll go away, and everything will be just as it was before. Yes . . . ? (*She laughs.*) Idiot! Take it! Snatch it! Seize it! What more do you want? Smoke it to the end, like a cigarette – pinch it out – tread it under your heel. Be human! (*She gently shakes him.*) You funny creature! A woman who loves you – a woman you love – fine summer weather. What could be simpler than that? (*She lays her head on his knees.*) You don't realise how hard life is for me.

PLATONOV. I shan't make it easier.

ANNA PETROVNA. And yet life is what I long for. Everything is alive, nothing is ever still. We're surrounded by life. We must live, too, Misha! Leave all the problems for tomorrow. Tonight, on this night of nights, we'll simply live!

PLATONOV. Let me make one last appeal. As a man of honour . . .

ANNA PETROVNA (*embraces him*). Don't be stupid, Misha. I'm never going to let you go. You're mine!

PLATONOV. One final plea . . .

ANNA PETROVNA. If I can't do it nicely I'll take you by force! (*She throws her kerchief round his neck.*) Come on!

PLATONOV. It'll end badly.

ANNA PETROVNA. You should write stern editorials in the newspapers.

PLATONOV. You'll see.

ANNA PETROVNA. You'd be good at that.

PLATONOV. Where are we going, then?

ANNA PETROVNA. To the old summerhouse!

SASHA (*calls sleepily, off*). Misha!

PLATONOV *and* ANNA PETROVNA *stop*.

PLATONOV. Sasha . . . I'd forgotten all about her.

ANNA PETROVNA. So had I.

PLATONOV. How could I just forget about her?

ANNA PETROVNA. It wouldn't be for the first time.

SASHA (*off*). Misha?

PLATONOV. I'll just get her off to sleep.

ANNA PETROVNA. Platonov!

PLATONOV. I can't leave her wondering where I am!

SASHA (*off*). Where are you, Misha?

ANNA PETROVNA. But that might take another hour!

PLATONOV. Two minutes! She falls asleep like a child if I stroke her head. Wait here!

ANNA PETROVNA. If you're not back in two minutes . . .

PLATONOV. I'll be back!

ANNA PETROVNA. . . . . I'll come in and fetch you!

Enter SASHA *from the house*.

SASHA. Misha?

PLATONOV. Here, my love!

Exeunt PLATONOV *and* SASHA *into the house. Enter* OSIP *from beneath the trees*.

ANNA PETROVNA. Who's that?

OSIP. See that stump there? Rotten. So it glows in the dark. As if a dead man had risen from his grave.

ANNA PETROVNA. Osip . . .

OSIP. My mother used to say that under every stump that glows in the dark there's a sinner buried. That's why the stump glows. To make us pray for his soul. I used to wonder how there could be so many glowing stumps in the forest.

ANNA PETROVNA. How long have you been there, Osip?

OSIP. Long enough.

ANNA PETROVNA. Were you spying?

OSIP. I thought you were some kind of saint.

ANNA PETROVNA. Used you to be in love with me then, Osip?

OSIP. If you'd have told me to walk into the fire, I'd have walked into the fire.

ANNA PETROVNA. You're not still in love with me?

OSIP. That's not my place to say. (*He weeps.*)

ANNA PETROVNA. Oh, and he's crying. Come on, we'll be friends again. You can bring me some more baby owls. Just so long as you promise me one thing . . .

OSIP. If I'd had a gun in my hands as I stood there!

ANNA PETROVNA. One thing, Osip: you won't ever hurt him. Promise?

OSIP. I'll promise this: if he should ever hurt you . . . (*He pulls out his hunting-knife.*)

Enter PLATONOV from the house.

PLATONOV. She's asleep!

OSIP disappears beneath the trees.

ANNA PETROVNA. Misha! We must go! Quickly! Before anything else happens!

She takes his arm, and they start into the forest.

Enter DR TRILETZKY, drunker than before.

DR TRILETZKY. Who's that? That Sasha? Sasha!·

PLATONOV *returns.* ANNA PETROVNA *remains hidden among the trees.*

PLATONOV. Sh! Sasha's asleep! You'll wake her!

DR TRILETZKY. Oh, it's you. Thought it was Sasha.

PLATONOV. Sasha's asleep.

DR TRILETZKY. Took Porfiry Semyonovich home, you see. Thought I'd just ask Sasha if I could sleep here.

PLATONOV. Well, you can't ask her, because she's asleep.

DR TRILETZKY. She's asleep?

PLATONOV. Fast asleep.

DR TRILETZKY. I'll wake her up.

PLATONOV. Don't wake her up!

DR TRILETZKY. Can't find my way home, Misha.

PLATONOV. Well, you can't stay here.

DR TRILETZKY. Sasha won't mind.

PLATONOV. Don't go in there!

DR TRILETZKY (*calls*). Sasha!

PLATONOV. Listen! Listen! The village storekeeper – he's ill. You've got to go.

DR TRILETZKY *flaps his hand dismissively.*

It's urgent . . . You've got to operate!

DR TRILETZKY. Operate?

PLATONOV. You know you like operating!

DR TRILETZKY. Can't operate now, Misha! It's the middle of the night! It's past the passenger!

PLATONOV. That wasn't the passenger. That was only the goods.

DR TRILETZKY (*goes towards the house*). Can't operate now. Haven't got my little bag.

PLATONOV (*turns him back towards the village*). Come on. You've got your penknife.

DR TRILETZKY (*heads back towards the house*). Have a little sleep first.

PLATONOV (*turns him round*). Have a little sleep afterwards.

DR TRILETZKY *begins to go off the way he came.* ANNA PETROVNA *emerges from the shadows, and* PLATONOV *goes to join her.* DR TRILETZKY *turns back towards the house.*

DR TRILETZKY. Think my little bag may be in here.

PLATONOV (*intercepts him*). Have you no shame? Have you no honour?

DR TRILETZKY. Not at one o'clock in the morning, Misha!

PLATONOV. What sort of man are you, Nikolai? What god do you serve? What are you doing with your life? Do you think you were put in this world just to eat and drink and behave like a swine?

DR TRILETZKY. I'm a swine, Misha, you're right.

PLATONOV. What are we all doing with our lives. (*He weeps.*) What god do *I* serve?

DR TRILETZKY. You're crying! Don't cry, Misha!

PLATONOV. What's going to become of us all? Dirt in the ground! That's all we shall ever make!

DR TRILETZKY. All right, Misha. I'll go and open him up.

Exit DR TRILETZKY *the way he entered.*

ANNA PETROVNA *emerges from the shadows again.*

ANNA PETROVNA. Has he gone?

PLATONOV. Yes, he's gone. Gone to save a human life. And what am *I* doing?

ANNA PETROVNA (*puts an arm round his shoulders*). *You're* going to save a human life. Your own life!

PLATONOV. It's not me who's coming with you, It's the devil at my back who says 'Go on, go on!' It's not me who obeys him – it's my weak flesh.

ANNA PETROVNA (*moves away from him sharply*). Oh, for heaven's sake! (*She strikes him with her whip.*) If you want to come with me then come with me. If you don't then to hell with it!

A shot off, followed by a wild cry of alarm.

He's going to kill you! (*She throws her arms round him protectively.*)

PLATONOV. What? Who? Where?

ANNA PETROVNA. Osip! He's fetched a gun! He's going to kill you!

She drags PLATONOV *into hiding under the trees.*

Enter VOYNITZEV *and* COLONEL TRILETZKY *from the forest. They are both carrying sporting guns, and are both drunk.*

VOYNITZEV (*sees smoke curling from one of the barrels of his gun*). Was that me?

COLONEL TRILETZKY. My dear chap, another inch and it would have been *me*!

VOYNITZEV. My ears are still ringing!

COLONEL TRILETZKY. I said, you almost shot me!

VOYNITZEV. Great shock to me, too, but don't shout, you'll wake him up. (*He prods* COLONEL TRILETZKY *warningly with his gun.*)

COLONEL TRILETZKY. Yes. Sh! (*He puts the gun to his lips.*)

VOYNITZEV. Sh! (*He does the same.*)

They cross to the house.

COLONEL TRILETZKY. Right outside his window!

VOYNITZEV. Biggest surprise of his life!

COLONEL TRILETZKY. Twenty-one gun salute!

They raise their guns to fire. Enter PLATONOV *from the shadows.*

PLATONOV. No! No!

VOYNITZEV. What the devil . . .?

They level their guns at PLATONOV.

COLONEL TRILETZKY. Halt! Who goes there!

VOYNITZEV. One more step and we'll shoot!

PLATONOV. It's me! It's me! Platonov! Misha!

VOYNITZEV. Misha?

PLATONOV. Don't shout!

COLONEL TRILETZKY. We're not shouting.

VOYNITZEV. We're shooting.

PLATONOV. Don't shout *or* shoot! You'll wake Sasha!

VOYNITZEV. Oh yes. Sasha.

COLONEL TRILETZKY. My little girl.

VOYNITZEV. Mustn't wake Sasha.

PLATONOV. What are you doing here?

COLONEL TRILETZKY (*to* VOYNITZEV). What are we doing here?

VOYNITZEV (*to* PLATONOV). We're looking for you!

COLONEL TRILETZKY. Show you my new gun!

VOYNITZEV. Give you a surprise!

COLONEL TRILETZKY. Twenty-one gun salute!

VOYNITZEV. Twenty-one gun salute!

They raise their guns to fire.

PLATONOV. *No*!

VOYNITZEV. Sh!

COLONEL TRILETZKY. Sh!

VOYNITZEV. Mustn't wake Sasha.

PLATONOV. Right, now will you get out of here.

VOYNITZEV. We want you to come shooting with us!

PLATONOV. Shooting? It's the middle of the night! It's gone the goods – it's almost the passenger!

COLONEL TRILETZKY. His wife – charming girl . . .

VOYNITZEV. Sofya. You've met Sofya.

COLONEL TRILETZKY. She told me to take him out and shoot him. Take him out and shoot him? – Take him out shooting.

VOYNITZEV. Very difficult to see anything to shoot.

COLONEL TRILETZKY. You could shoot owls, she said.

VOYNITZEV. Very difficult to see owls.

COLONEL TRILETZKY. He's drunk, of course.

VOYNITZEV. First time in my life, Misha! Oh God, I'm so happy! (*He embraces* PLATONOV.)

PLATONOV. Keep that gun away from me, will you?

VOYNITZEV. Oh yes. Mustn't wake Sasha.

COLONEL TRILETZKY. Creep quietly away.

VOYNITZEV. Indians on the warpath. Not a sound.

They begin to stumble away into the forest.

COLONEL TRILETZKY. I know what we can do!

VOYNITZEV. Sh! What?

COLONEL TRILETZKY. Serenade Anna Petrovna! Stand under her window and give her the old artillery serenade!

VOYNITZEV. How does that go?

COLONEL TRILETZKY. The twenty-one gun salute!

VOYNITZEV. Oh, the twenty-one gun salute!

They raise their guns to fire.

PLATONOV. Go away!

VOYNITZEV. Oh yes.

They guiltily place their guns against each other's lips.

COLONEL TRILETZKY. Sh!

VOYNITZEV. Sh!

Exeunt COLONEL TRILETZKY *and* VOYNITZEV *into the forest.*

ANNA PETROVNA *comes out of hiding.*

ANNA PETROVNA. Misha!

PLATONOV. Coming, coming.

SASHA (*off*). Misha?

PLATONOV (*calls*). Coming!

ANNA PETROVNA. Misha, yes or no!

PLATONOV *hesitates.*

PETRIN (*off*). So where is she?

ANNA PETROVNA *looks round to see who this is.*

Who knows? Playing duets with Platonov!

Exit PLATONOV *into the house.*

Out in the woods with the colonel!

ANNA PETROVNA (*to* PLATONOV). We might as well be in the centre of Petersburg!

She sees that PLATONOV *has gone, and goes back into hiding.*

Enter PETRIN, *supported by* DR TRILETZKY. PETRIN *is in his shirtsleeves, and is even drunker than the doctor.*

PETRIN. And where is our great lover of women? He's gone home with a heart attack! A moonlit night in June, and he lies down and has a heart attack!

DR TRILETZKY. Now you follow the rails, look. Be home in no time. No one around . . . I think I'm just going to have a little sleep at my sister's here.

PETRIN. No one could accuse me of impatience, Kolya!

DR TRILETZKY. Just step to one side when the train comes.

PETRIN. I own that woman! I own the clothes on her back! I own her stepson's underpants! All mine, Kolya! And what do I get in return? I get treated like dirt! Leant across by the servants! Spoken to like a pig!

PETRIN *starts away up the railway track.*

But thus far, Kolya! Thus far and no further! (*He stumbles over a sleeper and falls down on the track.*)

DR TRILETZKY (*calls, delighted*). Sasha!

Enter PLATONOV *from the house.*

Misha . . .!

PLATONOV. Well?

DR TRILETZKY. It's Gerasim Kuzmich! He's been with the village girls again!

PLATONOV. And the storekeeper?

DR TRILETZKY. The storekeeper?

PLATONOV. He's dying, Kolya!

DR TRILETZKY. Yes, well, the storekeeper . . .

DR TRILETZKY *retreats from* PLATONOV *back in the direction he came from.*

I suppose it doesn't matter if *I* die . . .

Exit DR TRILETZKY.

Enter ANNA PETROVNA *from under the trees*.

ANNA PETROVNA. Platonov! Are you coming with me or not?
Because I'm not going back behind that tree.

PLATONOV. All right. All right . . .

ANNA PETROVNA. If it's not your brother-in-law it's your
father-in-law. If it's not your father-in-law it's . . .

Enter SASHA *from the house*.

SASHA. Misha! What's happening? What are you doing out here?
Is that someone with you? (*She laughs.*) Anna Petrovna!

ANNA PETROVNA. Alexandra Ivanovna.

SASHA. What in the name of goodness are you doing here at this
time of night? You're dressed for driving . . . And you're
inviting us! Oh, what a lovely idea! It's such a beautiful night!
Do let's go, Misha! I'll get dressed!

Exit SASHA *into the house*.

ANNA PETROVNA. So now what are you going to do,
Platonov?

PLATONOV. I don't know.

ANNA PETROVNA. Well, I shall be in the old summerhouse. If
you want to see me you must come to me there.

PLATONOV. But what shall I tell Sasha?

ANNA PETROVNA. That's your business! I'm not going to lie to
your wife for you!

Exit ANNA PETROVNA.

PLATONOV. Anna Petrovna . . . ! (*He turns and goes towards the
house.*) Sasha . . .!

Enter DR TRILETZKY.

DR TRILETZKY. And another thing.

PLATONOV. You still haven't gone?

DR TRILETZKY. I'm going! One word of advice first, my friend! If you're going to preach at people then you must preach what you practise!

PLATONOV. Come here! (*He advances on him.*)

DR TRILETZKY (*backs away*). I'm going, I'm going!

PLATONOV. No, you're not. You're not in a fit condition to see a patient. Sasha will have to put you to bed.

DR TRILETZKY. Bed? Go to bed?

Enter SASHA, dressed, from the house.

SASHA. I've always longed to go for a drive in the moonlight! Where are we going?

PLATONOV. We're not going anywhere. You've got to put your brother to bed.

SASHA. Kolya! Oh, no!

PLATONOV. He can sleep in the classroom.

DR TRILETZKY (*bewildered*). Sleep? Lie down?

PLATONOV. Quickly, now! I think he's going to be sick!

SASHA (*leads DR TRILETZKY into the house*). And you'll wake the baby, so then I'll have to get *him* back to sleep.

DR TRILETZKY. Everything's going round. It's all turned back to front!

PLATONOV. I'll tell Anna Petrovna we'll come another time, shall I?

SASHA. Another time, yes, another time.

Exeunt SASHA and DR TRILETZKY into the house.

PLATONOV (*to himself*). I'm going, then. (*He begins to move irresolutely off.*) It's not as if I were the only man in the world to behave like this . . . (*He falls over PETRIN.*)

PETRIN. They all walk over me.

PLATONOV. Gerasim Kuzmich . . .

PETRIN. Not going to go on walking over me.

PLATONOV. You've been with the village girls again. (*He sits down on the rail beside* PETRIN.) We're all the same. One word from a woman, and that's all we can think of.

PETRIN. One word from me, and up the sign will go! 'To be sold at public auction'.

Enter SOFYA *from the forest, very nervous, her face concealed. She tries to see into the windows of the house.*

PLATONOV. Is that what our lives are going to amount to? One long procession of women?

SOFYA (*taps at the window and whispers desperately*). Misha!

PLATONOV. Sasha! My little noodle! That settles it! I must have been mad! (*He hurries across to* SOFYA.) Here I am, my treasure! I'll never leave you! Not for a moment! Not ever!

SOFYA. Misha! Oh, Misha!

PLATONOV. Sofya!

SOFYA (*throws herself into his arms*). I waited for you after the fireworks! Waited and waited! I was sure you'd come! I made my husband go out shooting with the colonel – they're both drunk – they'll shoot each other – I must be mad! You said you would, Misha! You promised you would!

PLATONOV. Would what?

SOFYA. Uproot us both!

PLATONOV. Oh yes.

SOFYA. Uproot me, Misha!

PLATONOV. Yes, but not here!

SASHA opens the window of the house.

SASHA. Misha!

PLATONOV (*to* SOFYA, *warningly*). Sasha!

SASHA. Was that you tapping on the window?

PLATONOV (*to* SASHA). No? (*To* SOFYA.) In the old summerhouse! (*To* SASHA.) Yes! Only me! (*To* SOFYA.) No!

SASHA. No?

PLATONOV (*to* SASHA). Yes! (*To* SOFYA.) Not in the old summerhouse!

SASHA. What?

PLATONOV (*to* SASHA). Nothing! (*To* SOFYA.) In the new summerhouse!

Exit SOFYA *into the forest.*

SASHA. I can't understand a word.

SASHA *closes the window.* PLATONOV *pulls* PETRIN *up into a sitting position.*

PLATONOV. Gerasya! Help me! What am I going to do? Which way, Gerasya? Which one – old or new?

There is the sound of a distant train whistle, and a tiny star of light appears on the horizon at the end of the railway track.

Train . . . ! Yes! I'll run to the station! Go away, and never come back . . .!

PETRIN. Never get her married to him now.

PLATONOV. But she is, isn't she? She's in love with me, too!

PETRIN. I'll take her to court.

PLATONOV. So this is happiness, then. This is what it feels like . . . But which one of them, Gerasya? Which one of them?

Enter SASHA *from the house.*

SASHA. Misha! Where are you? What's all this about a summer house?

PLATONOV *drops* PETRIN *back on to the track, and flees in the direction taken by* ANNA PETROVNA. *But he meets* OSIP *emerging from beneath the trees, and diverts to go off in the direction taken by* SOFYA.

Osip! What's happening? I don't understand . . . Osip, what are you doing?

OSIP *lies down across the level crossing. The headlights of the approaching train grows slowly bigger.*

You can't lie there! Osip, get up! The train's coming!

OSIP (*sobs*). He's gone to her! Gone to Anna Petrovna! And she loves him! She loves him!

SASHA. You're lying.

OSIP. God strike me down – I heard every word!

SASHA. He's left me, then! He's left me! Kill me, Lord! Mother of God, kill me!

The whistle of the approaching train. SASHA *runs towards it with outstretched arms.* OSIP *jumps up and runs after her.*

OSIP. No! No!

They stumble over PETRIN, *who sits up. They stop and turn round to gaze at him in astonishment.*

PETRIN. Yes! Yes! You'll see! Tomorrow!

SASHA *and* OSIP *drag* PETRIN *clear of the track as the headlight widens, and the roar of the approaching train and the scream of the whistle rise to a crescendo. The locomotive emerges from the darkness and comes towards us just as the curtain falls. The roar of the train and the scream of the whistle continue through the auditorium in the darkness, until the lights come up for:*

Scene Two

The combined schoolroom and living-room inside the PLATONOVs' *house. The wooden baulks of the level crossing now form the rough timber floor of the room. In the rear wall of the room are a window and a door;*

beyond it are the same tall trees of the forest as in the earlier scenes. There is a sofa in the room, a cupboard, a table with two chairs, and all the signs of a cramped, muddled and sleazy life. It is early evening.

PLATONOV *is lying on the sofa, fast asleep, with a straw hat covering his face.*

Enter SOFYA.

SOFYA. Platonov! Wake up! (*She shakes him.*) Misha! (*She takes the hat off his face.*) How could you put this filthy object on your face! Ugh! What a mess you are! Haven't washed, have you? And look at this pig-sty! It's only three weeks since your wife walked out. It would break her heart if she could see it now . . . Misha, I'm talking to you! Get up!

PLATONOV. Um?

SOFYA. Wake up, will you!

PLATONOV. Just a minute.

SOFYA. Now!

PLATONOV (*sits up*). Oh, it's you.

SOFYA. Yes, it's me! (*She holds her watch in front of his eyes.*) Look!

PLATONOV. Right. (*He lies down again.*)

SOFYA. Platonov!

PLATONOV. What do you want? (*He sits up.*) What is it?

SOFYA. Look at the time!

PLATONOV. Fussing away again, are you, Sofya?

SOFYA. Yes, I'm fussing away again! Look at this watch, will you! Now tell me what it says.

PLATONOV. Half-past six.

SOFYA. Half-past six, yes.

PLATONOV. Not time to get up yet.

SOFYA. Half-past six in the *evening*. Have you forgotten what we agreed?

PLATONOV. What did we agree? Don't talk in riddles, please. I'm not up to it today.

SOFYA. You have forgotten. What's the matter with you? Your eyes are red. You look as if you've been crumpled up into a ball and thrown away . . . You're not ill, are you . . .? What we agreed was to meet in the usual place. At six o'clock.

PLATONOV. Go on.

SOFYA. What do you mean, go on? Aren't you ashamed of yourself? You gave me your word of honour! (*She sits beside him.*)

PLATONOV. I'd have kept it, too, if I hadn't fallen asleep. You could see for yourself – I was fast asleep! I don't know what you're going on about.

SOFYA. Have you been on time for a single one of our meetings? Every day you give me your word of honour – and every day you break it! Why do you stop being yourself whenever I'm with you.

PLATONOV (*jumps up, and walks up and down the room*). So, here you are.

SOFYA. Are you drunk?

PLATONOV. None of your business.

SOFYA. And that's very charming, I must say! (*She weeps.*)

PLATONOV. Women!

SOFYA. And don't start saying 'Women!' I'm not some poor simple village girl, and I'm not going to let myself be humiliated like this. (*She weeps.*) My God! My God!

PLATONOV. Now that's enough.

SOFYA. It's barely three weeks since . . . Since that night! And already I'm only a shadow of myself! Where's the happiness you promised me? And where's all this going to end? Think, if you're so clever! Start thinking now, before it's too late! Sit down right here on this chair, clear everything else out of your head, and just think about this one single thing: what are you doing to me?

PLATONOV. I can't think. I've forgotten how to think. You think yourself! All your unhappiness comes from this irregular liaison!

SOFYA. I give myself to him, and he has the nerve to talk about an 'irregular liaison'!

PLATONOV. Oh, come on! We can't start quibbling over every word! I've ruined you; and that's all there is to say about it! And you're not the only one! Wait until your husband finds out!

SOFYA. You're afraid he's going to kill you?

PLATONOV. No. I'm afraid it's going to kill him.

SOFYA. He already knows!

PLATONOV. What?

SOFYA. Yes! I told him this afternoon.

PLATONOV. You're not serious!

SOFYA. Look at you. You're as white as a sheet. I don't know why I should love you. I must be mad!

PLATONOV. How did he take it?

SOFYA. Just like you. He was afraid. His skin went grey. He started to cry. Then he crumpled up. He went down and crawled on all fours . . . And he had just the same repellent look on his face as you have now.

PLATONOV. You've killed him! Do you realise that? How could you sit there and tell me it all so calmly? You've killed him! Did you . . . did you say it was me?

SOFYA. Of course. What else could I have said?

PLATONOV. You know what you've done, don't you? You've parted forever.

SOFYA. Forever, yes. What alternative did I have?

PLATONOV (*flaps his hand*). Well, you do whatever you think
best. You're a better person than I am. You've got a cleverer
head on your shoulders. You take the whole mess over! Just tell
me what to do! Get me up on my feet again, if you have the
power. And do it now, for the love of God, before I go out of
my mind!

SOFYA. We'll leave tonight.

PLATONOV. The sooner the better.

SOFYA. I wrote to my mother about you. We'll go to her.

PLATONOV. Anywhere you like! Just as long as we get away
from here!

SOFYA. Misha! This will be our new life, though! Do you see?
Trust me, love! I'll get you up on your feet again! I'll make you
work! We'll be proper people, Misha! We'll eat our bread in the
sweat of our faces. We'll harden our hands. (*She lays her head on
his chest.*) I'll work, too.

PLATONOV. What do you know about work?

SOFYA. Trust me, Misha, that's all you have to do! You raised me
from the dead, and all my life will be a thank-offering for that.
We'll leave tonight, then, on the evening train. Yes? I'll go and
get ready at once. You get your things together. We'll meet at
the usual place an hour from now. Let's say quarter to eight.
Yes? You will be there?

PLATONOV. I shall be there.

SOFYA. Word of honour?

PLATONOV. I said – I shall be there!

SOFYA. Give me your word of honour.

PLATONOV. Word of honour.

SOFYA. I don't want to have to come looking for you again . . .
Cheer up, then! (*She kisses him.*) We're going to start our lives
afresh, Misha! By tomorrow you'll be a different man. We'll be
breathing new air! We'll have new blood flowing in our veins!

PLATONOV. Of course we will . . . Did you say quarter past eight or quarter past nine?

SOFYA. Quarter to eight! Or we'll miss the train! I've got some money – we'll eat on the way. (*She laughs.*) And smarten yourself up a bit for the journey!

SOFYA *runs out of the house.*

PLATONOV (*to himself*). A new life! That's an old song! I've heard that one a few times! (*Pause.*) I'd better write to him. And to Sasha. They can have a little weep, and then they can forgive and forget. So it's goodbye to everyone, because tomorrow I'm going to be a different man! (*He opens the cupboard.*) What am I going to put my clean underwear in? I haven't got a suitcase . . . (*He takes one of the many bottles in the cupboard and pours himself a drink.*) Goodbye, old school of mine! Goodbye, boys and girls! (*He drinks.*) Your kindly old teacher, the swine, is doing a bolt . . . Was that me drinking? What am I drinking for? I'm giving up drinking! Well, this is the last drink I shall ever have . . . So, sit down and write to Sasha . . . (*He lies down on the sofa.*) Sofya really does believe it all, doesn't she . . . Well, blessed are they that have faith . . . As long as she hasn't told Anna Petrovna . . . Letter from Anna Petrovna somewhere . . . Ought to open it, see what she wants . . . (*Finds a number of unopened envelopes.*) *Three* letters from her . . . Haven't opened any of them. (*Finds more.*) Hundreds of letters from her! She hasn't stopped writing, ever since that wild and crazy night . . . (*He opens the letter absently.*) Just so long as I don't have to come face to face with her! She'd get the truth out of me in . . . (*He reads.*) 'If you don't answer this one, either, I shall come round there and . . .'

A knock at the door. PLATONOV *jumps up in alarm, then stands undecided. Another knock.* PLATONOV *conceals himself behind it as the door opens.*

Enter, cautiously, MARKO, *with his satchel.*

MARKO. Anyone at home?

PLATONOV. Who's this?

MARKO. Me, sir. That you, sir?

PLATONOV (*cautiously*). Yes?

MARKO. Platonov?

PLATONOV. What of it?

MARKO. Mikhail Vasilyevich Platonov?

PLATONOV. What do you want?

MARKO. From the magistrate, sir! (*He hands an envelope round the door to* PLATONOV.)

PLATONOV (*emerges from hiding, relieved*). From the magistrate? Oh . . . not *another* christening! (*He opens the envelope.*) Breeds like a rabbit, that man! (*He reads.*) 'You are hereby summoned . . .' (*To* MARKO.) Do you know what you look like, cowering away behind the door there?

MARKO. Yes, sir.

PLATONOV. Oh, you know, do you?

MARKO. Yes, sir.

PLATONOV (*reads*). 'You are hereby summoned to appear before His Imperial Majesty's Justice of the Peace . . .' (*To* MARKO.) What do you look like, then?

MARKO. Like God, sir.

PLATONOV. Like God?

MARKO. Made in the image and likeness, sir.

PLATONOV. Oh yes. (*He reads.*) '. . . before His Imperial Majesty's Justice of the Peace to answer a charge of indecent assault . . .' It's not an invitation!

MARKO. No, sir.

PLATONOV. It's a summons!

MARKO. Yes, sir.

PLATONOV (*reads*). '. . . a charge of indecent assault, which charge has been laid upon the complaint of Marya Yefimovna

Grekova . . .'! (*He laughs.*) Well, dash me! Good old Beetle-juice!
I didn't know she'd got it in her!

MARKO. Sign for it, then, will you, sir? Just here, sir.

PLATONOV (*signs*). When's the case being heard . . . ? The day
after tomorrow. I'll be there! She should have done this last
summer!

MARKO. Thank you, sir. (*He holds out his hand.*) Drink your
health, sir.

PLATONOV. You can drink it in tea. (*He takes the tea-caddy out of
the cupboard.*) Where do you want it?

MARKO *holds his pocket open.* PLATONOV *pours the tea straight
in.*

What a little champion she is, though! Never expected that! Who
have they got as witnesses?

MARKO (*sorts through the subpoenas in his bag*). 'Dr Nikolai
Ivanovich Triletzky.'

PLATONOV. The doctor? He'll be a comic turn! Who else?

MARKO. 'Sofya Yegorovna Voynitzeva'.

PLATONOV. Sofya Yegorovna? She won't be there! She's going
away . . . Oh . . . Oh, yes . . . Take Marya Yefimovna a
message will you?

MARKO. Marya Yefimovna – message. Yes?

PLATONOV. Tell her I'm very sorry . . .

MARKO. Very sorry.

PLATONOV. But I can't accept her kind summons because I'm
going away.

MARKO. Going away.

PLATONOV. Forever, tell her.

MARKO. Going away forever. Right.

PLATONOV. Say I behaved like a swine, but then I've behaved

like a swine with everybody. Say I should have been happy to kiss her again, with proper respect, before the whole world in open court.

MARKO. Like a swine. In open court.

PLATONOV. All right. Do you know where she lives?

MARKO. Good seven miles from here, sir. (*He holds out his hand.*) Can't walk seven miles on a glass of tea, sir!

PLATONOV. All right – a ruble. A ruble there, a ruble back, and a ruble for remembering it. Three rubles when you get back here and tell me you've delivered it! Off you go, then. Oh, and Marko . . .

MARKO. Yes, sir?

PLATONOV. That's what God looks like, is it?

MARKO. So I humbly believe, sir.

Exit MARKO.

PLATONOV (*to himself*). First time in my life I've ever been brought to book by a woman! Usually you treat them like dirt, and what do they do? – They hang around your neck . . . Oh, yes – Sasha. I was writing to Sasha . . . (*He finds the heap of unopened letters.*) No, I wasn't. I was hiding these before Anna Petrovna . . .

A sharp knock at the door. He gazes at the door, transfixed, then tries to stuff the letters away inside the cupboard. The door is flung open, and OSIP *enters. The letters come sliding out of the cupboard again.*

(*Over his shoulder.*) Anna Petrovna! This is a surprise. (*He turns and sees* OSIP.) Oh, it's you. What do you want?

OSIP *sits down.*

What's the matter with you? You look as if you'd been through all the ten plagues of Egypt. I feel as if I'd been through nine of them. You're nothing but skin and bone, though. Are you ill? What are you doing here?

OSIP. Saying goodbye.

PLATONOV. Why? Are you going away?

OSIP. Not me. You.

PLATONOV. Good God, so I am! But how do you know that?

OSIP. I just do.

PLATONOV. Clairvoyant, are you, Osip, on top of all your other skills?

OSIP. I know something else, too. I know where you're going.

PLATONOV. Do you indeed! That's more than I know! Well, this is something that interests me. Where *am* I going?

OSIP. You're going to hell.

PLATONOV. I see. Quite a journey. You're not planning to be the driver of the train that takes me there, by any chance?

OSIP (*takes out his hunting knife*). I used to have a lot of respect for you. Thought you were the great man . . . I've watched you these past weeks, though, you see. Slipping off into the forest at all hours of the day and night . . . Well, that's no business of mine, who the general's widow meets on her rides through the forest. But I saw something else tonight. I saw the young mistress come running down here. And I waited. And I saw her go running back again. So then I went and fetched my knife. Because I reckon you're making a fool of the general's widow, and I'm not having that. (*He stands up and seizes* PLATONOV's *arm.*)

PLATONOV. No! No! I've got a family! I've got a wife and child to support!

OSIP *raises the knife.*

Enter SASHA *through the front door.*

SASHA (*screams*). Misha! No! No! (*She tries to protect* PLATONOV.) Don't hurt him! Don't touch him!

OSIP (*backs away*). Oh, it's you. You're still around, are you. Can't kill him in front of you . . . Anyway, you're back . . . I *will* kill him, though! He won't ever get away from me!

Exit OSIP.

SASHA. Are you all right?

PLATONOV. Oh, my arm! He twisted my arm! (*He sits down on the sofa.*)

SASHA. Lie down. Put the cushion under your head. (*She settles the cushion for him.*)

PLATONOV. Don't fuss, my pet. I'm perfectly all right.

SASHA. Where does it hurt?

PLATONOV. I'm all right! Don't worry . . . He was going to kill me! He was! He was going to kill me! You were only just in time, Sasha! Another minute and you'd have been a widow! (*He kisses her hand.*) Oh, Sasha! Oh, my treasure . . .! Are you at your father's? How is he?

SASHA. He's all right . . . Misha, it's little Vova. That's why I came. He's ill, poor mite. He's running a terrible fever. The last two nights he's just cried all night. (*She weeps.*) Oh, Misha, I'm so worried! What am I going to do? If he died, Misha . . . What would become of us then?

PLATONOV. Yes . . . But God won't take our little boy away from you, Sasha. Why should he punish you? Look after him, Sasha, and I swear to you I'll make a man of him. I haven't been much of a man myself, I know, but as a father I shall be mighty! Oh, my arm! He hasn't broken something, has he . . .? Don't cry, love! (*He pulls her down on to his chest.*) You're home again! Why did you ever leave? I love you, lass! I love you deeply! My sins are black, I know, but what can we do? You'll just have to forgive me, won't you?

SASHA. Is the affair over, then?

PLATONOV. The affair . . . What a word to choose!

SASHA. Or isn't it over?

PLATONOV. What can I say? There never was an affair. It's just some kind of absurd nonsense. You should never have let yourself be upset by it. And if it's not over yet then it soon will be!

SASHA. When?

PLATONOV. Sooner rather than later, I should imagine. Sofya isn't the one for me. The ferment hasn't quite died down in her yet, but, believe me, Sofya won't be your rival for long . . . Sasha, what's the matter?

SASHA. Sofya? It's *Sofya* that you're having an affair with?

PLATONOV. You didn't know?

SASHA. Sofya? But that's terrible!

PLATONOV. Sasha, don't torment me any more! I'm in agony with my arm as it is! Why did you leave me, then? You mean, it wasn't because of Sofya?

SASHA. I thought it was Anna Petrovna! That was bad enough! But another man's wife! That's vile, Misha, that's wicked! I should never have thought it of you! Well, God give you happiness, the pair of you! (*She goes to the door.*)

PLATONOV. Don't talk like that, Sasha! I don't want happiness! Don't go, Sasha! (*He goes after her.*) Don't leave me! Could you truly never forgive me?

SASHA. Could you ever forgive yourself?

PLATONOV. That's an interesting question. (*He kisses her head.*) You don't have to go. I am truly penitent. And if you're not here it's going to be a dismal progression of vodka and squalor and men trying to murder me. If you won't stay as a wife, then stay as a nurse! All right, I've stolen my friend's wife – I'm Sofya's lover – and for all I know I may yet be Anna Petrovna's, too. You've every right to be indignant! But who will ever love you as I love you? Who will you cook dinner for? Who will you oversalt the soup for? (*He picks her up.*) Who's going to pick you up and carry you? How will you ever live without me?

SASHA. Put me down! My life is destroyed, and all you can do is joke about it! (*She gets away from him.*) You must know it's not a joke! How can I live without you? – How could I possibly live *with* you? (*She sobs.*)

PLATONOV. Off you go, then. And God go with you. (*He kisses her on the head, then lies down on the sofa again.*) I do understand.

SASHA. You've broken up our family. We were so happy and peaceful! There was no one on earth as happy as I was. What have you done, Misha? You'll never turn back now . . . Don't come and visit us. Father will bring Vova to see you . . .

She looks at him for a moment, then round the room, then goes out.

PLATONOV (*to himself*). Well, there's someone who's starting a new life . . . Oh, but my God, the pain of it, the pain . . . Poor little Sasha! She's a saint! She's got every right to throw the first stone . . . What was I doing? (*He takes a drink.*) I was going to write to Sasha . . . No, I was going to . . . keep Anna Petrovna out! (*He hurries to the front door and bolts it.*)

ANNA PETROVNA *appears at the window.*

ANNA PETROVNA. Are you alone?

PLATONOV *spins guiltily around.*

What are you doing? Don't you recognise me? Have you forgotten who I am?

PLATONOV. Anna Petrovna . . .

He crosses to the window, but ANNA PETROVNA *has disappeared.*

(*To himself.*) Quick! Before she comes back!

He hurries to the front door, unbolts it, and opens it to escape. In walks ANNA PETROVNA. PLATONOV *retreats in front of her.*

ANNA PETROVNA (*reproachfully*). Platonov!

PLATONOV. Anna Petrovna . . .

ANNA PETROVNA. Come here, Platonov. Why are you running away from me?

PLATONOV *attempts to stuff the letters into the cupboard behind his back.*

Never mind that. It's too late now to start tidying up. Come here!

PLATONOV *goes over to her. She gives him her hand.*

Why won't you look at me, Platonov?

PLATONOV. I'm ashamed of myself. (*He kisses her hand.*)

ANNA PETROVNA. What are you ashamed about?

PLATONOV. Everything.

ANNA PETROVNA. I see. You've seduced some poor girl, have you?

PLATONOV. Something like that.

ANNA PETROVNA. What are we going to do with you, Platonov? Who is it?

PLATONOV. You don't know?

ANNA PETROVNA. I'm asking you.

PLATONOV. I can't tell you.

ANNA PETROVNA. Perhaps we should sit down.

They sit down on the sofa.

Well, we shall find out who it is, young man, we shall find out. Why do you have to put on this hangdog performance in front of me, though? I know your black heart of old.

PLATONOV. Don't ask me, Anna Petrovna! Talk, by all means, but no questions. I'm not up to being cross-examined today.

ANNA PETROVNA. Very well. Didn't you get my letters?

PLATONOV. Yes.

ANNA PETROVNA. So why didn't you come and see us?

PLATONOV. I couldn't.

ANNA PETROVNA. Why ever not?

PLATONOV. You're asking questions . . .! I just couldn't.

ANNA PETROVNA. You knew we needed you. Sergey and
Sofya are behaving very badly. Terrible sulks and silences. You
wouldn't think they were still on their honeymoon. And all
because we didn't have our clever fool there to entertain us . . .
Or didn't you read my letters?

PLATONOV. Of course I read them.

ANNA PETROVNA. Sit up straight . . . Anyone would think
you were ashamed of what happened that night.

PLATONOV. I've been ill.

ANNA PETROVNA. You're lying.

PLATONOV. I'm lying. There's no point in asking me anything.

ANNA PETROVNA. What sort of mess is this? You're drinking,
are you?

PLATONOV (*spreads his hands helplessly*). It's the holidays.

ANNA PETROVNA. It's the same story as last summer, isn't it.

PLATONOV. I'll stop, I'll stop.

ANNA PETROVNA. Word of honour?

PLATONOV. Word of honour.

ANNA PETROVNA. On second thoughts I won't put you to the
trouble of keeping your word. Where's the drink?

PLATONOV *indicates the cupboard.*

You ought to be ashamed of yourself! Have you no character at
all? Look at the mess in this cupboard! (*She finds the letters.*) I see.
No wonder they had so little effect on you . . . Look at it all,
though! Your wife's going to have something to say when she
comes back! You do want her back, don't you?

PLATONOV. All I want is for you to stop asking me questions!
And to stop trying to make me look you in the eye!

ANNA PETROVNA. Which bottle is the drink in?

PLATONOV. All of them.

ANNA PETROVNA. All of them? It's like a distillery in here! We'll have to get your wife back. You'll just have to make it up with her as best you can . . . It was no part of my plans to get you divorced. I don't mind sharing you . . . Now, I'm going to empty all this foul stuff out of the window. Some vile backyard brew, is it . . .? (*She pours a little into a glass and tastes it.*) No, it isn't – it's good vodka! All right, then, we'll drink a glass of it first, shall we? Yes? Just a drop to wish it goodbye. Here . . . Make the most of it. That's all you're getting. And a drop for me . . . To the wicked of this world! Of whom you're one . . .! Not at all bad, this vodka. You have a little discrimination, at any rate . . . All right. (*She hands him bottles to carry.*) Out it goes . . . Pity to waste it all, though . . . One more drink first, yes?

PLATONOV. If you like.

ANNA PETROVNA (*pours*). The quicker we drink it the sooner it will be gone.

PLATONOV (*raises his glass*). Sobriety!

ANNA PETROVNA. Sobriety!

They drink.

Why don't we sit down? Put the bottles on the floor for the moment . . . Did you miss me?

PLATONOV. Every minute of every day.

ANNA PETROVNA. Then why didn't you come and see me?

PLATONOV. I'm dying, my dear, I'm dying! Dying of guilt and melancholy! I'm a soul in torment! Then you arrive, and what happens? – I feel a little better.

ANNA PETROVNA. Why can't you be like other people, you silly man? Why do you always have to be some kind of fallen archangel?

PLATONOV. My dear, what can I do?

ANNA PETROVNA. What can you do? You can stop drinking. You can stop lying here all day. You can wash a little more often. And you can come and see me. (*She gets to her feet.*) Come on! Let's go up to my house now!

PLATONOV. Go to your house? No, no!

ANNA PETROVNA. Yes, come on! Come and talk to Sergey and Sofya! Come and pick a few quarrels!

PLATONOV. No, no, no!

ANNA PETROVNA. Why on earth not?

PLATONOV. I can't.

ANNA PETROVNA. Of course you can! Come on – put your hat on!

PLATONOV. I'm not setting foot outside this house!

ANNA PETROVNA (*puts his hat on his head*). Don't be idiotic! (*She takes him by the arm.*) Now, then. Left, right . . .! Come on, Platonov! Quick march . . .! Oh, really, Misha!

PLATONOV. I'm not going. I want to stay at home, and that's that!

ANNA PETROVNA. I see. Listen, Platonov . . . Sit down . . .

They both sit.

Do you know what's happening today? Porfiry Semyonovich is taking the train into town, and tomorrow he's going to buy the estate. He's going to settle all our debts. So I shall have money, Platonov, and I'm going to lend you some, and you're going to go away somewhere for a month or two.

PLATONOV. Go away? Where to?

ANNA PETROVNA. Moscow . . . Petersburg . . . Wherever you like! All right? Do go, Misha. You absolutely must get away from here. Get out and about, see people, go to the theatre, have a complete change. And once the estate is sold *I* shan't have to be here. If you like, love, I'll come with you. Would you like that? We'll take drives together, we'll go for long walks. By the time we get back we shall be quite different people!

PLATONOV. It's a delightful idea. But, alas, impossible. I *am* going away, Anna Petrovna. I'm going tonight. But not with you.

ANNA PETROVNA. Well, please yourself . . . Where are you going?

PLATONOV. Away. (*Pause*.) Forever.

ANNA PETROVNA. Oh, nonsense! (*She drinks*.) Rubbish!

PLATONOV. It's not nonsense, my dear. I am going! And it will be forever!

ANNA PETROVNA. But whatever for? You funny man.

PLATONOV. Don't ask me! But this is the last time we shall see each other. Forget the blackguard that was Platonov. He's going to disappear off the face of the earth! Perhaps we shall meet again many years from now, when we're both old – old enough to laugh together and shed an ancient tear or two over the past. As the present will mercifully have become. But in the meantime – forget him. (*He kisses her hand*.)

ANNA PETROVNA. But what's happened to you?

PLATONOV. You'll find out soon enough. But in your horror when you do, try not to curse me. I shall have been punished already by my separation from you.

ANNA PETROVNA (*through her tears*). I can't think you've done anything so very terrible . . . And you'll never survive without me . . . I'm a little tiny bit drunk . . . We could all live so happily!

PLATONOV. Just leave me, my dear. Just say goodbye and leave me.

ANNA PETROVNA. One more for old times' sake?

PLATONOV. All right.

ANNA PETROVNA. If we're going to drink let's drink. (*She pours*.) You die if you drink. But then you die if you don't drink. (*She drinks*.) I'm one, too, Platonov. I'm a drinker . . . Another

glass? No, I mustn't, or the words will go. Then what shall I
have left? Oh, Misha, it's terrible to be an educated woman. An
educated woman with nothing to do. What am I here for? Why
am I alive? (*She laughs.*) They should make me a professor
somewhere, or a director of something . . . If I were a diplomat
I'd turn the whole world upside down . . . An educated woman
. . . And nothing to do.

PLATONOV. We're both in sorry case.

ANNA PETROVNA. Won't you stay? You do . . . love me,
don't you? You funny man. Don't you?

PLATONOV. How could any mortal man not love you?

ANNA PETROVNA. You love me – I love you; what more do
you want . . .? Why didn't you come to me that night . . .? That
wild night . . . Such a strange month it's been. Their honeymoon
month. A sort of honeymoon for all of us. A month of wild
honey.

PLATONOV. Please go now. If you stay I shall tell you
everything, and if I tell you I shall kill myself. (*He takes her to the
door.*) Goodbye. Be happy. (*He embraces and kisses her.*) We shall
never see each other again.

ANNA PETROVNA. That depends upon whether I can catch him
at the station.

PLATONOV. Catch him? Catch whom?

ANNA PETROVNA. Porfiry Semyonovich. He's getting the
evening train. He'll have all the money for buying the estate. He
can easily give me some of it. That's all we need, my love!

Exit ANNA PETROVNA.

PLATONOV (*to himself*). If only we could have gone away
together! What would it have been? A few weeks. No more.
What's that out of a whole lifetime? I could have seen Moscow
again . . . I suppose I could ask Sofya to postpone our departure
. . . We're going to spend the rest of our lives together – she
could scarcely object to waiting for a week or two.

PLATONOV *opens the front door to run after* ANNA
PETROVNA. *There on the doorstep stands* VOYNITZEV.
PLATONOV *falls back, abashed, and retires to the far side of the
room.*

VOYNITZEV. One gift and one gift only did God bestow upon
me in this life. One precious gift. And then he took it away from
me again.

PLATONOV *sits down at the table, and hides his head in his hands.*

What am I? I'm nothing. I'm not very clever. I'm no great figure
of a man . . . Whereas you have everything. Intelligence, looks,
spirit. But they weren't enough for you. You had to have the
one thing I possessed – my happiness.

He breaks down.

Give her back to me, Platonov! You've so much fortune in your
life! So much happiness! Give her back to me!

PLATONOV. If I had a gun I'd shoot myself.

VOYNITZEV (*laughs through his tears*). That's what I came here
for! To challenge you! Or even . . . (*He takes a revolver out of his
pocket.*) God forgive me, I don't know what I was going to do!
(*He tosses it down on the table between them.*) And what happens? I
break down and cry . . . I'm sorry, Misha! Hopeless, hopeless!
I'm sorry! (*His head sinks into his hands.*)

Enter GLAGOLYEV *through the open door, leaning heavily on a
stick, breathing with difficulty.*

GLAGOLYEV. Platonov?

PLATONOV *lifts his head out of his hands and gazes blankly at*
GLAGOLYEV.

Forgive me . . . (*To* VOYNITZEV.) Sergey Pavlovich . . . (*To*
PLATONOV.) Look, this is very awkward . . . (*He glances at*
VOYNITZEV.) Very awkward indeed. But I must know! And I
must know today! My whole future depends upon your answer
. . . Sit down, if I may . . . Walked here . . . Not as well as I
might be . . . (*He sits down on the sofa.*) Yes, well . . . You know,

of course, that I have long cherished certain hopes with regard to Anna Petrovna . . . In the last few days, however, I have been told certain things . . . It may be mere rumour . . . But they say that Anna Petrovna . . . Or rather they say that you . . . Or let me put it like this: I have, as you know, a great respect for women, but . . . Have pity on me, Platonov . . .!

PLATONOV. I know only one thing, my friend.

GLAGOLYEV. Yes?

PLATONOV. I know that there is nothing but corruption under the sun.

PLATONOV *picks up the revolver and goes out.*

GLAGOLYEV (*to* VOYNITZEV). Is this true?

VOYNITZEV (*lifts his head and registers* GLAGOLYEV's *presence for the first time*). What?

GLAGOLYEV. I realise how painful this is for you. But I must know! Has she – have they – do you know of any circumstances that might unfit her to be a wife?

VOYNITZEV *weeps.*

I see. I see. Thank you for your frankness. So much for love, then. So much for respect.

Enter ANNA PETROVNA *through the open door.*

ANNA PETROVNA. Misha! I can't find him . . . Oh, you're *here*! What are you doing here?

GLAGOLYEV. I have been taking a lesson from the schoolmaster. And now I am going forth into the world to put that lesson into practice. I'm going to start living before I die! One thing I shall never do, though. I shall never foul my own nest! I'll do my living in someone else's backyard!

ANNA PETROVNA. I thought you were going to catch the evening train?

GLAGOLYEV. I *am* going to catch the evening train! To Paris!

Exit GLAGOLYEV, *slamming the door behind him.*

ANNA PETROVNA. To Paris . . .? Sergey, we've lost the estate! What's happened? What are you doing here? What have you been telling him?

VOYNITZEV. Nothing. He was talking to Platonov.

ANNA PETROVNA. Platonov? And Platonov told him . . .? What did Platonov tell him?

VOYNITZEV. I wasn't listening.

ANNA PETROVNA. You weren't listening? You just sat there and did nothing while they took the estate away from you? God gave this estate to your ancestors! Now people walk in and take it away from you again – and you don't even ask them why!

VOYNITZEV. I don't care about the estate.

ANNA PETROVNA. Sergey! Where are we going to go? What are we going to eat? We're finished!

VOYNITZEV. I've lost something infinitely more precious to me than the estate. I've lost my wife.

ANNA PETROVNA. What do you mean, you've lost your wife? She was alive and well half-an-hour ago – I saw her!

VOYNITZEV. She's in love with someone else.

ANNA PETROVNA. Don't be silly. Concentrate on the estate . . . How *could* she be in love with someone else? There's no one in this miserable little place to be in love with! There's only the doctor. She's not in love with the doctor! There are only a few elderly landowners and a retired colonel and . . . Oh, no!

VOYNITZEV. Yes.

ANNA PETROVNA. No, no! That's not possible! I can tell you that for a fact!

VOYNITZEV. She's his mistress. She told me herself.

ANNA PETROVNA. Oh no. Oh no . . . (*She sits down.*) But what could he possibly see in her? And what were *you* doing, pray? You're supposed to be her husband! Have you no eyes in your head? You just sit there snivelling while they take the world away all around you! What sort of man are you? Anyway, Platonov isn't in love with her. He's seduced her, that's all. He doesn't love her, I can assure you of that! In fact I see now what he's running away from . . . He's leaving tonight. Did you know that?

VOYNITZEV. They're leaving together.

ANNA PETROVNA. Nonsense! Sofya's at home! I saw her!

The door is flung open. SOFYA *stands on the threshold, with a suitcase, hatboxes, ulsters, etc.*

SOFYA (*bitterly*). Your word of honour, Platonov! You gave me your word of honour!

She comes face to face with ANNA PETROVNA *and* VOYNITZEV. *Pause.*

ANNA PETROVNA. What fools men are! A flutter of the eyelashes, and their back's broken! I'm sorry, Sergey.

VOYNITZEV. I'm going to shoot myself.

SOFYA (*quietly*). Where is he?

VOYNITZEV. Where's my revolver?

ANNA PETROVNA. What could he begin to see in a little ninny like you? I'm sorry, but that's what you are – an insipid little ninny!

SOFYA. Where is he?

ANNA PETROVNA. And now you've lost him again!

VOYNITZEV. I've lost my revolver.

ANNA PETROVNA. Your revolver?

VOYNITZEV. I put it on the table.

ANNA PETROVNA. Your estate – your wife – your revolver . . .! Can't you keep your hands on anything?

VOYNITZEV. He must have picked it up, and . . .

SOFYA (*urgently*). Where is he?

A shot, off.

ANNA PETROVNA (*to* VOYNITZEV). You've killed him.

SOFYA (*to* VOYNITZEV). You gave him your revolver.

ANNA PETROVNA. You put it on the table in front of him.

SOFYA. You watched him pick it up.

VOYNITZEV. No!

ANNA PETROVNA. Then you cold-bloodedly sat here.

VOYNITZEV. No!

SOFYA. And waited.

VOYNITZEV. No! No!

ANNA PETROVNA. And kept us talking until . . .

Enter PLATONOV. *He crosses in silence to the table and puts the revolver back on it.*

PLATONOV. They've shot him.

ANNA PETROVNA. Platonov!

SOFYA. Are you all right?

PLATONOV. It was the peasants. They've shot him!

TWO PEASANTS *approach the window, dragging something that remains out of sight.*

FIRST PEASANT. Sitting on a tree-stump, he was.

SECOND PEASANT. Gazing at the old schoolhouse.

FIRST PEASANT. Didn't run. Didn't move.

SECOND PEASANT. Reckon he'd gone a bit soft in the head.

FIRST PEASANT. Want to see him?

They haul the dead OSIP *up above the level of the window ledge by his hair.*

ANNA PETROVNA. Osip!

SOFYA. Horrible! Horrible!

VOYNITZEV. Take him away!

The TWO PEASANTS *drop* OSIP *out of sight. They drag the body away.* PLATONOV *pours himself vodka.*

ANNA PETROVNA. Poor Osip! He used to bring me baby birds. He tried to kiss me once.

SOFYA (*to* PLATONOV). That could have been you, lying dead out there.

PLATONOV *drinks.*

VOYNITZEV. If he were half a man, it would be.

ANNA PETROVNA. Yes, now listen, Platonov . . .

SOFYA. It's after eight! You gave me your word of honour!

PLATONOV (*holds up his hand*). I haven't come back to listen to reproaches. I've come back because I discovered something important while I was standing out there with the gun in my hand. I looked at Osip lying there in his blood and I knew for certain: I don't want to die! I looked death in the face; and I chose life! I know you're all unhappy. But what about me? I've lost everything! My honour – my home – my loved ones! I know you're all suffering torments. But think of me, standing out there with the gun in my hand, agonising between life and death! I come back to you hoping to be understood – I throw myself on your mercy – and what happens? You attack me like wild animals! All right – I apologise! I beg your forgiveness! What more do you want of me? Wasn't that one accursed night and all its consequences enough for you? My arm hurts – I'm as hungry as a starving dog – I'm cold – I'm ill – I'm shaking with fever . . . I'm going to lie down. (*He lies down on the sofa.*) I'm not going out again. It's raining out there.

Pause. They all gaze at him.

SOFYA. Why are we standing here?

ANNA PETROVNA. Yes, are we bewitched?

VOYNITZEV. Platonov, are you running away or aren't you?

ANNA PETROVNA. And if so with whom?

Enter COLONEL TRILETZKY.

COLONEL TRILETZKY. She's taken poison! She's swallowed the matches!

PLATONOV (*sits up*). Sasha?

SOFYA. Oh, no!

ANNA PETROVNA. She's not . . .?

COLONEL TRILETZKY. She would be, if her brother hadn't found her. He's trying to save her. Mishenka, I beg you – go to her! Never mind what's happened. Just go to her and tell her you love her! Comfort her, Misha! Help us to save her!

PLATONOV (*tries to get up and fails*). Can't stand. Can't get my balance.

COLONEL TRILETZKY. Misha! Please!

PLATONOV. I'm ill, too, Father-in-law! I'm a sick man! I'm on fire! Water! Give me some water!

COLONEL TRILETZKY *hands him a jug.* PLATONOV *drinks straight from it.*

ANNA PETROVNA. He's drunk. I'll go.

SOFYA. *I'll* go.

ANNA PETROVNA. You?

SOFYA. I'll beg her to forgive me!

Exit SOFYA.

ANNA PETROVNA. Sofya! Come back!

Exit ANNA PETROVNA *after* SOFYA.

VOYNITZEV. Anna Petrovna! Sofya! Both of you! Don't make things any worse . . .!

Exit VOYNITZEV *after* ANNA PETROVNA.

COLONEL TRILETZKY. My only daughter, Misha!

PLATONOV. I'm a swine! I'm such a swine!

COLONEL TRILETZKY. My little girl, Misha!

PLATONOV. But, my God, I've been punished for it! Well and truly punished!

COLONEL TRILETZKY. Don't keep her waiting, Misha! She's sinking!

PLATONOV. I can scarcely hold my head up on my shoulders! Look, it's going to fall off!

COLONEL TRILETZKY. It's nothing, Misha. You've been drinking, that's all.

PLATONOV. No, I've got a fever. I've been out in the rain.

COLONEL TRILETZKY. It's not raining, Misha.

PLATONOV. I can't see anything. All I can see is little soldiers. Little green and yellow soldiers in pointed caps. They're crawling over everything . . .! I need a doctor! Get me a doctor!

Enter GREKOVA *through the open door.*

COLONEL TRILETZKY. Wait here, Misha. I'll tell Kolya. (*To* GREKOVA.) Look after him. He's ill. And Sasha's ill. (*To* PLATONOV.) I'll see if Kolya can leave Sasha for a moment . . .

Exit COLONEL TRILETZKY.

PLATONOV (*flaps his hand in front of his eyes*). All these flies everywhere! Clouds of flies! I can't see anything! Shoot the flies . . . (*He picks up the revolver.*)

GREKOVA. No! No! Please! (*She tries to take the revolver.*)

PLATONOV (*points the revolver at her*). Who's this?

GREKOVA. It's me!

PLATONOV. The doctor, is it?

GREKOVA. Marya Yefimovna.

PLATONOV. Can't see you. Flies everywhere.

GREKOVA. Beetle-juice!

PLATONOV. Beetle-juice? My mortal enemy! (*He points the revolver.*)

GREKOVA. No! No! I got your message!

PLATONOV. Message?

GREKOVA. I met him at the ford – I had the pony and trap – I've galloped all the way . . . I just want to say, don't! Please don't!

PLATONOV. Don't what?

GREKOVA. You said you were . . . going away. Going away forever. I knew at once. Please don't! (*She holds out her hand for the revolver.*) Please give it to me!

PLATONOV. I'm ill. I've got a fever.

GREKOVA. I'll look after you.

PLATONOV. Got to have water.

GREKOVA. I'll give you water. (*She picks up the jug.*) If you give me that.

PLATONOV. Water . . . Water . . . (*He exchanges the revolver for the jug, and drinks.*)

GREKOVA. Thank God I got here in time!

PLATONOV. I can't stay here. I've got to get to bed.

GREKOVA. I'll put you to bed in my house. I've got the trap outside.

PLATONOV. Quickly! Quickly! Help me!

GREKOVA *puts the revolver down, safely out of his reach, and goes to him.*

Hand! Give me your hand . . .! Oh, cold hand! Lovely hand!
Kiss your lovely cold hand . . .

GREKOVA. No, no . . .

PLATONOV. And your lovely cold cheek . . . (*He pulls her down
into his lap and kisses her cheek.*)

GREKOVA. You mustn't do that.

PLATONOV. I'm not going to seduce you, my dear! No fit state
at the moment. Can't even see you properly . . . Can't see you,
but I love you all the same. (*He kisses her hands.*)

GREKOVA. I know what happened. It was Sofya, wasn't it.

PLATONOV. Sofya, Zizi, Mimi, Masha . . . I love everyone –
and everyone loves me. I insult them, I treat them abominably –
and they love me just the same! (*He puts his arm around her.*) Take
that Beetle-juice girl, for example. I indecently assaulted her – I
kissed her . . . (*He kisses her.*) . . . and she's still in love with me
. . . Oh, you are Beetle-juice, aren't you. Sorry.

GREKOVA. You're all muddled up inside that head of yours.

She embraces him. He flinches.

You're in pain, too. Tell me where it hurts.

PLATONOV. In Platonov – that's where it hurts . . . *Are* you in
love with me, then? Are you really?

GREKOVA. Yes. (*She kisses him.*) I am in love with you.

PLATONOV. Yes, they're all in love with me. Once I used to
moralise away to them all, and they loved me for it. Now I
seduce them instead, and they still love me.

GREKOVA. You do what you like with me. I don't mind. (*She
weeps.*) You're only human, after all. And that's enough for me.

Enter DR TRILETZKY.

DR TRILETZKY (*cheerfully*). Misha! We've got a surprise for you!
(*He freezes at the sight of* GREKOVA *sitting in* PLATONOV's *lap.*

Enter SASHA, *supported by* ANNA PETROVNA *and* SOFYA, *and followed by* VOYNITZEV *and* COLONEL TRILETZKY.

ANNA PETROVNA (*to* SASHA). Come on, my dear. You know you want to see him.

SOFYA (*to* SASHA). You know *he* wants to see *you* . . .

The women halt at the spectacle before them.

VOYNITZEV. Terrible tragedy!

COLONEL TRILETZKY. But it's got a happy ending.

VOYNITZEV *and* COLONEL TRILETZKY *halt in their turn.* GREKOVA *hides her face in* PLATONOV's *neck.* PLATONOV *hugs her, unaware of his audience.*

PLATONOV. No fit state now. Never you fear, though – when I get better again I'll seduce you like the rest of them.

DR TRILETZKY *is the first to move.*

DR TRILETZKY. Misha! If I've told you once I've told you a thousand times . . .!

SOFYA. The revolver! Where's the revolver? (*She finds it and points it at* PLATONOV.)

GREKOVA (*jumps up and interposes herself between* SOFYA *and* PLATONOV). No! No!

VOYNITZEV. Sofya! It was all going to be all right!

ANNA PETROVNA (*tries to take the revolver from* SOFYA). Give me that! I'll do it myself!

GREKOVA. I love him!

SASHA (*left unsupported, sinks to her knees*). Kill me! Not him!

COLONEL TRILETZKY (*vacillates uncertainly between* SASHA *and the others*). Sasha . . .! Sofya Yegorovna . . .!

DR TRILETZKY. Misha!

VOYNITZEV. Sofya!

COLONEL TRILETZKY. Kolya . . .! Sasha . . .!

GREKOVA. We love each other!

SOFYA (*in a terrible voice*). Stand back! All of you!

Enter MARKO *through the open door.*

PLATONOV. Wait! What does *he* want?

They all turn and see MARKO.

MARKO. Three rubles.

PLATONOV. Three rubles?

MARKO. If you're happy, sir.

PLATONOV. Happy? My cup runneth over! Give him four!

In the instant while they automatically feel in their pockets and look around for four rubles, PLATONOV *jumps out of the window.* SOFYA *and the others rush to the window after him. As they do so there is the sound of an approaching train whistle, and they all turn, struck by the same thought. They run out of the door, shouting after* PLATONOV; *and the world falls apart. Amidst the gathering roar of the train the rear wall of the house moves aside and the lights go down. The forest and the railway line of the previous scene are revealed beyond, with everyone going away upstage, searching and calling* PLATONOV's *name.* PLATONOV *emerges from the shadows behind their backs. He steps on to the railway line and runs in the opposite direction – downstage – glancing back over his shoulder at them like a fugitive. Then he stops, blinded by the brilliant headlight of the train approaching from behind the heads of the audience, its whistle screaming. He staggers back a step or two, trying to wave the train away like the flies. Then sudden blackness, and the great roar of the train, its note falling as it passes us. The red tail light of the train appears at the front of the stage and dwindles rapidly into the smoke left by the locomotive. There is a smell of sulphur in the air.*

Curtain.